CASE DISMISSED!

CASE DISMISSED!

An Ordinary Jamaican Woman;
An Extraordinary Life

Gloria Cameron MBE

HANSIB

First published in Great Britain by Hansib Publications in 2016

Hansib Publications Limited
P.O. Box 226, Hertford, SG14 3WY

info@hansibpublications.com
www.hansibpublications.com

ISBN 978-1-910553-41-1

A CIP catalogue record for this book
is available from the British Library

Front cover photograph courtesy of Hazel Thompson
Cover design concept by Shadid Omar Muhammad

Production by Hansib Publications Limited
Printed in Great Britain

My heritage and lineage, reinforced by my family, gave me the fortitude to break into a system and change it for the better of my Caribbean peoples. The legacy I will leave can only be measured by time...

Dedicated to George B Greaves MBE who departed this life in March 2011. George was the Principal Community Relations Officer for Lambeth (1968 – 1989) and a war veteran who did not have to bark or display one-upmanship to gain respect, stampede his staff into every crisis confrontation or swayed by troublemakers and bounty-seekers.

CONTENTS

FOREWORD

The story of the life of a woman of vision, determination and resilience! Gloria takes her readers back to her childhood in the island of Jamaica which she passionately loves and where she was reared in an atmosphere of appreciation and enjoyment of her cultural heritage and love of community. She has given a brief history of the various groups of people who played a part in the early political development of Jamaica, including the war years, and the beginning of the mass immigration of people from the Caribbean to England. This is of great educational value for young people of Caribbean origin in the contemporary society, who have not had the opportunity to learn this history.

Gloria's participation in community life, her education and cultural experiences in the island, were the foundation and inspiration for her work among the Caribbean population during their early years of settlement in the area of London where she lived... She created opportunities for social events in order to relieve the strenuous lives under which most families lived; as her family grew she also involved them and their friends in utilising their entertaining skills.

I was privileged to meet Gloria in 1973 in Lambeth where she had been recently appointed Assistant Community Relations Officer with the special role of Development Work with Women. The social worker who recommended that I met her to discuss my research project, which was researching the effect of separation and reunion of Caribbean mothers and children, had enthused about the warm, friendly and helpful person I would meet, and I was not disappointed. Gloria's vitality, her knowledge of the community in which she lived and worked and her willingness to introduce me to some of the women who met the criteria for my research captivated me.

The nature of my research was not new to her as she too had experienced separation and reunion through the experience of immigration. I was grateful for her generosity in spending time to share her experiences with me and I was convinced that her memoirs would make for arresting reading.

It was a delight to see Gloria's dream of developing work with young children through the establishing of a Day Nursery/Family Centre become a reality. She pursued the work in her unique energetic and creative way, inspiring young carers and so assisted many families to see their children grow and develop in a safe and stimulating environment.

Gloria has written honestly of her life, her aspirations for herself and family and her dedication to helping the social and educational development of the Caribbean community in the Borough of Lambeth especially in the early days of settlement in London. She writes with the flowing style of a narrator and the book held my attention from the beginning to the end and called my emotions of joy and sorrow into play. I laughed and felt Gloria's excitement in new situations, shared her disappointments, and was sad and angry when unfair and unkind false accusations so needlessly inflicted upon her and family, brought an abrupt end to her dream of a lasting Child Care provision of quality for children in the borough of Lambeth. Although Gloria was unable to control some of the later events of her career which, through malice, were inflicted upon her, she remained a woman of honour and integrity and was not reduced by them.

I am grateful for the privilege and honour to write the foreword and have no doubt that other readers will be as captivated and enthralled by this book.

Dr Elaine Arnold

COMMENTARY

Since the arrival of the Empire Windrush in 1948, the whole story of Caribbean immigration to Britain has been told mainly through the eyes and not ears of academics and journalists. Important though they have been, these narratives that have made up the story have tended to be couched in a political, sociological, historical, literary and even behavioural framework. Covering a whole array of sub-subjects, from extolling the virtues of Victorian morality, musical and dance creativity, sporting, literary and other achievements, to documenting the dreadful, marginalised and racist treatment meted out to black families as they settled and made a life in the conurbations of London, Birmingham, Manchester, Bristol and wherever else a need for cheap labour existed, these narratives have been largely devoid of the inner life, feelings and struggles of particularly strong and courageous black women. They have lacked what might be called 'historical intimacy'; there is a sense that all that is personal and intimate, historically situated yet emotionally unfolding, has been blotted out of black history, together with the story of the struggle for survival, the story of sensitive and quiet resistance and constructive contribution to the making of modern Britain.

But this is not all. Many of these otherwise interesting, knowledgeable and necessary books, papers and articles – and especially those which have received much praise in both white academic and non-academic circles – have straddled a line between an unacceptable pathology on the one hand and a liberal expression of patronisation on the other. Although this may sound harsh, it needs to be stated in order to place Gloria Cameron's book into its proper and appreciative context.

The author provides a non-patronising, non-sentimental and certainly a non-pathological account of her experience as a Caribbean migrant mother living, surviving and bringing up six children in London. Her story begins with a non-romanticised and hence truthful account of pre-independent Jamaica. Explaining in a clear and unaffected style 'why we are here', and detailing the life of Jamaicans, especially those who settled in Brixton (and many did), her opening chapters provide a good historical account of that reality.

But on another level, a more profound and intimate one, Gloria Cameron's autobiography conveys a strong portrayal of legacy, in a vivid description of a father as a product of slavery and 'a mother who fathered me'. This degree of intimate experience, one shared by many black mothers, gives in part a deep insight into the source of physical and emotional strength, courage and tenacity that many black mothers exhibit. Paid and non-paid hard work, the bringing up successfully in Gloria's case of six children, the daily grind of figuring out how to manage bureaucracies (the social state) and/or fighting racially discriminatory authorities and the sheer effort required to maintain a modicum of self-respect and decorum – all these call for a strength of character and a singleness of purpose that has tended to go unnoticed in much of the literature on black immigration from the Caribbean.

This book cannot be read or appreciated without encountering this source of strength, modest pride and successful struggle which pervades each of its chapters. As an expression of survival in an often hostile, racist and, it needs to be said, sexist London Borough, it would not ring true to leave the story of the experience of a strong black woman as something that arises from strength of character alone. Gloria Cameron is in no doubt about this. Her description of what can be called the making and importance of Brixton culture, the many voluntary organisations she belonged to, her church and the support, spiritual and otherwise, she derived from belonging to an active and committed black congregation, and the charity work she undertook as an integral part of being a responsible and morally directed citizen – all were important in her own struggle. They provided not just support in a general sense: as a set of commitments, habits, associations or, simply, daily routines of life, they provided reassurance, identity, confidence and, together with the raising of her children, a raison d'être that made life feel and become whole.

This book, then, is more than a traditional autobiography. In many ways, it is one that recalls as well as validates the experience of many women of Gloria's generation. It will remind them that they were not alone in the struggle to survive in post-war metropolitan society. Perhaps more importantly, it is a book which talks to young black women today, as it glows with hope, with an understanding that there are ways through the difficulties society presents to black people in general and to black women in particular. Academics and researchers, too, will gain much from its pages, as each provides an orientation and, together as a whole, a black woman's perspective borne out of the 'intimacies' that make up the history of the marginalised and racially discriminated against who have survived. The importance and contribution of *Case Dismissed!* should not be underestimated or perceived as yet another autobiography: for it engages the mind, transcends the ordinary, touches the heart and records a history that has for too long gone unheard.

Dame Jocelyn Barrow OBE

PROLOGUE

Gloria Cameron! This is Your Life!

I woke up with a start as the voice of Eamonn Andrews, The TV Presenter, boomed out.

Of late, I have been having some flash backs shattering my quiet reflective moments and my mid-afternoon naps.

But some strident voices in surround sound soon drown out Eamonn Andrews with: *You going to Jail. You going to Jail. Thief, Thief.*

My heart would skip a beat.

Then I would find solace in the equally strident words of Judge Valerie Pearlman as she announces to all the world – *"You all have been found 'not guilty' and there is not a stain on the character of each of you."*

It is this journey from the heights of public acclaim to the depths of despair and disappointment and through the battles of attrition that I had to wage to salvage my reputation and self-esteem that are chronicled in the following pages.

The journey started in March 1957, when, at the age of 24 years, a bewildered naïve young woman strolled down the gangway of the S.S. IRPINI at Southampton Dock. With a United Kingdom and Colonies passport stamped for five years, I wanted to make my stay fruitful, profitable and unforgettable. Fifty-seven years later, I am still here in the UK.

This book is the story of what I experienced over thirty years living and working in the London Borough of Lambeth – embracing a community development role by leading and encouraging other black women, through tuition and example, to move away from the canteens and factories towards professional achievements, social mobility and equality. As women, a major feature of our existence in the early 1970s was being physically and socially trapped in our homes because our childcare needs remained unrecognised and not catered for. This motivated me to get involved with others to establish a Day Care Centre for the under-fives. It was this obsession to release women to play their part as highly useful members of the wider community that brought about my most bruising encounters with several individuals and organisations. Encounters that led me to fight for my very survival.

The last battle of that fight was waged in February 1989 at Southwark Crown Court – the lay magistrate and community development worker facing charges of fraud.

A few days following the completion of this trial, two black ring binders were given to me. I presumed that there was an expectation, from the donor, that I would eagerly peruse their contents. In fact, I could not bear the agony of re-visiting all the contrived falsehoods and lies nor re-living the many instances of fellow professionals ruining my personal life and professional career.

I remember getting home with the binders and putting them out of sight in a corner of my study.

Ten years had passed and on looking for a folder with my favourite poems, I came across the binders. I followed my temptation and started to flick through the pages. What I discovered took my breath away. My stomach churned, my fingers trembled and my eyes glistened as I continued to read the documents that covered such a painful period of my life.

It did not take me long to be convinced that the full story, contained in these ring binders and never seen by many, needed to be more widely known. If only to wash off the mud that did stick and that my silence all these years have solidified.

I decided to pen my thoughts now that I am in possession of a fair deal of the sequence of events that dominated what the 'Voice', a Brixton-based weekly newspaper, captioned "O What a Fiasco"

I have done my best to convey my observations, thoughts and feelings as I have experienced them. And to have done so with honesty, sensitivity and accuracy. This is not meant to be a comprehensive history or a full autobiography but a personal memoir that chronicles an extraordinary turn of events during my working life in the London Borough of Lambeth.

This is my life as I experienced it and my fight for survival.

ACKNOWLEDGEMENTS

This book may not have taken a community to write but that community has certainly afforded me the joys and sorrows recorded therein.

Before I thank anyone, I want to acknowledge the loss of a foremost enabler of my successful working life – George B Greaves MBE to whom I dedicate this book.

As I approach my 83rd birthday, it is difficult not to feel a sense of loss at the disintegration of our Caribbean Clan; the ever increasing frequency of the departure of one's colleagues and friends, hopefully to paradise. The efforts of Hansib to create a web presence to record the contributions that these members of our community have made post Windrush, intensified this sense of loss. So I want to pay my own homage to Gavton Shepherd, George Greaves & Astel Parkinson.

The smartest decision I made was to reconnect with Waveney Bushel, a retired Educational Psychologist, and to seek her help in giving me guidance in recording my experiences. She has the rear gift of understanding how to help another's voice to emerge and I could not have completed this book without her.

I would like to express my appreciation to Leonora Johnson and Vickie Bynoe-Samuel, my granddaughter, who did the initial typing, and in particular to Meverly Anderson MBE who came to my rescue with her skills and insight to type the bulk of the manuscript, thus saving my sanity.

My thanks and appreciation to a coterie of black women - Jocelyn Barrow, Elaine Arnold, Gerlin Bean, Mavis Clarke-Best, Lorna Hunte and Amelda Ingyang - who have been towers of strength throughout this journey. Their help, together with that of David Bryan, in recording sequences of events as they happened proved to be of immense importance as time went by. Their spirits have therefore shaped my message.

I am also grateful to Ansel Wong in helping me shape this message by editing the text for publication.

Without the receipt of the ring binders in which the false allegations, correspondence between conspirators, memos etc. were catalogued, I would not have been able to understand the full extent of the conspiracy which led to the demise of the West Indian Parents Action Group (WIPAG) Day Care Centre. My gratitude and appreciation go to my excellent legal Advisors.

Numerous people helped with the research that was very necessary because the organisation's documents were removed from the premises.

My heartfelt love, appreciation and gratitude go to the Prayer Circles in the UK, USA and Jamaica who never stopped praying for the truth to be revealed.

Jennifer and Gerlin Bean, demonstrating their love and concern throughout the entire ordeal, were the shoulders on which I often found comfort and solace.

My expression of gratitude would be incomplete were I not to mention the extended Caribbean Folk Culture family who have for nearly thirty years joined me in the exploration and projection of the rich cultural heritage of the Caribbean. Their unwavering support, dedication and expression of love are highly appreciated.

I wish to express my gratitude to my children - Franklyn, Chris, Christine, Jennifer, Richard and adopted daughter Paula - for their help and encouragement throughout my writing of this painful episode of my life. Without their patience and support, this episode of my life would have been completely lost to family and friends. They have forced me to grow beyond comfortable boundaries and have nurtured my attempts to explain the history they lived with me.

Finally, I am responsible for the interpretation expressed in this my memoir. These pages reflect how I experienced the events I have described. No doubt, there may be others – even competing views of the events. That is someone else's story to tell.

CHAPTER 1

IN THE BEGINING

Call her Gloria; She will live

The prelude to my birth, less than a century after the abolition of slavery in 1834, turned out to be the electric years of self-discovery and emancipation for the mass of African-Jamaican people who acknowledged the legacy of resistance that their ancestors had implanted. A new national consciousness emerged leading to a movement towards self-government and ultimately independence of Jamaica in 1962.

The rumbling sounds of the vehicles and the constant tooting of their horns grew louder and more frequent as drivers made their way along the main Spanish Town Road in Western Kingston.

This clearly suggested that the hustle and bustle of the market vendors, trading in foodstuff, were about to take on a lively air at the Coronation Market half a mile down that very road. The roosters in the neighbourhood yards crowed loudly, as though in response to the harmonious chirping of the birds, as they flew from branch to branch in the tall spreading trees, happy in their natural habitat. My mother was not feeling well but she did not want to alert my father to get the midwife until dawn.

However, struck by the excruciating pains, she got my father to fetch Nurse Austin. He did as he was told, speedily;

first getting Aunty Tiny, his sister, to prepare the necessary utensils for the imminent birth.

At 5.30am on Monday 27th June 1932 in the timber framed house situated at 54c Spanish Town Road, West Kingston, in the shadows of the Tivoli Cinema, a baby girl danced into the world to the tune of nature's tropical music. My parents were ecstatically delighted - "a girl"; their prayers were answered.

I was given the names, Florence Tina, both names inherited from Papa's sister who was deceased. Within months of my birth, my family moved to a house in Kingston Gardens near the Holy Trinity Cathedral along North Street, Kingston.

They were now settled; happy and content with their life and their bundle of joy, now a thriving one year old.

The period of August to October was the rainy season and people throughout the island, especially in the rural areas, would gather foodstuff in case the weather became severe and roads made impassable, because of swollen rivers and gullies. August 1933, however, brought about a frightening experience that was consistently retold to me throughout my childhood.

The rain started and continued moderately throughout the day developing into a storm during the night. The torrential rain and heavy winds lashed the entire Island leaving destruction in its wake.

On that frightful night mother was alone. She was awakened by the whimpering of the dogs and shouts for help coming from the other houses. She could feel her body being lifted as though she was floating on water and became very afraid, realising then that there was water almost knee high flooding the room. She wrapped me carefully in a blanket. In her confusion, she climbed on to the gable (the halfway partition of the room) with me in one arm.

The wind growled and whirled in its temper while she screamed for help. Below, all her possessions were almost submerged in the water. However, it seems that her cries were heard long before she had realised. The evacuation process in the neighbourhood having started, someone came to rescue her. By then she was quite exhausted and overcome with fear. In her own words, she could not recognise her own mother from a broomstick!

Manoeuvring through the water, the rescuer was able to get her out passing through the scattered debris to a place of safety across the Wildman Street gully where we joined other families who were already rescued. The women's faces reflected the anguish they felt in their soaked rooms. They lit a coal pot stove to heat the clothes iron to use to dry their soaking wet garments.

Days later when the rain had ceased and the murky waters in the gully had subsided, Papa went to see what had happened to his home and possessions. Nothing of consequence was found. The majority of families, including mine, were left with just the garments on their backs.

Suddenly the long rainy days vanished and again the earth was green and light, the sun shone gloriously and everyone's pre-occupation was to get their homes together again.

However, my parent's concern became more and more centred on my health. Medical examination confirmed that I was suffering from acute typhoid and I became a patient in the baby ward of Kingston Public Hospital, aged 14 months. The development was a traumatic experience for my parents who watched anxiously as my condition deteriorated. They were advised that I had developed pneumonia and that the possibility of my survival was questionable. Their distress became extreme. Hospital staff grew accustomed to my mother's wailing and weeping, especially when she arrived to find a screen drawn around my crib.

After months in hospital, my condition improved and a slow recovery commenced much to the delight of everyone. On that day, when the young man who had rescued mother and me visited, he commented on the marked improvement that I had made and as he stared at the weak fragile frame in the crib, he raised his head and with his palm hovering over my head he said to mother "Call her Gloria, she will live".

The name Gloria was adopted and has been widely used since then. It seems that my parents were looking for any symbol of hope to hold onto; this was it! 'Florence Tina' which appears on my birth certificate remains a part of my official identification only.

At the age of 14, I was introduced to a pint sized muscular man called 'Baboo' - an African-Jamaican with a typical Indian name. I listened attentively with much admiration as he relayed to me how he skilfully rescued us on the stormy weather night in August 1933.

My Father – Papa Clifford George

Papa was born to Angelina and William Hylton in the district of Cross in the Parish of Clarendon, Jamaica. He was named Clifford George, the second of six sons and two daughters of whom one was deceased at an early age. The family moved to Kingston in 1925 soon after the death of his father. The younger siblings continued their education, while my grandmother 'Gran', as I knew her, started employment with Seaga's, who were successful Lebanese textile merchants in down town Kingston. She soon became so versed in handling of textile and good customer relations that she was promoted to Senior Personnel in the store where she worked up until her retirement.

Papa joined the firm and became manager for one of their chains of stores. Soon he moved to larger premises along that same stretch of Spanish Town Road, close to the Coronation Municipal Market (so named, as it was built to commemorate the coronation of King George VI) and adjacent to the Metropole Restaurant.

The Metropole became the haven for up and coming politicians, serving Legislative Council Members and leading figures in the legal profession. Arlington House in East Kingston was the main branch of the Restaurant frequented by political activists and campaigners like Bustamante, the Trade Union activist and first Prime Minister of an independent Jamaica and J A G Smith, the eminent Barrister who prepared the text for the 1944 New Constitution.

During that era, the upwardly mobile people, whether in social, political or business terms, had their meals at these venues. Some stayed at the local hotel, many of whom were out of town members of the Legislative Council, in town for Council Sessions. These venues provided them with opportunities for the interchange of ideas and the airing of views from people who were becoming disenchanted with a Legislative Council whose members had to own property and were primarily male and who enjoyed extra-ordinary privileges in return for fostering Britain's economic interests.

The system was therefore strenuously criticised and challenged by those people who were becoming more and more politically and socially aware. These concerns were debated by the men who crowded Papa's store in the evenings after closing time. There was quite an array of them, easily distinguishable because of their attire, the way in which their hair was groomed and the differences in their linguistic ability.

Several other noticeable groups of people also frequented these venues. Amongst them was the followers of Marcus Garvey and his Universal Negro Improvement Association (UNIA), dressed neatly, wearing short cut afro hairstyles and walking with military precision. Usually they were good debaters with a fairly wide knowledge of Jamaica and its current affairs.

The Rastafarians were distinguishable by their dress, perceived by many as a bizarre fashion with the red, yellow and green colours dominating whatever apparel they wore. The majority kept their hair long and matted, leaving their beards equally long.

The Bedwardites were at the vanguard of a new religious order with a leader based in Gordon Town who saw himself as a prophet. It is rumoured he attempted to fly. Their membership were mostly females who wore scarves on their heads at all times and submerged themselves in the belief that they would be relieved from the burden of temporal poverty by ascending into heaven away from the oppression of the white man.

Other regular debaters included The Revivalist, few of whom visited the store, Shepherd Levi, his armour bearer and Sister Icy from the Revival Zion Baptist of the Spirit Church. They were forever buying reams of brightly coloured cotton materials, which were used as turbans or wraps, extending about ten inches above the base of their heads. The Shepherd who is usually the leader of the flock wore his robe festooned in a variety of colours with his rod of correction completing his regalia. This majestic man epitomised the biblical shepherd who was capable of casting out evil spirits from the lost and forlorn and who ministered to those who sought mystical help to relieve their illness or social problems.

These colourful characters and their ideologies were symbolic of the variety of strategies that many people felt were necessary to force the unbending nature and resistance of the ruling class to bring about a broader social change.

A dominant strategy, aimed at achieving constitutional change, was led by Alexander Bustamante and Norman W Manley in the mid-1930s. They intensified the struggle of some of Jamaican's earlier protagonists for freedom - William Gordon and Paul Bogle, who fought for the liberation of the black masses and Marcus M Garvey who appealed to the dream of millions of black people throughout the world, teaching them a sense of pride in race and culture.

My father was a strong-willed and strict disciplinarian who made no allowances for any form of activities, outside the home, in which he had no involvement. His humorous moments were quite sporadic and he ruled his domain (the home) with an iron hand. Nevertheless, he took his responsibilities as a father and provider very seriously. From an early age, I can remember him being engrossed in reading the bible for long periods on Sunday afternoons. I was soon given the task to read aloud to him. I did not like this task that became so unexciting I used to fall asleep.

As I grew older, it became clear to me that he was carefully applying the messages of the Holy Scripture to his daily life. But why, I have often wondered, he had never, as far as I knew, attended a church service nor was anyone in the household allowed. Why did he have an aversion to the Holy edifice? But I couldn't dare question his action. In those days, parents did not think that they needed to explain their actions to children. The old maxim applies here, children are to be seen but not heard.

However, my love and admiration for Papa were profound; his stylish mode of dress, the gold teeth in his mouth shone like looking down into Fort Knox. He was so proud and protective of them that he would not touch a slice of yam or a finger of boiled banana unless it had been crushed to a pulp and neatly presented. I used to watch Cotilda's colourful presentation, the yellow and white yam in its mound, the ripe plantain in its yellow splendour and the green banana in its cream coloured mound. Equally the rice and peas or plain boiled rice would look like a manicured lawn of rice grains pressed together neatly on his favourite plate.

Papa was an active and devoted member of the Universal Negro Improvement Association (UNIA) with the uniform rank of "Legion" and my Mother Dear served in the Black Cross Nursing Corps. At all times, he extolled the virtues of the black race. He often used the phrase "I am black but comely". His social life, as I can remember, revolved around Edelweiss Park along Slipe Road in the Cross Road area and Liberty Hall in King Street, Kingston, where UNIA had its Headquarters and meeting places.

Papa met and married Eugenie, known by everyone as Mother Dear. She came from Spanish Town in the Parish of St Catherine about 14 miles from Kingston, yet she was referred to by Kingstonians as the "country bumpkin". Her hometown was, however, significant in that it was, until 1872, the capital of Jamaica. There still remains to date the exceptionally fine "Georgian Square" with Kings House, once the official residence of the British Government's representatives to the island, the House of Assembly/Parliament and a commemorative statue of the British Admiral Sir Walter Rodney.

Eugenie left her hometown and made for the capital, the commercial centre of Kingston at a time when the urbanisation of West Kingston was at its height and the offer of work to the rural born Jamaicans was a major attraction.

The newlyweds set up their home in the heartlands of the cosmopolitan area of Down Town Kingston. I cannot remember for sure how old I was when I joined Papa's household. I have no memory of the journey from my mother's home or any circumstances that precipitated that move. It feels as though I had lived in Papa's home all of my childhood years up to age 14. I can, however, remember my mother's infrequent visits, the lovely gifts and the weekends that I spent with her.

My Aunty Tiny went to settle in Cuba and we eventually lost touch. However, there were three women in my life to whom I could relate and whose constant care and affection were ever present. Grandma Hylton (Papa's mother) whom I called Gran Gran, Mother Dear (his wife) and Clotilda (the housekeeper) who remained in the household throughout my childhood and was the main person to collect me from school during those formative years.

My five uncles were frequent visitors and although I loved them all, Uncle William was my adorable favourite and the only one with whom Papa would usually concur. It was therefore not at all difficult, when in later years, I chose to get married, despite Papa's disapproval, Uncle William was on hand to give me away.

However, my earliest recollection of being with Papa was my witnessing the meetings being held in the store. I later learnt that the discussions taking place were about the labour unrest in the Caribbean that first started in St Kitts in response to the employer's refusal to increase wages. This strike spread to St Vincent and Guyana where East Indian estate workers staged several serious disturbances.

By mid-1937, the Labour unrest had spread to Jamaica when the police using batons broke up a demonstration led by the unemployed and ex-service men in Kingston. Discontent continued and erupted in the riots at Frome Sugar Factory owned by the British firm, Tate and Lyle. This soon spread to the Kingston docks. The waves of riots and strikes, together with death and casualties of many people, attracted worldwide attention and led to major efforts to correct the injustices and to remove discontent from the society.

The leading person who supported and agitated for the workers was Alexander Bustamante who returned from work abroad to the island in 1934 presenting himself as a Spanish wanderer. He was a dynamic speaker who attracted attention to himself because of the remarkable series of letters he wrote to the "Gleaner" newspaper commenting on current affairs and expressing his opinions about the inequalities practiced in the society.

Together with a leading activist, the ex-Garveyite, Saint William Grant, they held meetings in parks and street corners. Everywhere they went the people would stop and gather round to listen, ready to act out their despair and frustration at what was described as colonial injustices. On the 23rd May, I can vividly recall seeing the distinct tall figure of Bustamante walking with an air of authority towards Papa's store, his unruly mass of silvery hair blowing in the wind. Bustamante and Grant stopped outside the store and a crowd of people gathered, waiting to hear what they had to say. But before long the police came and dispersed them.

Later on that same day, news had reached the store that Bustamante and Grant had refused to disperse from a street corner meeting, when requested to do so by the police. Papa and the men clapped their hands for joy; they admired Bustamante's bravery. But at the other venue in the Queen Victoria Park, named in commemoration of the Queen Victoria's reign, Bustamante climbed on to her statue to address a large mass of people.

Papa hurried from the store with me sitting on his shoulders to listen and to cheer the 'Chief' as Bustamante was affectionately called. His toughness and determination were hailed as he shouted with his arms around the neck of the portly statue of the Queen.

"The pot of discontent is boiling, today it has reached the brim, tomorrow it might over flow".

He was reading from the contents of a letter he had sent to a Member of Parliament in London. Papa was for ever repeating this phrase. It soon became a popular chant among the agitators.

The 1938 Strike

On the 24th May, which has always been celebrated particularly in schools throughout the island as "Empire Day", news spread across the island that Busta and his colourfully attired Lieutenant Saint William Grant had been arrested.

This created indignation among the masses. All services throughout the island were brought to a standstill with workers shouting, "No Busta, No Work". People took to the streets smashing the gas lamps that served as streetlights, overturning garbage bins and congregating at the street corners.

A state of emergency was soon declared by the Colonial Governor Sir Arthur Richards, resulting in armed troops, soldiers and the police patrolling the areas. Sadly, among other deaths a young mother and her child died from one single bullet, emitted from a long distance away by one of the British soldiers. I can recall my father holding me shoulder high to watch the cortege pass by on its way to the May Pen Cemetery, a small white covered coffin perched on the top of a large one.

People lined the main road to pay their respects, in a sad and sombre mood. Nevertheless, at the height of the upheaval when Busta and Saint William were held in custody, the African-Jamaican masses had in the process nurtured spokesmen who could lead discussions at the street corners and shop piazzas.

However, with the suspension of businesses because of the upheaval, Papa's debaters were always present, eager to discuss and update on the developing crisis. Busta and Saint William Grant were released on bail on the morning of the 28th May 1938, only four days after their incarceration, following the intervention of Busta's cousin, the renowned Barrister Norman

Washington Manley, who presented evidence and an affidavit on their behalf.

Thousands of people from the rural areas converged on Kingston in order to greet the 'Chief' and avail themselves for any task to which they could be assigned. My childhood recollections of this tremendous welcome and show of strength and allegiance, although I was aged about six years old, remain as vivid as ever.

The men bore Busta, shoulder high, high above the heads of everyone; the others waved branches cut from trees as they sang with utter conviction, "I will follow Bustamante till I die". The tramping footsteps and their resounding voices could be heard long, long after they passed the store. The song subsequently was hailed "Busta's song", usually sung just before he gave his address at the massive street meetings.

The British Government intervened by setting up a Royal Commission to look into the complaints. This brought about a much quieter mood, although incidents continued to occur. It can, however, be said that the upheaval gave birth simultaneously to Trade Unionism as well as Political parties serving as two facets of a single process aimed at achieving economic betterment, self-government, political independence and social reconstruction.

Papa's role in providing a focal point for people to voice their opinion about the inequalities and racial discriminatory practices made him a well-known person in the community. I also became equally well known. In some ways that was good, because the adults took care of me wherever I went and they watched my every move. However, sadly, I did not enjoy the freedom to join the children of my age and get up to a little mischief; I was constantly included into the company of adults.

That the significance of the 24th May 'Empire Day' should be historically marked as the beginning of Jamaica's modern era, when the labouring classes rose up in protest to say "enough is enough" surely fill me with immense pride.

The War Years (1939 – 1942)

The volume of Papa's radio was unusually high. People were stopping by and listening intently. I wondered what was happening and why their faces had gone blank. Some were waving their arms in disappointing gestures. The music stopped and the people began to converse. There was a sense of fear and I could not understand why people were looking sad so suddenly. An elderly woman was sobbing inconsolably.

I later learnt that Britain had declared war on Germany that meant that we were in the war. I was told that this lady had lost her brother in the first war and now feared that she would lose her sons in this one. There was, I can recall, a marked silence among the men, even those who were known to be noisy and talkative sat in a contemplative mood.

Each day brought with it more and more talk about the war, the subject became the highlight of most discussions. The radio became the focus, as people waited to listen to the bulletins that were regularly relayed.

In those days, very few people had radios in their homes, so it was customary to see crowds of people listening to the radios outside public buildings and businesses. Those with radios in their homes would turn the volume up to share news items with their neighbours.

As the war intensified, the young men who had volunteered their services to the war efforts became a familiar sight. There were those who joined the Royal Air Force (RAF) and the British Army. Although the slogan was "England expects every man to do his duty", many women rose to the challenge by joining the Auxiliary Territorial Services (ATS). While hundreds of recruits left the island to their designated outpost, there still existed a buzz in the city of Kingston. The soldiers' uniform became a status symbol. The Home Guards, established for local defence, and the American soldiers (an American base was sited on the island) were popular among the women who were fascinated with the uniform and the prospect of marriage.

The street singers, 'Slim and Sam', whose heydays were 1930s and 1940s, captured the mood at that time with their topical lyrics:-

O, the gal dem
Wouldn't go for a man
Except dem have occasion
To wear uniform
If you want to see them
Blow like a storm
Fool around dem bwoy friend
Whey wear uniform

I still recall the tearful eyes of some parents and wives and the endless talk about their everyday lives before the war began. They could then purchase foodstuff and clothing without having to adhere to the government controls. Foreign commodities became scarce, i.e. long grain white rice, a popular item that formed a staple diet, could no longer arrive from Hong Kong, neither flour, condensed milk, soap and cod fish.

The East Indian farmers tried growing rice locally and additional supplies came from Guyana but the quality was not so good, so at weekends the children helped to extract the untreated rice grains from its yellow pod. Sunday without rice and peas was unheard of among a vast majority of Kingstonians. So with no easy way of purchasing this scarce commodity the women often used their ingenious creativity by adding macaroni to the seasoned peas liquid, thus presenting a delicious rice and peas camouflage dish, and tasty it was too! Families would giggle when talking about their delicious Sunday dinner.

Jamaicans always have the tendency to laugh at their own dilemma, even when caught in a ridiculous situation, which rendered them helpless. Smiles and laughter of the needy do not always signify happiness. Our renowned folklorist, the late Hon. Louise Bennett–Coverley put this succinctly in her poem, 'Wartime Grocery':-

Aye you see me dah talk and laugh?
Mi no happy yaw Miss Vie
For how mi gwine ketch up mi body
If mi can't get condensed milk
And rice fi buy

I do not recall any bombings on the island. No desperate hurrying to an air raid shelter nor wailing voices. There were, however, regular sounds of the air raid sirens particularly at nights when the Air Raid Patrol (ARP) Wardens could be heard knocking on the gates in the neighbourhood and shouting in voices that conveyed a great sense of urgency - "Turn off your lights!" The commands were instantly followed and the Kerosene lamps and candles would be lighted. For those people who had neither of the former, a make shift concoction of a piece of cord or surgical lint was lighted while it swam in a saucer of water and coconut oil.

At first the air raid sirens, the shouting of the ARP Wardens and the shadows of the faint light near my bed gave me an exciting snug feeling. I would lie there all entranced watching the flickering light as it encircled the dark corner of its immediate space. I could not quite understand why the adults spoke in hushed voices, almost in a whisper.

As the war intensified and the sinking of the ships became prevalent in the Atlantic Ocean, Jamaica's importation of goods was discontinued, so were our chances of exporting our bananas, oranges, sugar and coffee. These commodities were piled up in the warehouses and had to be released to the local markets, where they were sold cheaply. Suddenly the Kingstonians started to make use of their own produce.

The street vendors passed around in the residential areas, shouting "Buy your green banana" and the mischievous children would call out teasingly "Meet me round the corner". There was one vendor who used to shout "Jamaica long grain rice" but everybody knew that with the acute rice shortages what she really meant was "Long finger green bananas" – those were the days!

Papa experienced the same problem - no form of textiles, shoe nor haberdasheries could be imported to keep the business going. He began to market locally made earthenware utensils colloquially known as 'Yabba' cooking pots, water pitcher, bowls, jugs and flowerpots.

Papa also became a local distributor, providing facilities for the storing and distribution of grains, i.e. peas, corn, rice and other locally grown foods for the retail trade. The wartime restrictions brought increased economic hardships and unemployment. Strikes were looming particularly among the dockworkers aided by Alexander Bustamante, the Labour leader. It is said that at a meeting with the would-be strikers, he made inflammatory speeches and utterances in violation of the Defence of the Realm Act. He was therefore detained, for 17 months, together with two other activists on the order of the Colonial Representative of the day, Governor Sir Arthur Richards.

Although the political activities were somewhat cooled during the later years of the war, Alexander Bustamante and

Norman Washington Manley QC (the two cousins), together with their respective supporters, were forging along with plans for constitutional change.

There were lots of discussions about the number of people who were brought to the island, many were refugees from Eastern Europe, particularly Gibraltar, escaping the tyranny of the war. A rehabilitation camp was established at Mona, the present site of the University of the West Indies.

Papa had always been keen to enlighten me on what went on in the island, so on a bright Sunday afternoon he took me to Mona, near Papine, St Andrew, to show me where the refugees were living and perhaps to get a glimpse of them. On our arrival at the Gibraltar Camp, we stood outside the large area, bounded by a high chain linked fence and peered through the gaps. Shortly afterwards a well-built African-Jamaican man with a machete in a sheath by his side greeted us and beckoned us to the gate. My father told him that he was curious and wanted to show me what a refugee camp looked like. He grinned, took his peeked cap off and scratched his head a bit and then offered to show us around.

There were rows and rows of wooden barracks with partitioned areas, consisting of army cots, chairs, tables and a large communal hall, with a platform at one end. We were told that the refugees were numbered for security reasons and allowed out each day between 8am – 10pm. Soon after the end of the war, most of the refugees left the island with the vast majority going to the USA.

Queuing at local shops and depots of large distributors for scarce commodities on Saturdays was an activity many children joined in. To return home, after waiting for several hours outside a shop, with the much-needed gallon of kerosene oil, rice, flour, soap and any other scarce items brought joy to the adults. The treat of ice cream, lolly and sweets gave us encouragement to return for more shopping the following Saturday. My main Saturday activity was, however, sitting under the counter or in the small room adjacent to the store reading my book but sometimes the noisy commotion made by the crowd of market women and peasant farmers distracted my attention.

While Papa and Mother Dear were busy attending to the impatient customers, I often stopped reading and focused my attention on what was going on. I found it quite fascinating to watch and listen to the country folks. The phrasing of their sentences, the vocabulary they used and their dress, was as varied as 'Joseph's Coat of many colours'.

I soon learnt to distinguish between people from different parishes, the dialect spoken with beauty and rhythm, their gestures, especially when greeting each other, their uninhibited laughter - all were like music to my ears. Equally, on becoming displeased about anything or with anyone, their hands would be put akimbo, the posterior pushed back, the chest moved forward and the most colourful speech would be projected from the injured person. The response would be equalled by the recipient. This verbal exchange is called 'tracing'.

Whenever the women's vocabulary got over the top, Papa would sternly show them to the door. More often than not, they would calm down but never without the occasional crossing of the eyes, kissing of the teeth, or threats like "a gwine meck me bwoy friend beat you til you sof". The other women would laugh loudly and everything would then be back to normal. I used to enjoy the humour; it was like going to the theatre.

Papa knew how to treat some of the outrageous customers, with a perfect blend of graciousness and distance.

Western Kingston during those war years, when I was a child, used to be extremely hectic on Saturdays. A vast majority of the rural poor, together with the urban uneducated and unemployed people, devised various ways of earning a living either by scuffling, deceit or being a sly rascal. The street singers of the 1930s and 40s in their social commentary responded to the everyday happenings with humour, self-mockery and deep understanding of the racial discrimination and poverty. Those characters, even today, are depicted in the folklore and Anansi stories of the island. Slim and Sam often stopped outside Papa's store to sing, among the hustle and bustle of the shoppers. Sam usually started the strumming of his guitar strings and Slim waited for his note to begin, some people passing by would crowd around them requesting the tune they would like to hear, with their pennies ready to buy the 'tract' (that is the printed words of the songs).

War songs were mostly tinged with humour, sadness and an unreserved determination for Britain to be victorious. So in those final days of the war, heart-warming news like –

'Troops land in France'
'Great success in Normandy'
'Allies trap 10,000 Germans'
'Mussolini Fall – Italy liberated'

would be included in their songs.

And then, that blessed day when news of the conditional surrender of Germany brought the World War 2 to an end – Jamaicans cheered. "The war is over" was on the lips of most people.

I had grown to look forward to the day there was news about the wonderful celebrations in Britain about Londoners crowding in front of Buckingham Palace cheering and dancing for joy. The King, Queen and the two young Princesses, Elizabeth and Margaret-Rose, waving from the balcony, the colourful parade marching by. I cannot recall any public celebration party in Kingston but no doubt the Governor and his fellow diplomats celebrated in style.

It is close upon four o'clock in the afternoon and Papa is about to close the store to customers. The eminent closure of the business day could be clearly noticed by the hustle and bustle of the last minute shoppers, children from the nearby Ebenezer School, which I attended, passing by. The teachers greeted Papa on their way home, and amidst all this is the spectacle of the casual gait of the men approaching Papa's store to begin their evening of deliberations. Most of the seven or eight men are carrying reading materials consisting of Garvey's 'Negro World' and 'Blackman' magazines. The main topic of the day included contents of the Daily Gleaner (Jamaica's foremost Newspaper) especially the pages 'Letters to the Editor'.

The constitutional proposals became the main point for discussion by Papa and his regular group members. The main aim of the gathering was to educate each other about political and developmental issues. Before long, I would be called upon to read the text of these books aloud for the men who were unable to read the written words, but who possessed an excellent power of grasping and internalising concepts that were being discussed.

I can recall stumbling over words I did not know on a number of occasions, or mispronouncing words unfamiliar to me, but I would be asked to re-read the sentence, break down the different words into syllables until the correct words were found. This exercise often left me wondering how they knew it was wrong. In time, I soon realised that by inventing words into the text I was making the sentence meaningless to their ears.

As I reached adolescence this every evening chore truly became boring and, much to Papa's annoyance, I began to bypass the store on my way home from school. Papa would be quite irate with me; the force of his dominance was frightening. His long lectures were centred on doing good to others and selflessness.

His fury, oh, frightened me, but the sound of my stepmother's voice, her gentle touch, concerns and care, which created a sensation of warmth and safety are fused in my childhood memory. Indeed, she was my best friend. It was as though we were inmates, living in a walled city, enjoying a much-needed breath of fresh air, whenever Papa was away on business.

CHAPTER 2

MY POST WAR 'GROUNDINGS'

With World War 2 behind us, and the newly inaugurated political parties – Jamaica Labour Party (JLP) and the People's National Party (PNP) - poised for attaining power from the imminent election results, everyone was in a state of euphoria. The place was alive, each party became a movement and the gatherings sang hymns, party allegiance songs, prayed and heaped verbal attacks on those in the other party. Two songs echoed throughout Jamaica, in mountains, towns and coastal plains. One was the allegiance song of the Jamaica Labour Party with the chorus "We will follow Bustamante till we die" and the People's National Party song "Trumpeters Arise" ended with "Land of my birth I pledge to thee, loyal and faithful true to thee". This pledge was accompanied by a raised fisted hand.

The young people, in general, chose the PNP. We were mesmerised by the changes that were taking place. Manley's evocation of a spirit of national unity, his appeal to history and to faith endeared him to us. His speeches echoed Marcus Garvey's call to break away from "the imperial version of history" and replace it with one that was Jamaican. He spoke of not only history but also of faith and destiny.

"We had a great struggle" he said, "to overcome a struggle with ourselves, with our own mental lethargy and with the inertia of our historical background". Constitutional reforms, he explained, was only the beginning, Universal Adult Suffrage was the means for bringing all the people of Jamaica into the political life of the country; and Self-Government was seen as a way of life and not merely as a transfer of power from Britain to Jamaica.

The reforms were essential for nurturing in Jamaicans a spirit of independence and a sense of responsibility. We were reminded of some Caribbean people who achieved this by revolution, for example Toussaint L'Ouverture and the people of Haiti and Jose Marti and the people of Cuba. Jamaica has heroes such as Cudjoe and Sharp, but their struggle was for freedom, not nationhood, nor the right to vote at elections nor the granting of self-government.

We used to applaud Manley with all the vigour we could muster.

My interest in public life was illuminated by a number of Manley's addresses to which our PNP Group, the 'Ukraine' in Hannah Town, Kingston, was ever present. His special unity of spirit and vitality of purpose stirred us to the deeper understanding of the forces outside and among us; they dominated our daily lives. He taught us to unite enthusiasm with reasonable action.

As I grew up, listening to the men's discussions in Papa's store and Manley's call for a spirit of National Unity, I could not avoid taking more than a casual interest in other aspects of community life around me. For instance, I became interested in the joblessness of women and the widespread suffering of children particularly in the rural areas of the island that led to the internal migration to Kingston and created the overpopulation of the City.

A number of women uprooted themselves from their various Parishes in search of the limited job prospects in the domestic service. These move, however, brought with it much hardship and emotional turmoil. Amidst all this, a group of educated women responded to what they saw. This was significant because at the time there were no mother figures, no female symbol of compassion in the dying plantation society. However, this small group of African-Jamaican women joined forces with Molly Huggins, the wife of the New Governor from England, to form the Women's Federation Movement in 1944 - a direct replica of the Women's Institute Movement in the UK with the Conservative motto "Our Homes and our Country".

Some of the African-Jamaican women had come into prominence as members of the Teacher's Union, Welfare Officers, Writers, Feminists, public-spirited upper class citizens and Champions of Children's Rights. They included Amy Bailey, Mary Farquhson, Edith Dalton-James, Ethlyn Rodd, Edris Allan (later Lady Allan), Lilly Mae-Burke, Una Marson, Gladys Longbridge (later Lady Bustamante) and Mary Morris-Knibb who also served as Chairperson for the Provincial Board of the Moravian Church of the Redeemer where I served on the senior choir until my journey to London.

During my early years, I took an interest in, and learnt about, those women who led the way in establishing a tradition of social concern by reaching out beyond the dividing lines of colour, race and class. They charted a worthy and indispensable role for women in Jamaican society working earnestly towards putting an end to the marginalisation of women. They understood that it was their task to invest womanhood with its proper meaning and dignity. The idea of women coming together to enhance the life of the less fortunate was greatly appreciated but the Mass Wedding Strategy, spearheaded by Molly Huggins, to force monogamy on Jamaica's black unmarried parents signalled the end of the popularity and appeal of the Women's Federation Movement.

Schooling and Education

I attended Brown's Private Infant School in Charles Street, West Kingston until I reached the statutory age of seven. I then became a pupil at the Co-educational Multi-Cultural Grade 'A' Methodist Church/State administered Ebenezer School where I remained until I was aged fourteen. Despite its nickname 'Ebenezer de Dumplin Squeezer', Ebenezer had a glorious tradition for passes in the Jamaica Local Examinations and successful scholarship to the island's secondary fee-paying schools. The school's records of children from working class families who went on to achieve academic success and successful positions were unique.

The staff comprised a body of devoted caring men and women who taught children from diverse races from across the socio-economic strata within the community. Mr E J Hendricks, the headmaster for a number of years, was nicknamed, 'Squire wid the bald head' and he had a passionate love for the English Language, English Literature, Poetry and choral music. I revelled in the poetry he encouraged us to appreciate and the prose he taught us to understand. Indeed, my love for words, their correct spelling and the joys of choral music were all his doing.

The students came from the Jewish, Chinese, Lebanese, Cuban, East Indian, Panamanian, Mixed Race and African-Jamaican communities. We said the same prayers and sang the same English, Scottish and Irish songs. There was no apparent stipulation made between the Jews and Gentiles. However, by the age of twelve years, differences became clearer. I suspect, fired by financial status, educational pursuits and the need to reaffirm their cultural identity, the Jews and the Chinese parents sent their children to their own specialist schools. The others, including a small percentage of African-Jamaicans, would be sent to fee-paying High Schools and Colleges and a recognisable number of children of East Indian and African-Jamaican origins would remain in the state system up to the age of sixteen. Some would pursue vocational training or nothing at all. Such was the colonial education system during my school days.

This magnificent two-floored timber building was situated on a corner plot which had a large manicured lawn, beautifully well-kept gardens with wrought iron railings around its perimeter bounded by Darling Street, Ebenezer Lane and Spanish Town Road. This was opposite the Coronation Municipal Market that was opened in 1937 in commemoration of King George VI ascension to the British throne. At the far end of the lawn and playing field were a large flagpole and a number of miniature trees, many owing their origin to the Empire Day Celebrations on the 24th May. This day was a Public Holiday throughout the Island when girls dressed in white 'midi' blouses and navy pleated skirts and boys in brown khaki shirt and matching short trousers sang out praises for King and Country. The Union Flag enthusiastically and proudly waved to the strain of 'Rule Britannia', 'Land of Hope and Glory' and

Flag of Britain proudly waving
Over land and distant sea
We salute thee
And we pray
God to bless
Our land today

At the section, 'we salute thee', each of us stood at attention and saluted the fluttering Union Flag. It was then hoisted on to the flagpole by the Headmaster, while the senior boys planted a tree on the lawn to mark the end of the ceremony.

The bell rang out, signalling the time for us to line up. We marched into school in pairs, with heads held high, shoulders up, in step with swinging arms in full military fashion. The boys in particular, as part of the keep-fit exercises, adopted to a form of militarism, each holding into place, sticks to represent rifles – we girls had so much admiration for their bold, determined steps, that at playtime we made every effort to emulate them.

It was sometimes before I really understood the meaning of the songs and indeed their significance. '*So after the teachers drill dem songs ina we head and hart, dem come out ina wi voice*', and sing I used to sing.

But the best part of the celebration for me, was when the dinner bell rang. Normally I am required to have lunch with Papa and Mother Dear at the store but on this special day Papa allowed me to remain for school lunch to join with the other children for the national treat of 'Bun and Cheese', sweetie and freshly made lemonade drink. This was a reward from His Majesty's Inspector of Schools for singing out our heart to Britain and providing a pleasing spectacle for the people who crowded and pressed themselves against the rails to watch the ceremony. They all clapped, the teachers clapped and said, "well done children". Their faces glowed with pride like Papa's carbine gas lantern.

Adjacent to the end of the lawn area and playground was the Ebenezer Methodist Church and Cemetery with the caretaker's cottage on the left. During those childhood days, together with others, we roamed the vast parcel of land situated beyond the cemetery, nicknamed 'Back-a-wall'. That area was exclusively populated by people of East Indian descent. Their environment being significantly different to all others, attracted us, because of the variety of fruits and vegetables they cultivated which we could get free of cost from our Indian school friends. Adults went there too, particularly at weekends to purchase freshly cut green vegetables.

Their detached houses were made from timber with identical features, large verandas and a pond in front of each house, from which water was taken in large watering cans to irrigate the soil. I remember too well the serenity of the area and watching the unhurried steps of the East Indian women in their white saris, as they tended the vegetable plots. More often, the men would be crouched on the veranda with their heads hanging forward and their hands tucked motionless between their knees or rolling their cigars that they made from the tobacco plant or sometimes they would be peacefully smoking away.

Come the month of late October to November on the darkest night of the year we were drawn to the main 'Indian Colony', as we often called it, to watch the Hindu celebration of 'Diwali'. Although we did not fully understand the language nor the significance of the symbolism, we enjoyed the sword fights and the singing and dance displays put on by the elegantly dressed bejewelled Indian women.

As I grew older, I was prepared for the Jamaica Local Examinations. I was selected along with a few children from other schools to attend the Examination Tutorial Centre; this was based at the Senior School adjacent to the West Race Course, part of which is now 'Heroes Park'. There, under the tutorship of Miss Olga Banks, I gained passes in the First and Second Jamaica Local Examinations. The Third year pass at that time served as admission to Teacher's Training College or other academic pursuits. But not being keen on teaching, Papa decided that I should go to St Martin High School in the Cross Roads area to prepare for Cambridge Examinations. My academic weakness in Foreign Languages did not augur well for my success and it became quite clear that I needed to change directions – indeed sudden regrettable changes did occur.

More Changes

These regrettable changes seem to come hard and fast.

Papa's bullying behaviour and controlling tactics soon became unbearable. His tantrums were displayed without any provocation and Mother Dear wanted a much quieter life, so they decided on a separation.

There I was again at the age of fifteen experiencing changes, a change to which I had not contributed. Suddenly, I was told to pack all my belongings, because he would be taking me to stay with my birth mother permanently. Although living with mother was a much easier and uncomplicated life-style that I felt I would like, I also felt that I was leaving behind an aspect of life that I enjoyed. My love and adoration for Mother Dear was unconditional and I did not really know my birth mother except for her fleeting visits, so the pain of leaving Mother Dear's care was over-whelming.

The current scripture lesson at school at the time was Ruth and Naomi – taken from Ruth, Chapter 1 verses 16-18 of the Old Testament. One day while Mother Dear and I were alone, I found myself dramatising the biblical story of Ruth's reluctance to part from Naomi to express my feelings of sadness, I so wanted to stay with her. In my bewilderment, I held on to her arm and repeated the verse that I had memorised:-

Entreat me not to leave thee
Nor to return from following after you
For whether thou goest
I will go
And where thou lodgest
I will lodge
Thy people shall be my people
And thy god, My God

I could sense the shock and the loss she was experiencing during those electrically charged moments. Locked in each other arms, it seemed the most comforting thing to do; we wept!

A few days later Papa took me to my mother's home where I remained until my marriage seven years later. Mother Dear and I met on several occasions until she immigrated to Cuba. We eventually lost contact.

My education continued at the West India Commercial College – Manchester Square, where I followed the Commercial skills option for girls who were expected to help their fathers in businesses or to seek Secretarial posts. I successfully mastered the subjects and attained passes (RSA) in Pitman's Shorthand, typewriting and bookkeeping.

In the meantime, I attended one half-a-day per week sessions at the Kingston Technical School, Hanover Street, Kingston and acquired skills in Domestic Science now called House Craft. However, I opted out of this course because Papa rated it as a 'waste of valuable time'.

During this period, one of Marcus Garvey's visions for the establishment of an institution for further education and training began to gain the consideration and support of academics, visionaries and nationalists. The plan quickly gathered momentum and by 1948, the University of the West Indies was cited in Mona on those areas of land on which the Gibraltar Camp stood. I recall with immense pride my voluntary contribution, at the age of sixteen years, when on summer holidays from college I went to assist with the volume of correspondence handled by the Extra Mural Department in preparation for the installation ceremony of Princess Alice and the Earl of Athlone as its first Chancellor.

Papa's insistence on me to spend every evening after college reading for the men, left me totally bewildered. I desperately needed to concentrate on my course work but Papa would not relent. His demands grew out of proportion, and sadly, my resentment spiralled. On some occasions, I did not report to the store after college.

One evening soon after my arrival there, without a word of warning, he removed his leather belt from his waist and thrashed me mercilessly in the store, in full view of the public. Of course, Mother Dear was no longer there to cushion the blows. Things came to ahead. Tried as I did, I could not, forgive Papa for this outrageous act. It left me feeling gutted and embarrassed. I felt that my self-esteem had been trampled on. I could no longer tolerate his bullying. I think he probably did touch a raw nerve by woefully underestimating the depth of my resentment and the volume of my emotions. At that time, I was two weeks past my seventeenth birthday.

As a result of this incident, our relationship developed into a painful and difficult one. For several weeks I did not visit him. Papa then had a conversation with my mother in which he stated his intention to send me to 'Liberia' where a group of his Garveyite colleagues had recently settled. He felt that there existed good opportunities for me to join in the much talked about development programmes with the Liberian people. Mother was in total disagreement with the idea and often dismissed the plan as "just a little madness". I immediately went into hiding from Papa. Not long afterwards, he ceased the payment of my school fees and maintenance. As a result of the foregoing, I stayed away from the store.

Earning a Wage and more...

With no school fees and no maintenance, I looked around for Secretarial employment and soon joined the new breed of African-Jamaican women who were beginning to emerge with practical skills and qualifications on to the job market. But the opportunities available were few and un-enticing.

Many young women were groomed for marriage. Others worked in the teaching profession, nursing or the Civil Service while some chased around for dead end jobs. Educational advancement at the time, for even those from middle-income families, was unreachable.

Two of my friends, who happened to be of mixed parentage, introduced me to the manager of a renowned photographic accessories establishment in Down Town Kingston that catered mostly to tourists. Having attended the interview, I was offered a post that it seemed was designed to keep me well away from the public's gaze. The manager was quite open about what he was doing - "I can't make the clientele know that you work here, or I would be in trouble" he told me, in an apologetic tone. I did not accept the position under such circumstances; this was blatant racial discrimination.

Like so many other black school leavers, I felt blocked at every turn. I began to think seriously about my next move when a letter arrived from my former College offering me an assistant teaching post at the College. I accepted out of loyalty and partly to fill the gap that existed in my life. Once I had settled in the role, I began to enjoy what I did and was further encouraged by the achievements of the students who, over time, produced satisfactory examination results.

My concentration on the role I played at the College was absolute or supposed to be. However, my raging hormones made me susceptible to an unusual form of activity that led me on the path of a fatal diversion. I thought I had fallen in love. I had no idea what that was supposed to mean. I joined the popular group of young people and in a very short time, I was struck with the realisation that I may be pregnant.

Finding out if one is pregnant was not a simple matter but eight weeks without a period you are fairly sure. I was nineteen years old and had no clear idea what having a baby would entail but I recognised that I was indeed a lost girl. If I had a baby, I would want to regain the status of a single woman after the baby was born. My mother soon suspected my predicament. Her disappointment was shown in an acute way but she seemed far more understanding and considerate to me than I could have ever imagined.

Much to my embarrassment, my mother met with the young man's parents to share the unexpected news. This was momentarily met with a tinge of sadness but was soon greeted with the joy of welcoming a first grand-child into their family. The offer of marriage swiftly followed but although I knew that there would have been disappointed family members on both sides, I could not be persuaded to go along with their plans. I said "no", as defiantly as I dared. I did not really think I was in love; in fact I did not really care.

I was, however, sure that I did not want to become the wife of a disdainful and authoritarian person, as I soon began to observe. The family was very supportive to my material needs, showing care, respect and understanding throughout. My best friend, Jas Gordon, encouraged me to go ahead with the marriage for the baby's sake and if it proved problematic I would only have to let it be known that he had left me - "better to be an abandoned wife, than an unmarried mother", she warned. I just could not warm to the idea. My mood moved up and down like a yo-yo, crying one moment, bent on self-improvement the next.

At last the baby arrived on 17th February 1951. Fathers weren't allowed anywhere near the delivery room. I got to the Recovery Room and there were mother and Sister Vassel, our neighbour, and senior sister at the Jubilee Maternity Hospital beaming and showing relief that I had delivered safely.

Returning home with my baby son conjured up mixed feelings. I was very happy that phase of my trauma was over but conscious of the curious eyes of people around and the stigma attached to the unmarried mother and her child that was still very strong in our society and very noticeable in terms of how you were seen by others. I therefore vowed not to be caught out in such a situation again. His family members were fascinated with the baby's features and boasted about the strong family resemblance. The conversation sometimes became annoying.

My mother's strategy in dealing with this mishap was to, in time, subject me to a heartbreak that I have re-lived on countless occasions. Mother's family and indeed most of whom retained the West African extended family tradition, usually took on full responsibility for the first off-spring of their children who were unmarried. The children would become a main stay of their household. The birth of my first child, a boy, was thus claimed. On the ninth day after his birth, I was allowed to sit on the veranda of the house with my baby, to receive the curious visitors, relations and friends. My mother then declared to all and sundry, "This one is mine". Although I was aware of the family practice, I took the announcement lightly. I thought she could not be serious, not in these modern times but her intention was real!

I returned to the West India Commercial College seven months later. Oh the relief was grand! The exhilaration I experienced made me feel like a new person.

By the beginning of October, I also resumed my social activities, so off I went to the St Bernard's Choral Society rehearsal just in time to participate in the preparation for the Christmas programmes. I threw myself in the things I had to do and enjoyed every moment doing the things I found interesting and rewarding – the work with my students, looking after the baby, attending rehearsals and participating in choral performances. There were a few new members of the Choral Society and among them was this fine looking man who seemed to have instantly started to shower an inordinate degree of attention on me. A platonic friendship developed over time. We often talked about our backgrounds, childhood, parents: experiences, ideals and aspiration.

I soon gathered that he had come from a small family group, comprised of one brother and a sister, two aunts, who were sisters of his late mother, cousins, one of whom is a member of the Chorale, and had invited him to join, and a father who left for the USA, when he was a boy at school, long before his mother departed. He talked about his guardian, whom he referred to as Auntie – on his mother's deathbed she promised her dear friend to take care of her three children, although she knew that this would have been a difficult task, particularly in financial terms. He was the eldest at 12 years old. He remembered this calm God-fearing communicant member of the local Anglican Church making every effort to get them to attend the church services on Sundays and single-handedly, through all her difficulties, to keep them in school. I empathised with him and thought that to a certain extent she was able to instil a measure of discipline in her charge despite the uphill task with which she was confronted.

Like all the other members, we shared a good jovial relationship meeting on Wednesday evenings and Sunday afternoons to perfect the programmed activities.

Months later, I arrived home after paying a visit to my aunt, on Mother's behalf. Mother was wearing a frown, she did not seem happy, so I wondered if she was anticipating an unfavourable diagnosis about her sister's illness, so I hastened to give her the information I had received from Auntie. Having listened to what I had to report, she smiled and I thought that was it. Then she said, "I want to have a talk with you, a serious talk with you".

My heart skipped a beat.

"I think you need to sit down", she continued. "Why did you send that young man to speak to me, without telling me your intention? I do not want any more surprises".

I was shaking like a leaf caught in a whirlwind. I managed to ask "which young man? Did he give you a name?"

"He say his name is Cameron, do you know anyone by that name?"

I sat there staring at my Mother dumb founded.

"What have you got to say for yourself?" she asked in a raised tone.

It was some minutes before I replied. I told her, "Yes, I knew the person but I did not ask him to come to speak to you. I had no idea why he came to my house. He is a member of the Chorale".

"I can't recall seeing him before", she quickly replied.

"He is new", I informed her.

I felt awful, I had no intention of upsetting my mother in this way. I wanted things to move smoothly without any unpleasantness and now this. I did not attend rehearsal for about two weeks. Then he wrote to Mother – I did not want to read the letter, I expected her to tell him "get lost" but it seems she was reluctant to go that far.

A further two weeks went by. I sat on the veranda breathing in the aroma from the flowers in the garden and was struck by that coming from the frangipane that was in bloom at the bottom of the garden. I willed myself to walk down there to look at it but the depressive heat that evening brought on a feeling of lethargy, I just wanted to sit and stare into space. I realised that a form of confusion was setting in and I needed to sort out this worry that was creeping into my world. I noticed that Mother had fallen into a snooze, propped up in her favourite chair, at the other end of the veranda – baby was fast asleep, as usual, at that time of the evening. There was stillness around, except for the hissing from the sprinkler in the garden. I looked towards the sprinkler thinking that it was time to turn it off when my eyes focussed on this Mr Cameron approaching the gate. I rose from the chair immediately, disappeared into the living room and exited over the back fence.

I immediately thought that if I went to my friend's house I could see him when he gets to the bus stop on his return from my house. I found the situation very hard to manage.

However, Mother was quite understanding and after a repeat of my disappearing action she called a truce, got us together to talk about the situation. This, of course, gave him license to turn up at my house, now that he had Mother's permission.

Herb Cameron visited regularly, his manner was quite captivating. I eventually grew to love and respect him – so did mother. He was eager for us to get married but unfortunately, he lost his job during the planning stage of the wedding so we had to halt the arrangements. It was a few months before we could resume the preparation. The wedding that took place at the Moravian Church of the Redeemer, Kingston; and the birth of my first daughter were almost simultaneous and yes I was an elephantine bride, eight months pregnant! In those days, there were still a stigma attached to illegitimacy and I wanted to get my child inside the fence of respectability before she was born. I managed it by five weeks!

But although I could have been more radiantly slender had I waited until the baby was born, that wedding day brings back floods of emotions, most of which I have reflected on over the years with pleasure. The two choirs, of which we were both members, provided what turned out to be a full Choral Service launching us on the road to a happy life. I was not at all keen to move away from home, it was one of the most difficult decisions for me to make. Herb had to join our household and that baby, my second, was a home delivery in Greenwich Town, St Andrew, in my bedroom at Momie's home. I had booked to have her at the Jubilee Maternity Hospital, but she arrived soon after a brief labour with little time to get to the hospital. The midwife who lived just three houses away was called. I had always told her that I preferred to go to the hospital and there she was smiling on her way into my room.

Mother, having prepared Herb for the experience, asked him "Do you feel up to it"?

"Definitely, yes Mummy", he said.

"OK you can help then. Just give me a drink."

He got her a drink of Wincarnis wine, a beer for himself and a cup of mint tea for me.

There were then busily making preparations according to the midwife's instructions - "Ooh", the pain. Midwife announced that I was ready!

At that point, Momie said to Herb, "You go and dig a hole in the garden near the Papaya tree because we are going to have to put the afterbirth in it and get some more hot water. Come, come, move fast. She is in heavy pain".

Poor Herb, I looked at him and he was so pale …. he looked like he was going to have the baby! But we kept our eyes on each other. In the end he was very much a part of the delivery. When he saw that the baby was a girl ooh! He went outside to tell the neighbours, I could hear the voices and when he came back inside he seemed so uplifted, he couldn't stop smiling, he was so proud. The baby girl was born in the early hours of the 10th February 1953.

Three months later, we moved into our own accommodation. I had to leave my son with mother because she was vehemently opposed to him being brought up in another man's household.

I had to slowly learn to master the mechanics of housekeeping. This did not come naturally for me. I think my saving grace was that mother told Herb quite soon after he showed interest in marrying me that I would not be able to launder those lovely shirts he wore, so he should give serious thoughts to what he wanted to do – because she did not want him to curse her when she had departed this life. She went on to tell him that my father would not allow me anywhere near the kitchen nor the wash tub – she further said "However, she can prepare a good tasty meal". He laughed, but clearly not deterred by what she said, he would not be put off. His reply to her was that he could get someone else to take care of the laundry. He kept his promise, because once we had settled in our home he found a woman who did the laundry, including my white choir outfits, for a very long period. During that time, I practiced on two of his older shirts until I gained his approval. He was very particular about the quality and presentation of the shirts he wore; he even took to wearing detached collars that he could take to the dry cleaners.

Our accommodation was a house designed for two families. The landlady and her husband occupied the other section and, luckily, she took me under her wings and became more like a guardian or adopted mother who taught me many things about life. Managing a home, budgeting etc. I think she grew to value our moral and social behaviour and before long, she became a member of our church, continuing her spiritual life there for many years after I left for the UK.

My third child, a son, was born on 28th June 1955. My mother and Winston, my first son, came to spend a few weeks with us and that was wonderful. We so appreciated the help she gave during that time. I was now aged twenty-three and a mother of three children, happy, contented and enjoying my spiritual, literary and musical involvement in the community.

CHAPTER 3

FAREWELL JAMAICA

Memories came flowing back as I reflected on that Sunday evening in June, when my husband and I strolled through the park on our way home from evening service. The sky had been gradually setting from pumpkin, tangerine into a deep aubergine colour of the night and now was studded with stars. I happened to look up and called Herb's attention to the brilliant canopy which sometimes goes unappreciated by those too busy to survey nature's beauty. The cool gentle wind blew, as we held hands relishing the closeness, love and devotion we shared as man and wife. We mused about some of the little things our children, aged three and one year old, often did and said in their innocence and shared joy of their development as normal parents did. Happiness was ours.

As we got closer to home thoughts of the main theme of Rev S U Hastings' sermon came to mind, his explicit reference to the many changes that were taking place in our little Island, some viewed with apprehension, others as necessary for the development of the people and island as a whole. He stressed that new phenomenon of the popular music and lyrics, as bordering on severe lewdness and the un-Christian behaviour of many people. Herb mentioned how touched he was when Minister led prayers for the hundreds of people who were migrating to foreign lands, week by week, not at all a new occurrence.

Jamaicans have always travelled to distant lands in search of opportunities and adventure, but the sheer increase in number not only of men as customary, but of women and children gave cause for concern. However, I consoled myself in the belief that we would not be caught up in that movement. But alas, before long fate intervened, when to my utter disbelief and amazement, my husband told me that he was planning to migrate to the United Kingdom.

"You can't be serious" I said hastily, "have I done something?".

He looked me straight in the eyes, observed my absolute shock and calmly said "Oh no, no, you have not done anything to cause this. It's just that I was having a conversation with my sister and she suggested that I should go to England, as others are doing to seek a better future. So as she gave me the money for the fares I have decided to grasp the opportunity".

This was a lot of information for me to take in all at once but I did not fail to realise that a foregone conclusion had been reached and that I was in no way part of that decision-making process that would inevitably affect the lives of myself and our children. I felt like a ton of bricks had fallen on my head, leaving it spinning uncontrollably. My mouth became parched and I was engulfed with fear and loss. My sister-in-law, by virtue of acting as arbiter in the direction of her brother's life, had for good or ill, ultimately changed mine.

He left the shores of Jamaica two weeks later for London, promising he would be back in three to five years at the most, as indicated on his passport. Despite the short notice there was a large attendance at the farewell party the night before his departure – an odd party, however, in that the guest of honour whose friends had come to toast his departure was physically absent. I later learnt from one of the family members that he was spending his last night with another person who shares our relationship. I was dumb founded!

The devastation of the sudden separation lingered for a long time. I looked forward each week for his letter, which was a great source of comfort and hope. Although my distress as a woman, wife and mother remained immense, I had to maintain a sense of normality. The Kingston Moravian Church of the Redeemer of which we were communicant members, the senior choir and the St Bernard's Choral Society served as my immediate community, affording my children and I material and spiritual comfort and immeasurable social interaction. I had barely settled into the routine of caring for my children, helped by my Mother's unwavering support, and immersing myself in social and cultural activities when nine months later he wrote to say that he will be purchasing my ticket so I should prepare to join him in London in six weeks. In that same letter he blamed me for spoiling his plan for our eldest daughter (my only daughter at the time) to permanently remain with his sister after the summer holidays. I knew nothing about this plan to split up our children.

In despair, I watched the letter fall to the floor. I always felt that he would come back. That is what he had promised; that was what I had expected - not to be told to leave my children behind to go off to a strange land! My emotions ran riot through my body.

Getting Ready to Leave

There were many important and vital decisions for me to make in very little time. In bewilderment and fear, my helplessness found solace in prayer; on my trembling knees,

I bowed down and conversed with my God, asking him for guidance, wisdom and understanding. I felt wrenched from my children in a similar manner when I was wrenched from my husband. My ancestors experienced being wrenched from their homelands in Africa to be bound and chained en route to America and the Caribbean. And here I was contemplating an unwilling move from Jamaica to Britain via the Atlantic Ocean.

The complexity of the preparation and actual departure from the shores of my beloved Island remains with me to this day. On this rare occasion I ventured on a solo trip to visit Aunt Jane, in the district of Thompson Town, Clarendon, where my Mother's family had made their home for over a century; a home I remember with pleasure. It was exciting to meet, sleep and discuss with several members of the extended family. Visiting the family cemetery was an education in itself, that in such a short time, I was able to read, ponder and reflect on the lives of my ancestors, many of whom I had never met, but the colourful stories often told about them gave me the feeling of having met them. For those whom I knew throughout my childhood, seeing their tombstones brought back poignant memories.

Towering above them all was the memorial to Great-Grandmother Richards and Grandmother Sarah Thomas affectionately called Cousin Queen by the folks in the district. She was an ardent member of the Baptist Church and although over sixteen stone in weight, she carried her body with dignity and pride. She strode for miles around the villages, hills and valleys tending to the sick, consoling and counselling the afflicted. Her strict, traditional upbringing of love and discipline was displayed not only to her own six children but also to anyone having to stay in her home and there were many!

The Jamaican family households always extended care and affection to children and young people whose parents, for some reason or other, were unable to care for them. That form of adoption was agreed through a verbal promise with trust as the by-word. The practice had no legal status, was unenforceable in a court of law, but was practiced widely throughout the island. This age-old extended family pattern may have, in some way, encouraged the early Jamaican migrants to the UK and USA to leave their children to the daily care and upbringing to a trusted adult.

Unfortunately leaving children behind to live and work thousands of miles away brings a crisis of separation and loss for all concern. The psychological effects of this activity had been grossly under-estimated. My three children, aged five, three and one year respectively, were to experience the same dilemma. I knew no other way. Reluctantly I packed my bags assured that my Mother would take good care of them while I look to the future. Those final days were hectic and full of my determination to absorb the pain I was feeling. Although I resented the cruelty of my fate, I had to keep smiling and certainly did. Going to England in those days was highly glamorised and those looking on expected me to be over excited. The St Bernard's Choral Society and its energetic conductor, George Martin, who incidentally was the best man at my wedding, organised a wonderful farewell party in my honour.

⌒

Following the speeches and the refreshment, members regrouped and did a rendition of the beautiful song, 'The End of a Perfect Day". Composed by the American, Carrie Jacobs-Bond, this song became a World War 1 anthem that

Paul Robeson recorded soon after World War 2. The words are so inspiring and had such an influence on me, it must be recorded here:

The End of a Perfect Day (1910)
Music and lyrics by Carrie Jacobs-Bond

When you come to the end of a perfect day
And you sit alone with your thought
While the chimes ring out with a carol gay
For the joy that the day has brought,
Do you think what the end of a perfect day
Can mean to a tired heart
When the sun goes down with a flaming ray,
And the dear friends have to part?

Well, this is the end of a perfect day,
Near the end of a journey, too;
But it leaves a thought that is big and strong,
With a wish that is kind and true.
Mem'ry has painted this perfect day
With colors that never fade,
And we find, at the end of a perfect day,
The soul of a friend we've made.

By the time they began the second verse, there was not a dry eye in that room. It certainly was not easy for me to say goodbye.

Morning worship on the following day was tinged with mixed feelings, everyone was sad to see me go but joyful that I would be reunited with my husband. Minister's sermon was quite appropriate for the occasion and the senior choir's rendition was inspirational and touching. A couple of days before I was due to leave, Auntie and my two cousins came from the country to see me off, a pleasant and loving gesture. She brought me a few large yams, dried sorrel, homemade chocolate, root ginger and pimento seeds. The ginger and pimento seeds were put in the bottles of rum. I was told that it was good medication for pain in the joints during cold weather. Also packed and sealed were some ceresee bush for tummy ache, my Dutch pot and some ground provisions.

The large suitcase was already packed but not sealed. A few hours before I was due to leave the house I was ordered to open the case so that Auntie could take a look at the clothes I was taking. She looked at every garment separately - my white dresses that I normally wear to church were quickly removed from the case.

"Why do you want to take these white clothes to England?" Auntie asked and I explained that I had been told to take all my clothes with me. She kissed her teeth with startling resonance, followed by her verbal disapproval.

"Carry white clothes to dat dey cole place whey no sun no shine? Foolishness, mi can give all dis to di pickney dem fi wear to church". And so I was divested of everything white in my suitcase. I was unhappy about this, but could not dream of arguing with my Auntie, especially that my Mother agreed with her taking them.

They consoled me by saying that when I got to England I would be able to replace them easily, "the things are quite cheap up there", they had said.

The sun was still high in the sky, on that February afternoon when I set out to visit my familiar area in Western Kingston where my teenaged years were spent. It was absolutely important that I see those people who had influenced my life as I grew up, before leaving the island. Mrs Mack who had always designed my clothes had to be given the opportunity to perform her task.

As I strolled along North Street, passing the St Ann Catholic School, I reflected on those early days when, as a teenager, our group of five friends used outside the school gate as a rendezvous during the long hot evenings. Our conversations and debates were focused on our island's history, community issues, influential figures and politics. We were quite interested in party politics and were followers of the People's National Party. Although we were not eligible to vote as we were under twenty-one years, we were a force to be reckoned with.

Our group, The Ukraine PNP Group, Hannah Town, attracted potential political candidates to the area because when it came to campaigning, they could count on us for positive feedback on the trends, level of support and even the suitability of potential candidates. My parents were not attracted to the Party Political Campaign meetings but I certainly was. Despite their foreboding, I would sneak out of the house at nights to cheer my favourites as they took the platform. The excitement was exhilarating. To us freedom, justice and hope were in sight.

But after all the excitement, Mother would be waiting for me behind the gate on my return to 'merry my bottom' but that did not in any way distract me from this informative pastime. We sometimes became mischievous and playful by teasing the array of unique characters who usually 'hang out' at their favourite spots, adding colour and humour with their peculiar ways of dress and eloquent use of the dialect.

Outside the school brought back some vivid memories of my teenaged years. The overweight chemist was sitting outside his drugstore as he had done for years, ready (as usual) for a little gossip and Mr Chung, the Chinese grocer, waved frantically as I approached the pavement.

The tenement yards were now in sight, the tamarind tree at number 38 hanged heavily over the fence; as a girl, I have enjoyed several glasses of frothy drink from that fruit. The Aurelia Bush, Love Bush and Ivy spread their glossy green and mauve foliage over the brightly painted wooden fences with people seated on their veranda, looking out to the lane and enjoying the cool evening breeze. Some young people were standing outside their gates, just hanging out. The evening shadows fell, twilight as it is called, the soft murmuring from the voices of neighbours were heard talking over their fences; in the tenement yards dogs were barking and children playing games - typical sounds one heard in certain areas of Kingston at evening time.

What made that particular evening untypical was the presence of an uneasy, dull feeling that felt as though something of a catastrophic nature was eminent. Darkness began to fall. It seemed so sudden and the sky had appeared to be darker than usual.

I began to feel a little fearful, so I quickened my footsteps and by then the temperature had increased. I could feel the perspiration steaming down my face. Mrs Mack, hearing my hastened footsteps on the tiled surface of the veranda, called out "come in, it's going to be pouring with rain soon".

I entered, exhaling my breath.

"It has gone really hot", I said wiping the perspiration from my face.

"See how the clouds have gone dark over the East, I am glad you got here before it started", she continued.

Mrs Mack was a slim muscular woman probably in her mid-fifties, a very popular designer/dressmaker. I was there to collect my dresses that I would be taking with me to the UK. Her ability to turn out the most exquisite designs was revered by fashion conscious women around Kingston. She turned out the blushing brides in elaborate nylons and organza gowns with real pride, and with the same elegance as she did in producing the festooned robes for the shepherds of the various Revival and Pocomania Churches. They were a pleasure to behold.

My dresses were not ready for collection but I did not make a fuss because I knew that she would spend the night applying her usual dexterity on her Singer sewing machine in order to complete the perfect outfit.

As she talked about some of the week's designs that had been completed we realised that it had become extremely hot. She looked up, our eyes met and there was an almighty rumbling noise coming towards the house. It felt as though the Blue Mountain, together with the Waurika Hill, had crumbled and was rolling down on the Liguanea Plain. The sound was moving closer and closer; the lights went out in a flash; the radio went off instantly. The room was pitch dark. One could feel tremors, strong, determined and sustained rocking the house from side to side, heaving and toppling furniture. We looked outside the window, to the Lane and saw the trees waving rhythmically, muted sounds could be heard coming from the houses nearby.

Everyone remained indoors because it is well known that during an earthquake fallen masonry could cause fatal injuries. Frightened and meditative voices could be heard chanting the scriptures, some people were shouting, "Lord have mercy, Lord have mercy". To our horror Sister Mattie, the woman who had been warning us all about the coming of the Lord since I was a child, was to be heard in the darkness up and down the Lane, she was wailing and groaning, "Repent, our soon coming saviour is here, the angels beckon". The voices were still, no one responded. So paralysed with fear, no one had the courage to heckle or jeer Sister Mattie, as they usually did.

I sat facing the sewing machine in the dim shadowing light of the glass lamp that is kept filled with kerosene oil, ready for use in case of power cuts. Its flame, like a beacon, made the prints around the circumference of the polished glass shade visible, in bold white letters with little flecks of gold. It read "Home Sweet Home."

The rumbling intensified but it soon passed us. The sensation, however, remained for a long time afterwards; coupled with fear that it might retrace its path later on. We both sat there, tense but thanking God that the experience had left us unscathed. Soon after the power returned and the streetlights glowed, that was an indication that the alert was over. In trepidation, I decided to make my way home in the quiet of the night; the atmosphere was hushed and much calmer.

The morning of my departure to London was cloudless, the sun shone gloriously as my heart sank, shaken by the thought of leaving my family, the lush beauty of my island's scenery and its lovely people. The Myers number three pier in Kingston Harbour teemed with a bustling crowd of well-wishers, dockworkers and a steady stream of would-be travellers preparing to embark on the SS IRPINI. This was an Italian ship, made popular among travellers to the United Kingdom, perhaps because its overall fares amounted to seventy-five pounds in those days.

The vigorous pounding of my heart and my heightened emotional state could not allow me to maintain eye contact with my children and Mother. I quickly embraced them and hurried off. I did not want them to see the streaming tears down my face. Even today, after 58 years, recording this outstanding regrettable action does not in any way minimise this experience. It was now my turn to show immigration my embarkation document. I walked up the gangway. Eventually I positioned myself high up, where I could see the people on the quayside, perhaps waiting to see the ship off. I could not avoid noticing how the sun's rays projected a colourful sparkle in the sea as the coconut trees swayed gently in the light trade winds. It was all so enchanting. A measure of calm enveloped me. The signal that we were about to sail was apparent. Having identified my bunk and sorted out my belongings, I looked out to see the thin line of my island home disappearing in the distance. My journey had truly began.

Getting to London

During the journey, like many other passengers, I was plagued by seasickness from the rough seas, the foul odour of the hot dank bunk and the indigestible food. Special thanks are due to the Captain of the ship who sometimes put us out of our misery by allowing us to cook our yam, sweet potatoes and dumplings. Through tuition, the cook soon improved the taste and texture of the meat dishes; more people began to enjoy the chicken dishes, although there were still others who continued the boycott fostered in the belief that they were being served seagulls instead of chicken. Two passengers in particular kept us supplied with smoked and corned pork.

Amazingly, the seasickness among many of the passengers abated, much to the delight of the stewards and all of us for the pleasure of having a cleaner environment. I met a delightful lady with whom I was privileged to share a bunk. She was in her late fifties, coming to join her only son, whom she told us, resided in the best area of London, on the tree lined street called Ladbroke Grove, a stone's throw from Buckingham Palace. I was very happy for her and silently hoped that I too would be living somewhere as prestigious. But deep down in my heart, I knew that this was but a dream because travelling to Britain was never really my choice nor any part of my life's plan, so my approach to the venture was an open minded one.

The long evenings on board the SS IRPINI were spent either doing organised group activities such as sing song, storytelling, dancing and sometimes just making conversations. After the bar was closed some of the men would join us, usually to tell some rude bwoy stories and after much laughter we sometimes sat out on deck and relished the cool sea breeze for a while before we dispersed to our separate bunks.

Sunday services had a special feel to it, a chance to dress up, join in the lusty singing of hymns, specially chosen by us the passengers and to reflect on God's love for his children. The sermons were often touching and relevant to our situation as immigrants venturing to settle in a place away from our familiar homes.

The SS IRPINI stopped for a day at Trujillo where some passengers embarked, The 15 days voyage was coming to an end. Parting from those with whom precious thoughts, ideas, hopes and dreams were raised, proved somewhat difficult; many of us were highly emotional as the ship made its way to Southampton on that final day. For some, uncertainties occupied their minds, for others sheer joy, but the mixed emotion was all expressed visibly through lots of tears.

The SS IRPINI was due to dock at the Southampton Pier on a pleasant afternoon in March 1957. I hastened to the deck high on the side of the tall ship to have my first view of the country where I had hoped to take up temporary residence, a slightly fresh gust of wind greeted me, up went my gold coloured linen dress, its circular embroidered skirt, depicting a tree laden with coconuts, fluttered in the wind. Holding the skirt down with my left hand, I quickened my steps. The sound of several hurried footsteps became more and more audible, visibility of the land mark became much clearer, and our quiet anticipation gave way to a tremendous applause, clapping of hands and stamping of feet. We danced to the music of our emotions and then automatically we were on our knees giving thanks to God for allowing us a safe passage across the Atlantic Ocean.

Soon we went through the immigration processing procedure and having put away my travel documents, I was assisted with my luggage to the train by a white porter. My first of many surprises was to see white men unloading the ship, doing heavy manual work like black men did at the docks in Kingston, Jamaica. I was certainly not prepared for this sight.

The dock was a melee of people, boxes and suitcases dotted around like debris after an invasion, but the porter with his strong muscular arms skilfully moved the trolley along unaffected by the swirl of people around him. Sensing that there would be more culture shocks and surprises awaiting me in this strange land, I entered the train as directed and settled down in a comfortable upholstered seat.

The reverberation from the train's engine became more intense and it became clear that its departure was imminent. The smooth movement of the train was tranquil. I readjusted myself in the seat, reflected on the life I had left behind, mused, and thought of the many train journeys, albeit inland, that I had made with Papa. One such journey I recall quite vividly. A journey to the rural area of Cross, in the parish of Clarendon where he was born.

There in the fading day light, on my first day, I sat greedily sucking at the sweet orange coloured juice of a St Julian mango. My cousins were more interested in their games of 'hide and seek' and 'chebbie chase' rather than the eating of fruits which grew in abundance around them. To me a Kingstonian, this mango was a special delicious treat plucked straight from the trees above my head. Looking around, I was attracted to the luminous white smoke coming from the fires on which the evening meals were cooking, just drifting away slowly in ghostlike fashion across the valley. The chatter and laughter of the people's voices echoed from a distance. Uncle Amos from the closest neighbouring field whistled a rhythmic tune to 'home in' his cattle which had been grazing in the pasture throughout the day.

However, like the delicious taste of the mangoes, the cool evening breeze added a degree of tranquillity that reminded me that I was away from Kingston because it was situated on the Liquanea Plain where the heat from the sun's ray lingered far into the night. One evening soon after the rain had stopped, Papa took me for a ride on the donkey towards the mountain. I was a bit frightened when I heard the deep croaking frogs and the splash-splash of the donkey's feet in the puddles. Sometimes I imagined seeing a thin kind of human form in a distance which conjured up the existence of what the country folks called 'duppies' (ghost). But then I would get excited at the magic of the fire-flies, 'peanie wallies' as they were commonly called, thousands of them in a wave of light moving ahead of us as though they were propelled by a gentle wind, lighting up the surrounding areas and then suddenly disappearing in the darkness.

My teenaged visits to the country with Papa gave intriguing insights into the work and life style of the people. We used to walk through the chilly mist of the early morning, the dew clearly visible on the green vegetation, across the valleys to see family and friends. Many would be already at work on their garden plots which surrounded the huts and cottages. The hardwood floor-boards meticulously stained with tree bark and polished with bees-wax and buffed vigorously with coconut brush, gleamed brightly in the shadows of the daylight. On the larger fields or 'grung', the women were preparing to cook the meals for the workers, most of whom had come to give their neighbours a day's work free. Traditionally, the favour would be returned at a later time.

Soon the activities would begin; the men and boys laid out the pimento to dry on the barbecue and some picked the scarlet coffee berries to be dried, packed and milled or grounded in a mortar. The fragrances from the logwood and orange blossom greeted us as we made our way to the morning digging. I would watch the men with their hoes, diggers and machetes in their strong arms rising and falling to the rhythm of the tropical digging songs. This gave me a great thrill.

Those rhythms, I soon learnt, were fashioned by our ancestors, as a response to their harsh work schedule on the plantation, after they were uprooted from their homelands in West Africa and the alienation they faced during the full force of enslaved labour. When an oversized ground provision is lifted out of the soil much excitement is created, the roar of laughter, the frolicking and dancing echoed through the dense thicket of the vegetation. At such times of the year, the whole countryside is awash with provision; some would be for sale and export but many were destined for the church altar on Harvest Sunday.

My greatest delight, however, was to be given a mug of freshly made hot chocolate drink, the globules of fat floating on top of the thick cinnamon spiced liquid, followed by lunch and a variety of fresh fruits, giving this town girl a most unusual experience of rural life. The adults' conversations did not escape my ears, they talked about helping the young adults to acquire their own plots of land to build their houses, joining the Burial Scheme Society which would be responsible for their burial needs and participating in the ever popular communal saving activity called 'Pardner' in Jamaica or 'Sous Sous' in Trinidad; all aimed at encouraging that degree of independence, 'providing fi di rainy day'.

The day's activities soon drew to a close as twilight approached and Papa was ready to leave the green pastures for home. I was quite worried as the hills and valley faded away in the descending twilight. As we walked with our hands in a lock, partly to steady my steps on the rocky road, but also to calm my fears, I asked Papa, "How are we going to find our way to Auntie's yard?"

Papa replied in his most reassuring voice, "Foot know track, dem wi get us home" – meaning that although the darkness seemed impenetrable, his feet knew the journey and would lead us home.

We reached the yard in a short time afterwards, where a logwood fire was burning with the aroma of roasted cashew nuts filling the air. Almost everyone was avidly cracking and eating the nut while some children and adults pranced around in the shadows. Sitting on the kitchen steps were those engaged in the telling of stories about the infinite cunning of Anansi, the spider man of the Caribbean and West Africa. Some were guessing riddles with the magical beginning 'riddle mi dis, riddle me dat, guess mi dis riddle and perhaps not'.

The hysterical laughter subsided with everyone giggling as the younger children, who were engaged in a game of 'moonshine darlin' and other ring games, joined the adults, almost signalling the end of the recreational activities. Prayer was then led by one of the elders and everyone began to prepare for bed. The dim lamp light soothed my tiredness and like a lullaby tune I fell asleep in no time.

The train to London was now travelling faster, I could not get Papa out of my mind, memories upon memories clouded my head. I thought about the countless times when Papa would take me to spend the school holidays with my Mother. Suddenly I am living in a different environment with quite a different regime. They were free, easy, do-as-you-like times. No pressure on me to do anything in particular. I wore the latest fashion and Mother did not hesitate to have my kinky hair straightened.

My holiday would often come to an end as suddenly as it had started.

It is strange how in moments of crisis the mind whips back to childhood. Oh so many memories, so many thoughts haunted me, as I sat in the solitude of that rumbling train. I felt so alone although there were other passengers there. I pondered over those incidents which characterised my childhood and promised myself never to consciously put my own children through such experiences.

I thought, here am I taking a journey to Britain, not because I wanted to, but because I had to. Going to Britain therefore meant that I had to compromise my position and bury my pride in order to prevent the disintegration of my family. This was a responsibility I did not care to abdicate. Herb had always indicated that he wished to keep his family together and provide for them so that they could enjoy a better life than he had experienced as he grew up. He had always remarked that "growing up as an orphan in colonial Jamaica of the 1920's was no bed of roses".

The rumbling train journeyed through the countryside and seemed to be passing through a populated area. A glowing wave of optimism overtook me and the uncertainties which had overwhelmed me slowly faded. I began to feel a sweet release as positive images paraded before my eyes. There was a remarkable hush in the carriage except for faint muffled voices, people had become tired and many were asleep. I tried to keep my eyes open in a desperate attempt to see the area. I marvelled at the brick designs jutting out of the roofs of the houses, as far away as I could see. Later I learnt that they were chimneys designed to expel the smoke from the coal fired heating.

As I scanned the horizon flashing past me, I heard a slow steady build-up of snoring, accompanied with a heavy weight on my shoulder. Mrs Puzzey, my new found friend, had fallen asleep with her spectacle hanging precariously from her nose. I removed it gently, not wanting to disturb her slumber. Feeling relaxed but still experiencing the sensation of the tossing of waves and the intense creaking and bobbing of the ship, my mind focused on my Mother and my three children who were left in Kingston. Suddenly I was enveloped in grief and try as I did, I could not hold back the burning tears which cascaded down my cheeks like a swollen river, emitting its unwanted contents. I must have fallen asleep soon after because Mrs Puzzey was nudging me with her elbow to wake me from what she called a 'nightmare'. She told me that I was crying in my sleep. I felt better after that snooze so I decided to go to the rest room and freshen up.

I smoothed on my Madam Rose Leon 'Bloom of Youth' make-up onto my face, then huddled in my seat of the Waterloo bound 'boat train', alone with my thoughts. The journey had another twenty minutes. I tried hard to relax but the eager anticipation of seeing where I would be living and meeting my husband, from whom I had been separated for nine months, caused me an anxiety which did not seem anywhere near subsiding. I have always been particular about where I lived and how I lived. A comfortable home to me was one of the greatest luxuries in the world. The unknown was proving to be quite frightening to me.

CHAPTER 4

WELCOME LONDON

The boat train arrived at Waterloo Station in London as scheduled. The porters were there already to transport the luggage to the large meeting area where relatives and friends of new arrivals were waiting. As I walked out with the porter and my two pieces of luggage, I spotted my husband who was looking quite anxiously at the females passing by, as they looked anxiously for whoever they expected. I rushed impulsively towards Herb and with outstretched arms he gathered me to his bosom, squeezed my forearm and kissed me profusely for a considerable time. This left me feeling quite embarrassed; as such a public display of emotions was alien to me.

An old family friend had accompanied Herb to meet me and as we greeted each other with people pushing all around us, I introduced my husband to my newly acquired friend, Mrs Puzzey.

The smoky smell and grey gloomy light of London greeted me as I walked out to the taxi rank where the black taxis were lined up in a long steady stream. They took up the passengers and luggage with a quiet precision as if rehearsed. It was now our turn and as soon as we were settled in our seats, we talked non-stop until we got to the house. There was so much to talk about. In the meantime, I continued to peer through the darkened glass window of the taxi, but everything and every place was far from being discernible. I, however, could not miss noticing that the London streets were much wider than ours, seemed darker and the buildings appeared high and oversized.

We were nearing our destination and the family friend was still with us. Within minutes, we were alighting from the taxi outside a house, 11 Myatt's Road, London SE5, opposite a building with a sign that read, 'Advance Laundry'. I was ushered into a room on the first floor of the house. My heart sank, "Is this it?", I asked, looking at Herb and his friend who were already sitting comfortably on one of the two chairs in the room. Herb sat on the bed staring absent-mindedly at the circular lace like pattern reflecting on the ceiling from the paraffin heater.

A single light bulb hung from the ceiling that cast its glow in the dark corner of the small room where his friend sat. I asked for the bathroom and was mortified to be told that a toilet was outside the house and that there was no bathroom. A chill went straight through my body. Not wanting to show any sign of my unease, I remained calm and hoped that his friend would see it fitting to leave but he just stayed. I had no idea why he was waiting. I watched Herb's countenance change from accepting the unwelcome presence of his friend to a gradual emerging wearisome body language. I kept my eyes on him because I wanted to see if he was going to give him that sign – the one we Jamaican's used when we wish to be left alone. As a child, Mother used it regularly to send me out of ear-shot when adults were having a conversation. Will Herb resort to this subtle admonition?

I kept my eyes on him, waiting to see his head turn a little to one side while he looked his friend in the eye and swivel his own eyes towards the door – but no, he did not want to seem insulting. Herb eventually started to unpack the luggage which contained the 'goodies'. Suddenly his friend came alive on seeing the J Wray & Nephew bottles of over-proof rum. He had no interest in the other things and as soon as some of the rum was poured into a bottle that he could take away with him, he was ready to depart a very happy man. We kept in touch for many years until his wife joined him from Jamaica and they moved on to the USA.

As much as part of me wanted to argue, there was no urge to get into that. The reunion was very touching and emotionally charged that my overwhelming desire for my husband took precedent over and above every other issue. It was as though nine months without him had diminished my memory and seeing him again in the flesh, I was simply bowled over by his good looks. I just gazed fixedly at him utterly appalled by the unstoppable wave of love and lust that washed over me. "I missed you, I really missed you", he whispered.

A hot melting sensation had begun deep down inside of me, his tenderness, a soothing balm to my smarting sensitivities and a body already out of control, seething with a feverish needy passion. The silence around hummed as the burning hunger he had ignited with his touch exploded with ecstatic pleasure.

The daylight showed itself through the curtains as I stretched, yawned and rolled over in my new bed with my husband next to me, smiling and seemingly happy and pleased with himself. He had already planned for us to visit a few friends. He went out to prepare the breakfast at about 9.30am while I spent the time remembering the events of the past and preparing myself for the not too easy road which undoubtedly lay before me. He soon came in with a tray loaded with delicious breakfast which I avidly enjoyed.

I could hear the loud voices of people, then whispering, and before long music was coming from every corner of the house.

It was as though the people on the three floors of the house were having a tug-of-war. The radiograms sounded as though they were on full volume, each playing its own tune - a mixture of hymns, Jim Reeves evangelical tunes and a very suggestive calypso. One woman was singing very loudly. It was quite a din and I was never able to determine whether this was meant as a welcome or it was a normal Sunday morning occurrence.

The discomfort was immeasurable, a far cry from Sunday morning in Kingston, Jamaica. We decided to get out of the house earlier than planned. So having prepared ourselves, dressed and ready, I was ushered out of the room to be introduced to the other tenants who were by then overly anxious to see me. Their overall reaction and comments which they did not disguise was hair-raising. One of them declared that I was so young, the other echoed, "she look like a pickney". I knew from that moment that not only were the amenities in the place unsuitable but that it would be virtually impossible for me to survive living with such insensitive people.

My first Sunday in London with friends was a glorious one. The weather was fine, the company of friends was stimulating and encouraging. On our way home I saw a black man about six feet tall, wearing a flowing blue robe with a small fitted cap on the crown of his head; his gait was so dignified that I could not have missed this outstanding figure. I asked Herb who this man was, the reply was whispered in my ear, "He is an African". I had no idea that an African could have been six feet tall, as my history book, "The World and its People", portrayed an African as a short man with his bow and arrow by the riverbank. I stood for a while staring in awe at the figure. This man so reminded me of Papa and his friends, especially when they were attired for their activities at the Liberty Hall or Edelweiss Park, United Negro Improvement Association (UNIA) meetings.

My dissatisfaction with the lack of a decent living accommodation drove me to continue to press my husband to find alternative accommodation. For months I could not have a good bath, I had to have a 'wash', as my colleagues at work used to call their weekly ritual. This situation drove me in desperation to find the London Borough of Southwark's Public Baths in Camberwell Green. Having paid the entrance fee and all the preliminaries undertaken, I was shown to a cubicle where the water was already running in the bath in preparation for my use. It seemed clean, in fact there was no time or inclination for me to investigate its cleanliness, just the sight of the running water seemed like heaven to me. I thought of my homeland Jamaica, the 'Land of Wood and Water', and laughed at myself. I rubbed and scrubbed my skin with vigour, I was enjoying my bath as though it could never end, when I heard a sudden gurgling of water. I quickly climbed out of the bathtub and noticed that the water from the bath was rapidly receding down the drain. I soon realised that my allotted time had expired and it was time for me to vacate the space.

I got dressed and walked out of the warmth of the building onto the pavement. A cold wind blew with piercing intensity through my body, this strange force left me feeling as though I was floating on air, in fact I felt lighter. I quickly pulled my overcoat snugly around me and hastened my steps towards Camberwell New Road. As I passed the London Transport Bus Garage on the right, entering under the overhead bridge, I was startled by an almighty rumbling that appeared to be crashing over my head. I stumbled and caught hold of a post on the wall, petrified. I was sweating and shaking in utter distress. My situation was soon noticed by a passer-by, an elderly lady who stopped and asked, "Are you OK Duckie?" I was too numb to reply – I had no idea that trains ran overhead, so my immediate thinking was that a war had begun. Then this lady had called me "Duckie" which I knew meant that the person was foolish. On reaching home, I was feeling so wretched; I climbed into bed and cried inconsolably.

By the following day my body ached, the pains became unbearable, I was taken to the doctor who confirmed that I had caught a cold and was running a high temperature. It was many weeks before I felt well again.

London – The Centre of My World

When I first arrived in London I felt like a lonely child in a large unfamiliar place. It was expected that one should be thrilled coming to the great City of London, centre of the world. I was at a loss as to what to do with my time except to get on the upper deck of the red buses, heading for the City - just to look at the buildings and the people, taking great care not to miss my landmark. Everywhere looked the same. I tried not to use Barclays Bank as my landmark, after discovering that there were many on the bus routes, when on one occasion I alighted from the bus in the wrong area.

The red buses and the red telephone kiosks were the most cheerful objects, they stood out like beacons! Many of the buildings, especially in the East End of London and the City, were war damaged ruins; their cellars were filled with holes and muddy water. Everywhere seemed so dark, drab and silent. It was unlikely that I would come across any black person except African male students who wore their hair parted in the centre. They were almost always carrying a loaded briefcase and would eagerly introduce themselves. The familiar line was, "I think I have seen you somewhere before". I often wondered whether it was the African resemblance to which they were drawn or it was really a 'chat up line'.

Today they are no longer a familiar sight. Cafes and restaurants were sparse so the chains of Lyons Restaurants were the high point for an eating place among ordinary people. A number of black people were employed in their kitchens, so one felt at home when eating there. The steamed steak and kidney pudding and vegetables, poached eggs on toast and fish and chips were my favourite dishes.

We used to frequent Lyon's Corner House in St Martins Lane, near Trafalgar Square when we were on sight-seeing trips or, nearer to home in Brixton, we went to the local restaurant along Brixton Road near the Acre Lane junction. The Pubs, however, were the more popular social centres, particularly for the men. Each Pub has what they called their 'regulars'.

All Pubs were regulated to be closed at 11pm and indeed all other social functions ended then. It was customary to try at all cost to be home by 10pm. By then the streets were literally empty. If you were seen on the streets beyond 11pm, it would be strongly assumed that you were on your way home from the pub. This was never a place of interest to me, because in the society from which I came, women who frequented 'pubs' (bars in our culture) are regarded as 'loose beings'.

For many years I used to wait for Herb across the road from his local pub, 'The Coach and Horses' in Coldharbour Lane, Brixton, until he had consumed his last drink. I would not accompany him in there, 'dead or alive'.

I did not fail to notice how silent the majority of the people were in their houses with crowded furniture and crowded patterned wall paper. If one was lucky, you could even see the silent peering eyes through the lace curtain as you pass by on the streets. There were really two things in those early days which gave me a clear warm feeling out of the grey, cold silence. They were Herb's return from work in the evenings and another tenant's radio to which I would listen intently.

To live in London, particularly during the Autumn/Winter months, seemed so unhealthy to me. Coal and paraffin were the principal sources of our heating. Grime and soot came in through the windows and covered everything. Our paraffin oiled heater did not only serve our heating needs but in the absence of somewhere to hang the washing, a clothes-horse (a fold away wooden frame) was placed around the heater, where the clothes were hung for drying and a kettle placed on top of the heater to keep a supply of hot water.

During the winter months, London would suddenly be enveloped in a cloud of dark fog with freezing temperatures. I can recall when in 1959, living in a basement bed-sit in Avenue Park Road in Norwood, South London, a marked annoyance for me was the dripping pipe emitting its water against the wall of my room. Freezing as soon as it settled, it was like torture. Having enough paraffin to keep the heater going for every hour of the day was a must.

On one occasion, when on my way from purchasing the paraffin, I got lost. I could not work out the direction from which I had come because the whole area, as far as I could see, was suddenly under a cloud of darkness. It was two o'clock in the afternoon, but no one on the road was recognisable, the footsteps on the pavement were quite audible and only the lighted cigarettes or blurred lights from the passing vehicles were visible. This fog sometimes developed into smog when one is unlikely to see one's own feet or hands.

When the temperature plummeted, people would invariable throw more coal on to the fire to keep it going; the domestic chimneys, the power stations and the exhaust fumes from the vehicles poured out soot, increasing the accumulation of smoke that was ultimately trapped closer to the ground. This affected normal breathing, causing coughs, splutters and gasps for breath, especially among the elderly. The Clean Air Act of 1956, which allows only the use of smokeless fuel for open fires, had not been operational in a big way, as it is now.

Within a decade, however, there began to appear coffee bars, Indian Restaurants, Chinese Restaurants and Italian Ice Cream Parlours. Colourful and stylish clothes began to replace the black and the greys. I no longer had to send back home for lingerie. The buildings also began to look brighter and amidst all these changes was the steady flow of new arrivals from the Caribbean islands. The London of the 1950's-60's has now vanished and it is hard to believe it had existed – no one who has known only today's London can imagine what London was like then.

My London Memories

My memories of these times are still etched in my consciousness and as I recall some of the more distinctive experiences, I can only marvel on how things have changed.

I remember my first real encounter with our local shopkeeper. I entered the shop and stood there and waited. I waited and waited. I was in no hurry, there was plenty of time. If there was little time, I did not know where to find the next corner shop. The shopkeeper did not look in my direction, despite the ringing of the doorbell when I entered. Strangely, he did not seem to have raised his head, he made no eye contact whatsoever. I shifted my weight from the left foot to the right a few times and waited and waited. There was one other customer in the shop standing before me but she was certainly in no hurry. She had not yet started her shopping because she was engrossed in giving the man behind the counter up-to-date news about the recent addition to her family and the array of knitted garments she had completed for the new baby. He was, of course, interested; one could tell the difference. I looked at her in amazement. A short gaunt looking middle aged white woman wearing a pair of pink fur trimmed bedroom slippers, her mousy hair was adorned in several multi coloured plastic rollers held firmly in place with a thick black hairnet. I thought what a stark contrast the sight of this woman is to the many others whom I had seen in the short time since my arrival.

Standing there, I recalled the migrant service officer's comment to me, when she saw my London address, she said "O, you will be living in a mixed area". Is that what she meant?, I wondered. The woman continued to peer around the shelves, her eyes lit up on seeing the display of new flavoured crisps. Pointing at them, she said "I'll have some of those". Then she suddenly remembered that one of the ham knuckles in the bacon section would be a good purchase, so she rushed back to select the one she wanted. She looked at various items, selected some, hesitated, then decided against any more items. The shopkeeper was piously calm, as his eyes and attention followed everywhere she went. I listened to her and watched her looking around the obviously familiar shop for more items. I shook my head and wondered if this experience was a taste of things to come.

Waves of nostalgia overtook me. It was quite acute. Where I came from, we acknowledged people's presence and it was considered rude to do otherwise. I was now beginning to feel like a shadow of myself and seriously thought of leaving the shop but I did not really know any other corner shop where I could possibly get a loaf of bread, so I waited and waited. My impatience subsided when in a high squeaky voice she announced, "That will be all". He added up her purchases. She again inspected each item and thrust them into her shabby canvas bag.

"Thanks a lot Mrs Pullen", he said with a bit of humour in his voice.

"Thank you Mr Parker", she replied, "Give my regards to your wife".

They both smiled as her wrinkled stocking feet shuffled through the clanging door.

It was now my turn. I could not fail to notice that full eye contact had been established, his pious mood had now changed to an impatient matter of fact approach: "And what would you like madam?" he asked.

"A large loaf of bread", I replied, forgetting to add please to my request. He walked over to the other end of the shop, picked up a square uncut loaf and stood it on the counter. My jaw dropped, I stood there aghast. I have never seen this before. I expected my bread to be wrapped. I looked at him, then on the loaf of bread and muttered, under my breath, "But your hand was in the till just a while ago".

Not knowing what to do, I bravely asked, "Have you got any other loaf?" He gave me a puzzled look and informed me that the other loaves were just the same as the one on the counter.

"Could you wrap it for me, please?", the words tripped off my tongue before I knew it.

He gave me a long sulky stare, leaving me with the feeling that I was particularly singled out for this awful treatment. My body responded by feeling overheated and the tears steadily trickled down my cheeks. He noticed my confusion and quickly said, "We do not wrap bread here Madam; you should have brought a paper bag or a towel with you". Reaching for the loaf from his outstretched hand, I thanked him and left the shop, not to ever return there again.

I was learning fast what adjustments I had to make in order to live in London.

My First London-born

I was told that visiting the Department of Employment Labour Exchange was a very important pre-requisite to finding a job. One day I went to the Ferndale Road Labour Exchange in Brixton to register my availability for work. Following the officer's interview, I was asked to attend the Somerset House in the Strand, WC1, and the Dulwich Hospital, South London, to be interviewed by those prospective employers for the position of shorthand typist. Somerset House was then the Central Records Office for the registration of births and deaths and the Inland Revenue Collection Office.

I prepared myself for these most important dates by listening to the wireless, particularly to gain a grasp of the inflection in the speech pattern of the English people. Tinged with a degree of nervousness, I attended the interview. Firstly, I was seen by a middle aged man who spoke kindly and moved through the interviewing process with ease and understanding. He took me through exercises which included general knowledge and comprehension. I was then asked to meet a young lady who would dictate the Pitman's Shorthand test. At this stage my nervousness had subsided and I began to feel more at ease in the environment.

I was taken aback when the dictation started. The words to my ear sounded as though they were plucked from a different language. Pitman's Shorthand goes by phonetic sounds and what I was hearing was entirely foreign. My other skills were accepted as satisfactory but although I could prove a certificated speed of 120 wpm, I was politely asked to return in six months, when it was felt that I would by then be able to understand the speech pattern of the average English person.

The second interview at Dulwich Hospital went amiss because my husband's friend advised against me going to work at a hospital. His reason being that I would have to work at weekends! This would prevent me preparing my husband's Sunday dinner, so I was forbidden to attend that interview. Amazingly in those days one did as one was told.

Eventually I took employment at the Advance Laundry in Fredrick Crescent, SW9, across the road from where we lived. My duties were to maintain the stock control and inventory of the garments coming in and going out to the various outlets. All hopes of returning for the second interview at Somerset House faded. I was stuck at the laundry. I was pregnant.

Overtaken by unhappiness and home-sickness, the desperation to return to Jamaica became intensely acute. Overwhelmed with discomfort and uncertainties, I drew on my early Christian teaching and the beliefs this teaching had instilled in me. Remembering the first verse of Hymn 298, in my Moravian Hymnal, I closed my eyes and threw my whole being into the reverence of my God. I prayed:-

"I cannot do without you
O saviour of the lost
Whose precious blood redeemed me
At such tremendous cost
Thy righteousness: thy pardon
Thy precious blood must be
My only hope and comfort
My glory and my plea"

I asked him to give me perfect strength in my weakness. I clung to his promise that he would not forsake his own. With these thoughts in mind, I collected myself. I soon realised that there was no room for self-pity. The clock could not be turned back, just as it is with "the spoken words, the spent arrow and the neglected opportunity". The journey ahead had to be faced, I reasoned to myself.

My son was born a week before Christmas 1957 at Lambeth Hospital, Kennington. In those days patients were required to remain in hospital for no less than ten days. The memory of spending my first Christmas, after arriving in London, as a patient in hospital has always brought back pleasant memories of the excellent National Health Service at that time. Patients were afforded the time to rest, as babies were brought to the ward only at feeding times. One could not help admiring and showing respect to the staff who reciprocated in a pleasant and caring way. Meals were served with precision and those patients who were allowed to walk around were served meals on a long dining table set out in the middle of the ward. I cannot recall feeling that I was a new comer.

Adjusting to the care of a new baby without the help from family members was not an easy task, especially as mine had the tendency to sleep all day and scream all night. So in order to minimise the sound, I had to walk around the room with him on my shoulder and make sure that we stuffed old garments under the door in an attempt to muffle the sound of his crying. The landlord soon started to complain. He used to say "Cho you baby cry too much, you will have to give me my room". Our difficulties had only just begun!

Looking for a job was put on hold, while I waited to return to the hospital for the six weeks post-natal examination. The urge to earn a wage was very strong as the desperate feelings to ensure that my children in Jamaica were financially supported haunted me daily. The contents of my Mother's short, curt letters spoke volumes. "Greetings in the name of the soon coming Christ" was the usual salutation followed by, "I received what you sent, things here are very expensive so let me hear from you by return of post". Nothing about how my children were getting on in school, no information about how they were and specific questions to her in my letters went unanswered. I was left feeling gutted on reading those short non-informative letters.

I often sat quietly, just to summon the courage to assess my situation. Then I would grit my teeth and try to develop the will to face my new world. The push to find a job was enormous, I went job hunting.

Working for London Transport
By early February, nearly three months after the birth of my son, I was offered a position as Assistant Cook for London Transport. Following the training sessions at the Baker Street Centre, I was assigned to the London Transport Bus Garage, Camberwell Green, SE5. Like the majority of West Indian women, I joined the steady stream of mothers in the early hours of the morning making my way to the uncharted sea of the child minders' world. The dingy room with the paraffin oil heater positioned in a corner and no sign of a toy in sight did not leave me at all comfortable and assured. I handed over my baby to the woman who had impressed me a few days earlier as a pleasant and caring person.

On that particular morning I could not help noticing that pleasant and caring mask had disappeared and had been replaced with an utterly solemn funeral face. I left my baby, to make my way through the cold crisp air, to report for 'early turn' duty at the nearby garage. The woollen knitted gloves that I wore to warm my already numb fingers served as an handkerchief to mop up the warm tears which trickled down my cheeks.

My arrival was greeted by the manager of the canteen. Fitted with overall and cap, I joined the other staff members who were elderly white ladies. They acted quite friendly towards me and willingly showed me how to translate theory into practice. Except for the constant jibe from one of the staff members, I soon settled into the routine of the kitchen. Her persistent jibes became regular, daily chants like "cold enough for you ducky?", "Warm enough for you ducky?" "You don't need to wear your shoes today ducky".

It was a blessed day when the chef intervened. He shouted at her in a most indignant tone, "Put a sock in it Emma". His command was loud and clear. Her response was immediate. She looked at me with a sheepish glare. I ignored her facial grimaces, accompanied by the sticking out of her tongue. I viewed her as a true trouble-maker and gradually I began to experience some peace, directing my attention to the duties.

The bus crews came in quickly in order for them to re-join their buses in the break-time allotted to them. "Time is of the essence", the trainer used to say. Their orders mostly consisted of welsh rarebit, dripping on toast, toad in the hole, bacon on toast, bubble and squeak, etc. The early turn duties were more welcomed, especially for me with a young baby, because duties came to an end at three o'clock in the afternoon. Then I was on my way to collect my baby and spend some daylight hours with him. But on the 'late turn' duties work began at two o'clock in the afternoon, finishing at ten o'clock at night – an uncivilised way of life I often thought.

Whenever I was on such a duty, Herb was expected to collect the baby and carry out his paternal duties. On one particular occasion I was assigned to work at another garage further away from home. The direction dictated that I would need to take two buses and I should get off where the second bus terminated at the Sidcup Bus Garage, Kent. I had no idea of the distance, nor of how long it would take me to get there. It was bitterly cold and soon it began to snow. My heart skipped a beat when whilst waiting for the second bus along Lewisham Way, I experienced the touch and sight of cloudy, white frozen rain as it descended over me. As I waited under the bus shelter my fascination with this unusual weather condition soon abated. I began to worry about how I would be able to walk in this white mound that had settled around my feet, on the pavement and indeed everywhere my eyes could behold.

The number 21 bus arrived and I walked timidly to join it to my destination. I arrived late, but they were so short of staff the delight on their faces suggested that my lateness was excused. It was quite a busy evening in the canteen. The men joked about the weather, tucked into their snacks, made up their time sheets, glared at their watches and hurried out of the canteen to re-join the buses. The evening went quickly and it was time for me to get on a bus just outside the garage headed for Camberwell Green. The snow fall had now developed to something more like a blizzard; as a result, the buses were terminating half way into the journey. I was advised to wait outside the New Cross Bus Garage for another bus that might continue the journey to Camberwell Green.

I stepped out on to an area heavily blanketed with a high mound of snow lining the pavement. Thick, dark fog swirled around and visibility in the area was almost nil. Buses came along at intervals but they too were terminating at New Cross Bus Garage.

I mustered the courage to ask a passer-by for the time, he rolled up the cuff of his overcoat, flicked on his cigarette lighter, guarding the flame caringly with his left hand, as he held it closely to the face of his watch whilst moving on, he said "five and twenty minutes to one o'clock". I worked out quickly what he meant. My heart throbbed, I was fearful, I felt as though a dark cloud was steadily devouring me, far more than the darkness which surrounded me whilst I stood under the bus shelter. I watched the heavy snow drift piling onto the pavement, overshadowing every object in sight. The cold wind blew with a pronounced ferocity.

I was now shaking with fear, no one else passed by. Gripped with a longing for my homeland and the familiarity that I knew, I wept. I wet myself. I stood there numb with fear marking time with my frozen feet in response to the overwhelming shudders which went through my body. It was sometime later that I spotted a dim headlight piercing through the thick foggy darkness. My closer observation revealed that it was an approaching double-decker red bus whose destination read, 'Paddington'. Yes, it was going all the way. "Thank God", I whispered. I got on the bus, sat uncomfortably, wet and shivering. It was now fifteen minutes past one o'clock in the morning.

There was no means by which I could communicate my whereabouts to Herb. In those days we did not have the use of such facilities as telephone in our bed-sits. That was not viewed as a necessity, more a luxury. Trudging through the snow drifts on the pavement and listening to the crushing sounds beneath my feet I promised to save up some money quickly to return home, "no, this is too much for me", I murmured. Releasing the lock on the front door of the multi-occupied house brought with it an enormous sense of relief, a feeling of being safe again only that the temperature inside was almost the same as outside except for the absence of the ferocious wind.

The communal areas of our house were never heated, so the paraffin oil heater reigned supreme by emitting its heat and faint glow around our room. The kettle was sitting on top of the heater, ready for me to brew a cup of tea, which I desperately needed to aid the thawing out process. I reached for it immediately.

My baby was sound asleep. I looked at him with longing eyes. I missed him so much. But for the need to earn in order to supplement the maintenance for the other children, I would have stayed home with him. I prayed and wished for what I really wanted. It was not long before that wish came true. From that morning I learnt how well Herb could read my silent thoughts and manipulate the outcome he wanted.

That morning, he reiterated his disagreement for me to take on the job so soon after the baby's birth. He also stated his displeasure in having to collect and look after him when I was on late turn duties. He moaned and groaned about the nature of the job I had chosen to do. Then in a tone, as if instructing a wayward child, he commanded, "When you report for duty tomorrow, tell them that you will be leaving and would like to have your card at the end of the day".

I did not respond, then in quite a firm tone of voice he asked, "Have I made myself clear?" I nodded in the affirmative.

My three months with London Transport came to an abrupt end and I was again cast in the role of a housewife dependent on my husband, a position I truly detested.

I was quite unhappy with my everyday life of carrying out domestic duties and nothing else. Much of our free time was spent on sightseeing trips, mostly to Central London. To get on a double-decker red bus and sit on the upper deck to look at the large buildings and watch the moving throng of people on the pavements was a great pleasure. It was like 'watching the world go by'.

On a very cold Bank Holiday in April, we were on our way with the baby to get on a bus when I suddenly felt ill. I felt like I was going to faint and asked Herb to take me home – a flurry of snowflakes had started to float, feather like to the ground. He was hesitant but had little choice because I was really ill. I later discovered that I was pregnant.

My whole world fell apart. I was in total despair. One particular evening, overcome with disappointment, I buried my face in a pillow and was having an agonising cry. I did not hear Herb's approach until he had entered the room. My distress seemed to have worried him greatly because he became quite emotional and tried to get me to stop. Feeling quite weak, I sat up in bed. He bent and took my hands from my lap and lifted my chin until he could look into my face. As the tears had not yet subsided, he wiped my face and threw his arms around me. I hid my face against his shoulder.

He asked me to promise that I would stop worrying about what is inevitable. Resting his hand on my tummy he said, "There is a life that is blossoming here, let's give thanks". Herb's support and encouragement helped me to see the brighter side of life.

My daughter was born at the Lambeth Hospital on 13th December 1958.

I looked admirably at my son, fifteen months old, sound asleep in his blue cot, his peaceful round shaped face peeped out from under the warm white blanket. His sister, three months old, was lying in her pram, warmly clad, just a few feet away on the other side of the bed. The rest of the space in the room accommodated a yellow Formica top table, a pair of chairs and a wardrobe. The kitchen utensils were packed under the table because of the lack of space in the passageway between the rooms which was designated as the kitchen that I shared with two other tenants.

Overtaken by loneliness, which descended on me like a dark cloud, I was in a reflective mood. I needed a breath of fresh air. Quite often a walk around the block or a stroll in the nearby Myatt's Park would suffice but on this particular Wednesday evening I was feeling profoundly lonely and anxious. A wave of longing for the warm Jamaica environment from which I had removed myself engulfed me – my longing for the social, cultural and spiritual activities, which gave me reverence, peace of mind and stability, were losses which I struggled to come to terms with.

Overwhelmed with despair I recalled the occasion when I visited Papa, with Uncle William in tow (in case I needed a referee), to tell him my intention to travel to the UK. The recall of his distraught voice came back to me as an eerie echo. "England? Why England?" he asked. The expression on his face disclosed his horrific thoughts. For a few seconds we faced each other in silence, I knew perfectly well that he would not have been impressed with my intention, but as an adult, he could do nothing about it. However, as always, I listened to his customary lectures. In his usual slow, clear and sustained voice, he said, "Britain is a racist society that often treats her colonies with long range contempt".

He paused and I thought, "Oh, that's a short lecture today".

But in a faltering voice, he continued, "It will be interesting to see how the Negroes will be treated when so many are living in her yard. Remember to keep the principles for which Marcus Garvey fought uppermost in your mind and reflect his teachings throughout your daily life".

Needless to say, I was much moved. I met with Papa once before I left Jamaica and that was the last I saw of him. I really wished he had lived long enough to hear of my journey.

I could hear Herb's footsteps, climbing up the steep creaking, winding stairs leading to our second floor room. He was normally home from work by 7pm on Wednesdays, earlier than most evenings when he did some overtime work in order to supplement his low wages. Wednesday nights were special, he attended the St John's Interracial Club that met in the St John's Anglican Church Hall in Angel Town, Brixton. Having repeated the usual ritual of setting a basin of warm water in which he could immerse his often cold feet, he would settle down to a meal then get ready and be off for a good two to three hours. That particular evening I watched him making his way down the creaking stairs, he looked back and waved to me. That wave must have pulled something in me because my stomach lurched and I could not hold back the desperate longing that I was feeling to socialise. I asked the tenant next door to baby-sit for me and when she happily agreed, I felt as though I was riding on a cloud.

I got dressed quickly and looked at my babies. Satisfied that they were sound asleep I put out the flames from the paraffin heater and opened the windows for a while to expel the strong fumes. I then tiptoed on the noisy linoleum covered floor and gently closed the door behind me. My neighbour met me at the door and went in to see my babies, assuring me that they would be quite safe. Walking freely through the door, without the double buggy, helped to put a spring in my steps.

St Johns Interaction Club

The April wind blew coldly. With a piercing chill, I wrapped my pink coat more snugly around me. My aim was to find the Interracial Club. Following the route Herb had always talked about, I got to the intersection of Lilford and Ackerman Roads. Turning left along Loughborough Road, I saw some white boys standing under the street light. I was filled instantly with fear and wondered if those were a group of 'Teddy Boys'. I had often heard the men talking about the attacks from young white men who resented the idea of blacks taking up residence in their 'land of hope and glory'. It was said that some hung about in the Notting Hill area of West London on 'nigger-hunting sprees' and that they had plans to visit Brixton.

Gripped with fear, but not wanting to turn back, I began to walk slowly keeping my eyes on them. I thought, a black woman walking the streets of Brixton alone at 8.30pm at night was not at all a clever idea. My fears dissipated instantly when a black man came out of a nearby house and called out some form of greeting to the boys who acknowledged the man by waving. Just seeing a black person allayed the fear and gave me a sense of protection.

I could now see the alleyway leading to Angel Road where the large block of council flats was being built; a mixture of terraced and semi-detached houses were now in sight. With the stillness in the air and a quiet thudding in my stomach, I thought, "What if he isn't there?" On recognising a green Austin Cambridge car parked a little way along Angel Road I knew that I was close by. The owner, Headley Johnson, was a frequent visitor to our home and for many years worked tirelessly for the social and cultural development of our people in the borough. In those early years, 1959, he was the only member of the club who owned a car and his willingness to help to transport the housebound, visiting speakers, transporting members from various events and undertake any other tasks delegated to him was a much needed and appreciated contribution.

I was now at the door of a wooden structure, with clusters of creepy bushes almost covering the entrance. A warm magnetic atmosphere greeted me. There were about twenty five people in the not too decorated hall with its dusty floor, several broken canvas seated chairs lying around and a piano which I am sure had seen much better days. Teas and biscuits were served by a chirpy white lady, to whom I was introduced. Mrs Covell was an expert ball room dancer, a pastime that was easily recognised owing to her fleeting movements and upright gait. Her husband, a serious looking, well-built man, was the Treasurer. Two Jamaican ladies, Mrs Christine Morgan and Mrs Sylvia Cooper, whom I learnt were communicant members of the St John's Church, were instrumental in the setting up of the club aided by Rev Roy Campbell, the Church of England Chaplain who was appointed by the Government of Jamaica to offer Jamaican Nationals welfare counselling through the Migrants Advisory Service.

The women were busily talking with a group of new arrivals from Jamaica and Trinidad – passing on information and generally making them welcome. I could not, however, help noticing three black men positioned at the extreme end of the hall. They displayed an epitome of organisational ability and importance. They were Joseph Hunte, Courtney Laws and Oswald Simpson.

Before long, a couple arrived. The lady was cheerfully greeted by the other women, her husband a serious astute man joined the men's debating group which by then had become heated. I soon became quite attached to this couple, Jimmy and Gwen Byfield. They eventually gave tremendous support to the idea of pursuing cultural awareness sessions to the growing numbers of young people who were joining their parents from the Caribbean and looking for activities outside of their often cramped homes. It was felt that this area of interest would be more acceptable and understood by the children far more than the weekly debates about the proposed Federation of the West Indies, Racial Discrimination and the mechanics of the integration process. Herb's reaction to my unexpected presence at the Club was good - once he was assured that the children were being looked after by the neighbour.

I quite enjoyed my experience at the Club and arranged with the neighbour to help me out on future Wednesday evenings. On one visit I joined in what was called a business meeting. I soon realised that the majority of the members and regular visitors were male. They were the office bearers; they led the discussions and came to whatever decisions they wanted. They led the delegations to the Borough Council, whenever there were issues of concern within the black community, i.e. housing, racial harassment, disputes with neighbours and between landlords and tenants. I soon developed a keen interest in the issues that were debated at these meetings, gradually taking on tasks that the men were too busy to undertake. I was then asked to accompany them as part of a delegation to meet the Mayor and Alderman of the Borough.

It was not long before I was elected as the Recording Secretary for the St John's Interracial Club whose Presidents had always been the vicar of the church – its main aim was to 'reach out and provide a voice for new comers to the Borough of Lambeth'. Appreciating that my African-Caribbean people did not know the purposes and functions of the various institutions within the borough, we regarded the dissemination of such information as falling within our remit.

In order to contact a wide cross section of the immigrant population we went out on Sunday afternoons to knock on doors, give advice and find out about their concerns. The police were complaining that many of the newly arrived immigrants were coming to the station seeking their support and help for issues which were clearly outside of their jurisdiction. Our work was made even more relevant. The lack of meeting places for the young people from the Caribbean who were joining their parents in growing numbers became more and more acute. It was therefore important for us to provide suitable activities at the church hall in order to harness their energies in positive pursuits. While we grappled with this growing problem, there was a variety of other issues occupying our attention.

By 1962-1963, numerous complaints were surfacing from the police as a result of the rapid growth of basement clubs that were being used for social and drinking purposes in the central Brixton area. Also, there was a proliferation of weekend parties held in the multi-occupied houses much to the disgust of their white neighbours.

These weekend parties were an important feature in the social calendar of the community. They offered a timely respite from the struggles of the working week and were an antidote to the pent up frustrations and insecurities of living in Lambeth.

The rhythmic movements of the dancers, the cacophony of laughter and animated conversations; all experienced behind firmly closed doors felt, to the outsider, like precursors to trouble and impending disorder.

Relationships between our community and their white neighbours were at breaking point.

It was not surprising then that officers of the Council sought the services of the St John's Club to assist in reducing the rising tensions. We agreed that three of our male officers would visit the parties on Saturday nights and ask the host to lower the volumes of the music as soon as 11pm approaches. Most people were co-operative. This led to an agreement about acceptable behaviour and noise control. In so doing, the parties were concluding much earlier because once the volume of the music was lowered, it became bereft of its pulsating, invigorating rhythm and less attractive to the dancers.

The basement clubs were far easier for the authority to obliterate because of the Licensing Act 1961. The successful objections made to the authorities against the issuing of licences were very effective, resulting in a total closure of the basement clubs in a very short time.

During the summer of 1964, I became more acutely aware of the noticeable influx of West Indians in the area. It was not difficult to understand the problems that were surfacing. Many of them needed help to understand the public services and acquire knowledge of correctly accessing them. Accommodation seemed to be the foremost problem. From my own experience, I had no doubt that they were met with suspicion and reserve, because their colour was noticeable.

We saw this as a community problem, so through the work of St John's we visited West Indians in their homes by knocking on doors on Sunday afternoons to engage as many as possible in conversation, giving advice and information.

We also took the opportunity to invite them to our Wednesday night meetings at the Club. In doing so we were attempting to relieve the isolation that many of them were experiencing. Local Liaison Committees were set up by the Council for Social Services and the Council of Churches, both of mainly white membership. The Liaison Committees were not voices of protest but voices of conscience of the establishment, built up in the belief that the newcomers needed only help and friendly guidance and that there was nothing fundamentally wrong with the host community. However, a growing racialist lobby, individual's experiences of racial discrimination and the findings of Social Surveys, all began to give warnings that a substantial reservoir of racial prejudice existed. This caused us grave concern.

Challenging Lambeth Council

The outbreak of rioting in Notting Hill in West London in 1958 and similar disturbances in Nottingham, both with racist undertones, were stark testaments of the deep seated and alarming fissures in the communities where Caribbean people settled. A true reflection of how the Government of the day viewed our presence was reflected in the hurried enactment of the Race Relations Act 1962.

The government's intervention to tackle the rise of racism, particularly in the public sector, and to arrest the growing unease between communities was to put forward proposals contained in the White Paper, 'Immigration from the Commonwealth 1965' which embodied the British policy in relation to people from the New Commonwealth. Despite opposition from politicians, social commentators, churches, people from various sections of the community and delegates who voted against it at the Labour Party Conference in the autumn of 1965, the Policy was adopted.

The White Paper proposed to take away citizenship rights which had always distinguished commonwealth immigrants legally from aliens. It excluded children aged under 16 years from joining their parents, except in proven cases of special hardships. It endowed general powers in respect of entry to Immigration Officers. Even the man on the street who would have normally ignored the significance of the issues raised realised that the subject matter had grave consequences for these immigrants who left their families in the West Indies with the hope that, in time, they could work and save in order to enable a reunion with their loved ones in the UK.

The second section of the proposal was geared towards 'integration' and the setting up of a new National Committee for Commonwealth Immigrants (NCCI) to co-ordinate the work of the Liaison Committees throughout the UK. These proposals were not readily embraced by the mass of commonwealth immigrants. As a result, the Liaison Committees, with its focus on nurturing the 'good will' of the host community, had now taken on the role of dealing with the 'ill-will' of this community. Their work attracted a great deal of criticism and they were vilified and viewed with suspicion by a cross section of the community.

During the protests that followed, a small group of us in the declining St John's Interracial Club turned our attention to Lambeth's policies in relation to the welfare and social problems of the West Indian community. We had lived in the borough for well over ten years, but until then Lambeth had not treated 'immigration' as a major public issue. The muted voices of the first generation West Indian residents, to which the Council had grown accustomed, became louder in their objection to being treated as an invisible entity. Demands for action from Lambeth were made by the active forces within the Liaison Committees and the St John's Interracial Club. Towards the end of 1966, the Council eventually set up an Official Liaison Committee. A document was produced, 'Immigration from the Commonwealth', as a follow up to the Government's White Paper.

This document revealed the appalling condition of Lambeth's housing stock. It stressed that there was no hope for the Council to rectify the acute housing need unless it was handled at Central Government level and with assistance from the Greater London Council (GLC). The document also suggested that it was the immigrants who had made the Council's task impossible. On a whole Lambeth's frantic plea for help resulted in attention being focused on a Borough which had come to be regarded as a barometer for race relations in Britain.

The Jamaican-born Chairman of the St John's Interracial Club, Courtney Laws, an ingenious, energetic man who became the backbone of the organisation, was among the first to recognise the shift in emphasis, from a Welfare Work Model to a Voluntary Community work ideal. Unable to gain the organisation's agreement and support to focus on the Community Work ideal, he resigned his position as Chair.

The shifting perspective of race relations within the community made it quite difficult for us to focus on particular aspects. There were so many concerns. For example, at that time the residents who held leases on the houses in the Sommerleyton and Geneva Road areas of Central Brixton, known for its poor housing conditions and high concentration of immigrant families, were served with 'Dilapidation Notices' by Lambeth Borough Council, i.e. requests was made for the properties to be put in acceptable structural order in accordance with the conditions of the lease. This resulted in a 'standoff' between the residents of the area and Lambeth Council.

The majority of the landlords, most absentees, were Maltese and West Indians. Courtney Laws, now firmly committed to community development and self-help, took on the cause on their behalf and established the Sommerleyton and Geneva Community Association. He effectively got the Council to adopt a more caring responsible attitude, to undertake a programme of housing rehabilitation rather than the suggested 'Dispersal Plan'. The organisation focussed on the housing and social needs of the residents in that immediate area. Representation was made to the Council for support to deal with the stressful situation which arose from the upheaval. There were many psychiatric cases, neglect of children and an increase in anti-social behaviour.

Towards the end of 1966 we acquired a partly occupied house from the Council in Geneva Terrace to operate a Pre-School Play Group. Some members, including myself, prepared ourselves for this new role by attending a training course at London's most prestigious Adult Education institution, Morley College in North Lambeth.

A prefabricated building was made available to us to hold meetings with the residents. Here counselling sessions and recreational activities were organised supported by Lambeth Mobile Library Services. One of the most outstanding contributions we could have hoped for was the total commitment of a dedicated team of social workers from the Borough's Social Services Children's Department. Families were rapidly falling apart and tremendous support from the Department was given to the families as well as to us, the workers, who tried our best to 'stem the tide'.

The Council's housing stock was in grave disrepair, except for a few freehold properties in which owner occupiers resided. White residents who had lived in the area for many years before the immigrants arrived watched the social and physical decline of the neighbourhood - floor-boards in houses disappearing into dust and the roof of houses becoming so porous one could view the stars on a clear night. However, there was no racial conflict between the host community and the immigrant groups. The new comers felt that to be white was to be privileged and since they could not regard themselves as such, sharing an environment with white people who like themselves were equally powerless to effect change, became a way of life.

Later, with the Council's rehabilitation of some of the houses and the eventual demolition to make way for a new type of accommodation, some residents were re-housed. Mission accomplished.

One unique aspect of Courtney Laws' role and value was that he would walk daily through the streets and market place of Central Brixton where everyone knew him and where he knew everyone. He played a valuable role in pioneering Lambeth's very first free Legal Advice Service and he provided housing for the elderly. It was sad that his later months were dogged by wholly unfounded allegations of mismanagement which emanated largely from jealousy and conspiracy within the Community. Courtney Laws OBE, being the innovator he had proved to be, set up the Brixton Neighbourhood Community Association which served the community in a number of desirable ways for many years up to his death in July 1996.

My Own Housing Crisis

The landlady offered to take care of my two children during the day. You can imagine my delight not having to take the children out daily to a child-minder. A few weeks passed and

I became content with this excellent arrangement when two incidents occurred which militated against the continuation of my day care bliss. The child-minder explained that the baby was sick on her new candlewick bedspread. I apologised profusely and took the bedspread to the launderette.

Then one Sunday afternoon, having completed my chores, we went to have an afternoon nap. There was a knock on the door. I woke up, staggered to the door and was confronted with the landlord and three other people. He said, "I want to show these people the room".

My husband and the children were fast asleep. Instinctively I said, "sorry it is not convenient for you to look around now, perhaps…".

Before I completed the sentence I was sent flying, whilst he pushed into the room with his friends in tow. Naturally an argument ensued that culminated in him telling us that we must vacate the room by Friday.

I will never beg anyone to reverse their decision when my position becomes untenable; we searched diligently for alternative accommodation with bath and kitchen. Most multi-occupied accommodation offered a shared cooker on the landing, sometimes opposite your room; a kitchen sink might be available up or down a flight of stairs and no bathroom. The week went quickly and when we thought that all was well, having paid a week's rent on another accommodation, we began packing.

On the evening of the removal, the mini-van arrived and as Herb started to put the things in the van, a young man asked, 'Where we were moving to?'. On telling him the address, he looked puzzled and asked, "Are you sure you got that room? I know someone who is moving into that very room tonight".

We were dumb founded. Then the young man suggested that Herb should stop removing anything else out of the room and go to the other place to find out for certain whether or not they were expecting us. The baby's pram was quickly put back inside the room while the van driver was asked to suspend the removal activity. Herb hurried off. He returned shortly afterwards, anxiously and nervously, putting our possessions back in the room before the landlord realised what was happening.

Herb later told me that when he got to the house it was in total darkness. On knocking the door, someone came and handed him his money before he could utter a word. The voice through the darkness said, "The room was already rented when you came".

As he walked away from the door, feeling weary, angry and dejected, a van drew up with the new tenants. But our situation was made worst by our landlord's and his prospective new tenants' anger because in anticipation of us leaving that night, the latter had arrived to take our place. It was a humiliating night that I will never forget. The landlady banged on our door for the rest of the night and when her husband returned in the early hours of the morning from his British Rail night shift, he continued the disturbance.

The following day neither of us could think about going to work. It was room hunting at all cost. Someone recommended that we go to Number 50 Gresham Road, a stone's throw from Brixton Police Station. There we found a comfortable basement room. Comfortable, in that it had potential. The kitchen was painstakingly fitted, flooring and walls tiled and to be shared with a single male tenant. I could not be sure what was the true colour of the cupboards nor the tiles; the air was foul, it reflected the presence of an un-kept canine but I felt that a thorough clean up with some strong detergent and wire brush could bring about some good results. I offered to take the room.

The landlady could not believe what she was hearing. She looked at me long and hard, smiled and asked, "You really want it?" I said, "Yes". She had no idea how desperate we were.

That very evening we returned to the place with a bucket and cleaning materials and hours later my kitchen, with its midnight blue cupboards, floor tiles and white wall tiles, stood out in its splendour. A close escape from homelessness was so far averted. However, it was not long before my homely bliss was again interrupted. The landlady announced, out of the blue, that her daughter, who had lived away from home, would like the accommodation. So it was time for us to move on.

A couple that we knew from Jamaica, whom we visited quite often, were being faced with the same predicament regarding their housing situation; three children in one bed-sit, so they asked if we could lend them some of our savings so that together with what they had they could purchase a property. We readily agreed to lend them £250, almost all of our savings, and they offered to rent us one of the large rooms at their newly acquired home in Josephine Avenue, SW2. We were very happy for them and settling in was not at all difficult because the wife and I attended the same commercial college and the husband and I were members of the same choral society, so we more or less had common interests.

Baby number three came along on the 9th March 1961 and with three children under five, I could not hold down any employment.

My previous job paid £12 per week; child minding cost £4 per week, plus food and toiletries. Economically that was a no-no and to be honest I did not possess the energy or inclination to go off to work and leave my children so I decided to remain at home. Herb supported this decision, although it was evident that we would have to make sacrifices and forward planning for the future.

Honesty and trust would have to be the hallmark of our everyday life for things to work out successfully. But it later appeared much to my regret that we were agreeing to take that road for different reasons – I wanted to spend the time with my children during their formative years, despite the lack of material things. He wanted that too, but in addition he wanted to ensure that I was permanently unemployable – thus becoming completely dependent on him for my every need.

This I could not promise and I started to complain about his complacency in securing proper accommodation for our growing family. My concerns became even more acute when I was not allowed to take my children to play in the back yard. Have you noticed that I used the term 'back yard' instead of garden? It was a bare yard without a sight of weeds, let alone plants. I could not fathom the significance of it being made into a no go area for my children. We took them to the nearby Brockwell Park as often as we could – I recall us purchasing a second-hand three-seat couch that served as their play area, positioned in a way that they could look out from the window.

The children learnt to walk on the tip of their toes so as not to disturb the tenants who occupied the ground floor rooms. Such strain, anxiety and uncertainty of my everyday life in Britain plus what seemed like endless cold and sometimes rainy days, encouraged me to remain indoors. At least I was away from the stares and gaze of some of the people. I felt strange and unwanted, sometimes I consciously felt being dissected by those curious eyes, even small children called me 'nigger' and put out their tongues at me. When out with the children the women would linger by the side of my double buggy, waiting for an opportunity to feel the texture of their hair – their curiosity was so noticeable.

My boredom was somewhat alleviated when the St John's Interracial Club asked me to take on some secretarial duties. I can recall dealing with correspondence in preparation for the King George the V Memorial Jubilee celebration event. The Trinidadian members led the carnival style procession from Clapham Common through to Central Brixton – culminating with a musical fair at Brockwell Park. I was very happy to use my skills as a stenographer with this group and so extended my role beyond that of a full-time housewife.

Challenging the Boys in Blue

A chilly wind of change, within the Metropolitan Police 'L' Division, blew frostily cold towards the immigrant population. By 1963, the Police were openly entering the homes of Caribbean families on the pretext of searching for something but not presenting a search warrant. Engaging with some officers, for whatever reasons, would often elicit abuse by way of racially derogatory comments and on challenging such attitudes, resulting in being placed under arrest for assault on the officer or obstruction.

Other popular responses from the boys in blue were their willingness to enter parties and social gatherings, confiscating the drinks on the allegation that drinks were on sale. In one instance, the Police entered a wedding reception and although it was obvious what the occasion was, they took away the cake and the drinks and the gifts to the Police Station. The Chief Inspector, in his naivety, pointed out that all efforts to get the people responsible to remove the articles from the premises had failed. The family became frustrated with the insensitivity of this police intervention and decided to seek legal advice.

When the case was heard in court, it was proven that the occasion was in fact a wedding reception. The Police, however, maintained that they were at a loss to understand the speech of a West Indian, especially in cases of emergencies via the telephone, because of his excitable nature and unclear language.

Whenever there was a complaint against white attitude and behaviour, members of the West Indian community would be often viewed as the troublemaker.

I recall being one of the Box Office attendants at a dance organised by the Interracial Club on 26th December 1964. The tickets were sold out. The assembly room at Lambeth Town Hall was full to capacity of nearly 450 people but there were still a crowd of people waiting for admission. With regrets, having refunded money to the disappointed ticket holders, the door was duly closed. Many people lingered on the pavement.

Two Police officers on patrol in the area considered them as causing an obstruction and asked them to move on. It took some time for them to clear the area. Reinforcement was summoned including two dog handlers who charged at the crowd, resulting in the manhandling of some people and a member losing buttons from her coat as a result of the dog charging at her.

This incident was recounted in a pamphlet, Nigger Hunting in England, written by Joseph Hunte and published by the West Indian Standing Conference in 1966.

A formal complaint was made to the Chief Inspector and after several weeks a reply came back saying that the "physical contact that occurred amounted to no more than a hand on arm for guidance. If through mischance the dog removed buttons from the lady's coat with its paws, this is very much regretted". He concluded, "I regret that you had cause for complaint but I am unable to find that the Officers acted other than properly in the execution of their duties".

As an eyewitness to the incident, this reply from the Chief Inspector left me seething.

Numerous other cases come to mind where the Police openly displayed unfair practices. Young Black males seemed to be the target for such practices. Under the terms of the Vagrancy Act, these young stallions from our community were often seen as acting suspiciously whenever and wherever they congregated. More often they were identified by the clothes they wore. The Crombie styled overcoat that was the fashion for boys was usually the apparel the Police linked to identify those acting in a suspicious manner.

Commonly referred to as 'Sus', this practice touched the hearts and souls of parents and activist alike because a growing number of children were collecting criminal records like medals for outstanding sportsmanship. The 'campaign for the revocation of the Act was vigorously pursued by the North Lewisham Project, spearheaded by Mavis Clarke-Best, a community worker, who was able to mobilise a large National Campaign to repeal the Act which was on the Statute Book since 1824. This was successfully achieved in 1981.

Getting on the Property Ladder

I became very dissatisfied with my situation in Britain and would often go into deep thoughts about my living accommodation that I considered to be pretty awful. I used to take a daily stroll to the Newsagents to purchase the Evening News and on Fridays the South London Press in order to read the ads for 'Houses for Sale'. I would marvel at the properties for sale, a number of which were being sold with sitting tenants partly vacant; the latter were protected under a Housing Act and had a right to remain in occupation of that particular portion of the house that their controlled rent entitled them to occupy. These houses were less expensive, but might not offer adequate space for one's own family so I had no interest because I learnt that these situations were fraught with frustration and difficulties.

I quite liked the idea of purchasing and when it was brought to my attention that we could purchase a house for £2,500 on a £250 deposit, I was enthused so I started to talk with Herb about the possibility. He was not at all interested. He thought that such a move was completely above his means; he was terrified to embark on such a business.

"How could I afford a house? Woman you must be mad", he would angrily shout.

I eventually approached our landlord and asked how soon he would be able to repay our loan. This was about eighteen months after the loan was made. He told me that he was expecting his 'pardner draw' in two months. I immediately began to plan quietly the way forward.

On receipt of the money, I put the plan into action. My searches in the Real Estate columns became more intense while our landlord and landlady's behaviour became less friendly than before making us realise that an early exit was necessary. In the meantime, Herb sought another room to accommodate the whole family while I was busily looking around for a property, even viewing a few. I knew that I could not survive in yet another bed-sit so my determination got stronger and stronger.

One day on perusing the South London Press, I came across an advertisement for a three bedroom house with two reception rooms and kitchen. I spared no time to contact the agent in order to view the property. Being satisfied with what I saw, my only disappointment was that the WC would have to be entered from the side of the house. It was effectively an outside toilet and there was no bathroom but there was a large cupboard adjacent to the kitchen that I felt could be utilised for a shower room.

I could not wait to tell Herb about this little house. We went to view it together and he was more or less inspired enough to seek more information from the agent. I will never forget that day when we went to see the agent to sign the agreement to purchase the property. They were offering to secure the mortgage for us and we were required to use their firm of solicitors. Herb called me aside and nervously announced that he did not want to purchase any property, he wanted to rent a room.

I could not believe what I was hearing. My patience gave way to a rapidly developing rage, fuelling such anger that I was not aware could have come from me. I became totally irresponsible, throwing chairs, books and anything in the office that I could put my hands on to pelt him with. I had completely lost my cool. The emotions, pent up in me for months, had finally surfaced. My tears flowed and I shook like a leaf caught in a turbulent wind.

The middle-aged lady in the agent's office was now nervously twitching; perhaps for the first time in her life she was experiencing the rage of a distraught black woman. The agent came over to me and was desperately trying to calm me down while Herb moved towards the door, calmly looking on. Eventually I felt calmer, although my body still shook at intervals. Herb then agreed to go ahead with the purchase. I knew that he was not doing this because he felt it was the right thing to do in view of our circumstances but as a way out of the embarrassment.

On our way home, he said to me, "If you cause me to lose my money on your stupid idea you will never hear the end of it".

I cannot remember making any reply to his threat because my heart was busily humming a melodious tune. In twenty-eight days, I would be receiving the keys to 8 Danes Road, SE5.

The days ahead were filled with the planning and preparation for our removal. The house was already redecorated and would be acquired with vacant possession. A few days before the expiry of the twenty-eight days, a letter from the solicitors arrived which informed us that an additional £120 to cover the cost of obtaining the mortgage would be added to our final expenses that should be paid on the completion date. Not expecting this further cost, I felt as though my world had fallen apart. This was not at all good news. "How on earth are we going to find this money?" Herb asked.

I had no immediate answer; no idea came to my head. My heart sank and I thought this is it; he is now going to lose his money if we cannot complete the transaction. The tears trickled down my face. I started to pray; I cried out "Lord show me the way". Herb heard me and he knew I was broken hearted. I was surprised to hear him suggesting that we go to Brixton to see if we could find anyone to help us. We were out of the house the following morning.

It was a bright sunny Saturday and a number of people were engrossed in their shopping at the Granville Arcade in Brixton market. We stopped to talk with one of Herb's work colleague. No, we wouldn't seek his help. We continued along Coldharbour Lane. On reaching the intersection with Atlantic Road, we saw a black man coming out of Barclay's Bank. He seemed in a hurry. Strangely, Herb and I focused on the man almost at the same time. Herb walked forward and engaged him in conversation. I immediately joined them. Herb had identified the man as resembling a large family who lived in Fairy Hill, Port Antonio, Jamaica. He remembered when as a boy he used to go up the hill to fly his kite.

The man was overjoyed to see someone who knew his family so the conversation took off in earnest. He wanted to know how long we were in London and how things were for us. The golden opportunity had arrived, Herb explained our dilemma. He listened carefully and sympathetically then said, "Oh I can help you man, come with me, I am living up Saltoun Road". We followed him gingerly. By the time we got to his house, my breathing had become a little laboured, so much so that his offer of a glass of water was very welcomed. We talked for a little while and then he counted out one hundred and fifty pounds and handed it to Herb. We offered to give him a receipt but he refused to accept. We then wanted to give him a note, to say when we would repay him but he would not accept that either. In a very lighthearted manner, he told us to repay him when it was possible for us to do so.

A friend introduced us to 'Denwoods', a furniture store in Camberwell Green and with credit from them we were able to move into the property, with the essential household gadgets, on the 9 June 1961. Our children aged five, four and three months for the first time could be accommodated in their own room. Quite often, I would mouth the biblical phrase, "God moves in mysterious ways, his wonders to perform".

Mr Buckley, our benefactor from Fairy Hill, became a regular and much welcomed visitor to our home and promptly handed back our loan repayment to our children as a present. In order to provide much needed funds, it was necessary to rent the largest bedroom to a couple.

We had no central heating; so during the winter, warmth came from the flame of the paraffin oil heater that was mostly lit during the evenings. The bed sheets were linen and cold but the weight of many blankets was reassuring. After you had been a little while in bed, it would begin to steam with damp that was oddly pleasant. In the morning ice crystals would have formed on the inside of the windows, the ledge was the ideal place to leave the jelly to set for the following day's dessert, as there was no refrigerator. The linoleum covered floor was so cold that you would waste no time to get dressed in the mornings and hurry to the kitchen.

Despite all this, we were very happy with how things were progressing. Before long, our little house had fast become an open door for social and cultural activities. The acquisition of our home coincided with a very important and historical era in British history, a low point for people in the Caribbean who were planning to immigrate to the UK. The Commonwealth Immigration Act 1962 was in the process of making its way on to the Statute Book; in this period also, Jamaica became an Independent Nation within the Commonwealth of Nations.

Many Caribbean people, especially Jamaicans, rushed to Britain in a desperate attempt to (as we termed it then) 'beat the ban'. Prior to this Act, there were no controls on the movements of Commonwealth people from the British Colonies. Our little house provided an 'oasis' of peace for many depressed but hopeful brothers and sisters, many of whom I had never met before but came to me via introductions. They used to escape from the loneliness of their bed-sits, particularly on Friday nights, to a social atmosphere where they could join in heart-warming activities, make friends and become part of a group. The laughter in our little home was infectious, despite the dreary atmosphere outside, sometimes punctuated with a welcome smile and kind words from some people within the host community.

We gathered at weekends, talked about our experiences, ate West Indian food, drank cups of tea, listened to music, sang songs and sometimes grew serious when acts of racial discrimination and racial attacks were being reported. At such times, we would crowd around the 'Formica top table', our elbows upon it, with faces near to each other and talk in low voices. Yes, I remember all that and many other things too.

Our own personal experience of securing places to live and cope with the challenges of surviving worried me a lot. Despite this nomadic existence, we tried to be good tenants but it seemed that we simply did not fit in. Having purchased a small property on a mortgage in mid-1961, we were able to lead a more settled life providing for the children in a more comfortable environment. I was stung by the urge to replicate the settled, social happiness I enjoyed in my homeland.

Our Struggles for Equality

I therefore began to extend my knowledge of Caribbean folk culture to members of the St John's Interracial Club by organising social evenings at the Club and 'at home' events in my front room. This led to the formation of the Caribbean Folk Group in 1963 with weekly rehearsals on Friday nights.

Further inspiration came from Mr Leslie Garwood, the Public Relations Officer for the London Borough of Lambeth. He was the Council's link with the community and as we were newcomers to Brixton, he was the person to turn to for advice and guidance. At that time, the 'Integration Strategy' was a much talked about idea. When Roy Jenkins, as Home Secretary, defended the idea as not a flattening process of assimilation but as equal opportunity, accompanied by cultural diversity in an atmosphere of mutual tolerance, I gave it some thought. How was I going to turn this cultural diversity into an advantage, rather than a handicap?

On one of Mr Garwood's many visits to the Club, he came over to me, after one of my performances, and said, "The Council are planning to set up an Arts and Recreation Department. It is thought that there exists a great deal of talent in the borough and we would like to give exposure to people's talent by way of asking them to give public performances in the Town Hall". I looked aghast at him. He then said, "Would you like to get some of the members together and teach them some of your songs? You could even do a play". My reaction was. "A play? Teach them?"

I didn't think I could. These were adults. My only experience was with organising children in my neighbourhood in Jamaica to put on yard concerts, to entertain the adults, particularly the elderly, using a lot of imagination to keep the naughty children out of trouble. I gained a lot of confidence from the Schools and Social Literary Forum but to work with adults, I was not quite sure.

However, after serious thoughts I decided to take on the challenge. I visited Boosey and Hawkes, HMV Oxford Street and other West End stores that were stockists of recorded music from the Caribbean. I thought of presenting a one-act play for the first half of the programme and folk songs and dances for the second half. Finding a Caribbean play proved very difficult. At that time, the West Indian Students Centre in Earls Court could not help in finding a script but they were able to introduce me to a fantastic pianist, Joyce Wade, a Jamaican student who was here studying at London University. We eventually decided to do Harold Pinter's 'Slight Ache' that virtually had two speaking parts, the third character being dumb.

The second part of the programme included folk songs from the Caribbean, dialect poetry and suites of spirituals. I desperately wanted to create a good and lasting impression of the presentation both of educational and aesthetic value. Costumes for the folk singing group were vital for visual effect but it was not possible to obtain the official 'bandanna' outfit. In 1963, there were a number of young women still in possession of their flared skirts adorned with embroidered or painted Jamaican sceneries, the fashion in those days, and a must for most women immigrating in the late 1950's-1960's. We were fortunate in assembling enough garments for the cast.

Stage props for the play was another much needed visual effect. The garden, according to our interpretation of the script, would be the most enchanting prop to acquire but how could we achieve this? Determined to make this presentation as authentic as possible, I visited the Commonwealth Institute in High Street, Kensington to look for music scores for some of the songs we were planning to present. The Institute proved to be an excellent resource. Where there was no music scores, I was able to borrow recordings.

On my way back to the underground station, feeling well pleased with the materials I had obtained, my eyes focused on the display windows of the two large department stores on either side of the entrance to High Street Kensington station. 'Barkers' and 'Derry & Toms'. And there my eyes feasted on a most magnificent garden display in the front display window of Derry & Toms. My excitement was kindled with the idea of having this garden set, sun loungers, ornamental grape harbour, artificial flowers in large decorative pots. The set was most beautiful. I thought, and I thought and with determined strides, I took the lift to the top floor, garden furniture department. I remembered the good Jamaican adage "look for one good face smady" meaning "look for a pleasant person".

I looked around at the personnel and selected a lady who seemed pleasant and approachable. I greeted her and told her that I would like the store to loan me the use of the garden display in the downstairs window to be used as a prop for the play 'Slight Ache' by Harold Pinter. I pointed out that the flowers and plants mentioned in the script were represented in the display and that it would enhance the depiction of that garden on stage. She smiled and seemed quite receptive to the idea but asked me to wait while she went to seek out the manager.

Soon a well-proportioned middle-aged man came up to me, extending his right hand. Having shaken hands, I repeated my request. I gave him the date of the event and the venue,

Lambeth Town Hall, Brixton. My heart was now racing while my emotions were jostling with each other for prominence. He readily agreed to loan me the entire set for the dress rehearsal and performance and offered to transport them to and from the venue.

I stood there happy but shaking with amazement. I thanked him heartily and promised to send him complimentary tickets and the programme, showing the acknowledgement of our grateful thanks for his help. As I left the store I wanted to shout for joy, I wanted to express how wonderful it was to be treated as human and with respect. In those early years, such gestures did not come easily. I looked around for a black person to share my experience with but alas, although it was the rush hour period, there was none in sight.

My entry into the voluntary sector was thus bolstered by this little success. I had no illusions of the tasks that lay ahead if we were to become an important player in our development as a community. Confronted with a goal, not only beyond our means but beyond our powers of definition, we struggled to formulate a strategy and to work out what it meant in terms of action. Such words as 'Grant-aid' were unheard of. While a few people were willing to put their sixpences towards the purchase of writing paper, envelopes and stamps, mistrust and a lack of self-help drive prevented many from making their contributions.

A number of groups were emerging, each with their own ideology. The politics of 'race' had spilt over to Britain from the USA, headed by a group of academically trained young people whose preaching about the "disenfranchisement of the black race" by the colonial powers soon found support from the young people in particular. The Black Panthers UK and the Black Liberation Front, with their Black Power sentiments, were the precursors of a combative and communal struggle that took on like wild fire, particularly among the young and the students.

The Pentecostal Church movement also grew as did the Rastafarian movement. In addition, there were some individuals who aimed at attaining a party political voice, while others preferred the interracial way by marrying into the host community.

A group of us from the declining St John's Interracial Club continued to meet in each other's home to discuss and highlight a number of the situations that the local community were experiencing. We could not realistically confine ourselves to welfare problems, neither could we become a 'political pressure group'. Our perception of the situation at that time was that none of the political parties had yet recognised the immigrant community as a viable entity or perhaps they were gripped with the fear that association with the newcomers could cause their political suicide. Every issue, be it housing needs, discrimination in employment, the education of West Indian children, incidence of violence and Police abuse, posed its own dilemma. There was no clear direction from any source as to a way forward. Everyone was groping in the dark on an untrodden path to tackle racial discrimination that was soon to be regarded as the symptom of a national disease.

Our small group eventually decided to engage itself in a mixture of welfare activities and pressure group tactics. We had become so motivated in the struggle for equality that not even the lack of a centralised leadership within the community could diminish our resolve.

The Education Debate

By the early 1970s, concerns were surfacing about the persistent educational underachievement of West Indian children in the British school system. Culture, language differences and parent's unrealistic expectation for their children's attainment were some of the reasons given by educationalists for this failure. In 1969 I had become a member of the North London based Caribbean Educational and Community Workers Association (CECWA). A conference was organised to look at the educational attainment of the West Indian child in the British school system. This was led by John La Rose of New Beacon Books, Waveney Bushell, a psychologist and Winston Best, a teacher.

The main paper was presented by Bernard Coard, a teacher from an East London school, with experience of teaching in the United States. His paper detailed the way in which the system operates. This is strictly in accordance with a Euro-centric approach and in total ignorance of the background and culture of the West Indian child. Through this system, a disproportionate number of West Indian children were systematically consigned to the schools for children with special learning difficulties. We were so fired by what was said at this most informative conference that Bernard Coard was encouraged to publish his presentation, together with the recommendations. A pamphlet, "How the West Indian Child was made Educationally Sub-normal in the British School System", was published by New Beacon Books amidst wide publicity.

This was new information that West Indian parents were receiving about their children's education. It explained why their children were attending 'special schools' and the true meaning of the word 'special'. Parents expressed feelings of shock, anger, distress and being let down by the British system. Gradually parents formed into groups and started to discuss ways of combating this treatment of their children. The authorities on the other hand felt that they were correct in placing the children in 'special schools' given the fact that they were following the anthropologist theories of the intellectual inferiority of the black race.

Bernard Coard was, however, blamed for criticising the authorities for their negative attitudes towards the children. While the debates about Coard's findings raged, I invited him to Brixton, in the Borough of Lambeth, where a number of parents were already discussing some of the problems they were encountering in the schools their children were attending. His delivery highlighted some of the situations with which they could identify. He recommended some actions to the parents that were easily attainable in that they only required a measure of parent participation in the life of the school and an unreserved interest in their children's progress with the teachers could help to bring about a healthier relationship between the home and school.

Coard's advice became a challenge to many parents who began to visit the schools with the express purpose of having first-hand information about their children's progress. The St John's Interracial Club was instrumental in enlisting the help of Waveney Bushell, an Educational Psychologist from the London Borough of Croydon, also a Member of the CECWA and Ros Howells, a Community Worker from the London Borough of Lewisham, now The Baroness Howells of St Davids OBE. Their support in attending the Parent Education sessions in Brixton to advise, stimulate and encourage dialogue with, and amongst, the parents resulted in their acquisition of better knowledge of how to get involved in the life of their children's school.

A consciousness about the importance of helping children with their schoolwork and providing them with an atmosphere at home, which is conducive to learning, soon became evident among many of the families I visited.

The notion of encouraging the setting up of supplementary schools and reading groups was actively pursued. 'The Gresham', a project of the Council for Community Relations in Lambeth, was foremost in attracting funds from the Inner

London Education Authority for the delivery of a learning programme that sought to confront not only under achievement but develop positive self-esteem and empower parents to be more active in their children's education. The Ahfiwe School, as it was called, became an early resource for assisting children with homework facilities and tuition in a variety of subjects, out of school outings and outreach work with local schools. This innovative learning programme was pioneered by Gerlin Bean, a Nurse and Community Development Worker, the Rev. Anthony Ottey and Ansel Wong, a trained teacher.

There were a number of parents whose inhibitions prevented them from engaging with the teachers of thier children. In such cases, workers and volunteer teachers from the Ahifiwe School accompanied them to the schools in a supportive role. As their confidence grew, they developed increased awareness and soon were able to participate in the wider community issues. Later, Marcia Wright and an army of volunteers, many of whom had greatly benefited from the work of The Gresham, continued the work until the demise of the Council for Community Relations in Lambeth in 1989.

Housing & Schooling: Sorted!
In view of the Borough's poor and inadequate housing stock which was evidenced by the large percentage of dilapidated boarded up properties, squatting of houses deemed as not fit for human habitation and the increase in multi-occupied dilapidated tenement houses, Central Government could no longer continue to ignore the growing housing crisis. By 1964, the Urban Renewal Programme was being debated, culminating in the Government's decision to put into effect the Compulsory Purchase Order Act 1966. This Act would affect the owners of properties in those areas where the housing stock was nearing its structural life and where demolition and

the building of new houses would benefit far more people than would be displaced by demolition.

These areas were not publicly identified but, in view of my interest and experience of working with the owners and occupiers in Geneva and Somerleyton Roads and Loughborough Park, I contacted the Housing Manager, Mr Harry Simpson, with whom I had a good working relationship. I wanted more information on the Urban Renewal Scheme. He invited me to his office where I was afforded the opportunity to look at the map and diagrams of the areas that the Government's proposal would affect. Danes Road, the quiet cul-de-sac on which my little house was situated, was very much part of the scheme. I was moved with mixed emotions; joy, as I wanted to sell the house, tempered with anxiety, as Herb's refusal, could result in uncertainty that the Government's compensation, under the scheme, may not be enough to allow us to purchase a house on the open market.

I soon developed an obsession for information about the scheme. I wanted to be equipped with the knowledge of how to deal with this 'Compulsory Purchase Order'. I learnt that one could not object to the making of the order on one's property and the only thing for me to do was to await communication from the Borough Council who would be implementing the Central Government's Order. I could not wait to discuss this, my findings, with Herb, but my excitement and curiosity about the outcome of this Order was met with disinterest and put aside as something which might happen in the distant future.

A few months went by, long enough for me to have put the situation on the back burner, when a brown envelope, franked with the Lambeth Borough Council's logo, dropped through the flap of my letterbox. "Oh, oh", I shouted as I opened the letter, eager to read its contents. It pointed out the compulsory nature of the Order, an offer price of £2,500 and it expected complete vacant possession of our property. I sat for a while, glued to my seat pondering the reality of our situation. I rejected the offer, explaining that the mortgage on the property would be redeemed leaving us with little capital to enter the housing market at the current prices.

The Council's response was swift. The purchase price offer was increased by £500 with an offer of re-housing the family in a Council owned accommodation. We were agreeable to being re-housed on a Council Estate until it emerged that black people were being allocated to the most unpleasant estates in the borough. I did not want that for my children and decided to fight vigorously against making such a decision.

Coinciding with the Urban Renewal Plan and the dispersal of the people to other areas, the borough boundary to the South Western section of Streatham changed, taking parts that were formally within the Borough of Wandsworth.

Lambeth, in an ambitious renewal scheme, was in the process of buying a considerable amount of privately owned properties much to the annoyance of the over-whelming white residents of Streatham.

On the night in November 1966 when the Urban Renewal Policy Statement was presented to the full Lambeth Council meeting, a number of members from the St John's Interracial Club, including myself, took our seats in the public galleries. A delegation of white residents from Streatham had come to protest at Lambeth's decision to buy their homes. They brought with them a petition with 1,200 signatures.

It was clear that the Council had already made a decision in principle and was prepared to justify it by argument and reason. As a result, the Policy Statement was unanimously passed and so the Leigham Court Estate was made part of the

Urban Renewal Scheme. It was earmarked to rehouse a cross section of the community, including owner-occupiers from the Flaxman area of Lambeth. I left the meeting with high hopes of finding accommodation suitable for my family. With the Council's purchase of Danes Road completed, we were asked to indicate the area in which we wanted to be allocated. Well, trust me, I elected to reside in Streatham.

The first offer came quickly. A two-bedroom first floor maisonette was allocated to us. I went to view it and wasted no time in rejecting the offer making it quite clear in my letter to the Officer that I was being removed from my three-bedroom house with a garden and adequate sleeping arrangement for my five children. I concluded by asking that the Council, in its allocation strategy, consider the importance of treating families as a unit, which deserve accommodation according to the number of family members, regardless of their ethnic origin. I was just thinking that I had a fight on my hands when a letter arrived to inform us that a house comprising four bedrooms, three receptions and the usual amenities had been allocated to us in Streatham. Keys were available from the Housing Office. My quiet murmurs of "Praise the Lord" accompanied me to the Housing Office.

Having collected the keys, I made my way to Barcombe Avenue, Streatham Hill. As I walked down the Avenue, my spirit soared high! Just the type of neighbourhood I would like my children to grow up in. Number 111 stood out to greet me. A house on three floors with large bay windows, I released the lock and walked into the hallway. The place represented everything I had wanted as accommodation. I looked in every corner, then sat on the step and pondered.

I could hardly wait to share the excellent news with Herb and the children. We all went to view our dream home that very evening. The following day, without any hesitation we accepted the offer of becoming a tenant of the London Borough of Lambeth, taking up residence in July 1967.

In the days prior to the removal, I wanted to undertake essential preparations for our moving in - laying floor coverings, hanging curtains etc - but this was not to be. Herb could not convince the Bank to deposit the Council's cheque, made out to both of us, into his personal account. After much delay, he had to adhere to the Bank's procedure so he was not at all a happy man and could not bear to see the happiness coming from the children and me.

On that bright July day when the removal van arrived and all the household gadgets were loaded, I went back inside to make sure nothing was forgotten. I stopped short in my track, glanced in the cupboard adjacent to the kitchen which I had earmarked six years earlier for a shower room and had instead become the junk room. Low and behold, the galvanised bathtub was still leaning against the wall. I got the children to help me to move it on to the van. I could not bear to leave this bit of history behind.

I gently closed the door, and slowly moved away in full recognition of what was indeed the end of an era.

We made our way to Barcombe Avenue where by then the removal van, with our possessions, was waiting. Organising the home and sorting out the children became my main focus. The summer sunshine was glorious so we spent a lot of the waking hours outdoors.

The garden was on two levels, so the children could not play their favourite ball games safely, so the Hillside Park at the other end of Barcombe Avenue served for such activities.

I could hardly believe that the days were beginning to get shorter, a sure indicator that autumn was fast approaching and preparation for finding schools for the children was to be given serious thinking. I was looking for vacancies to place one child in the infants, two children in the juniors and one at secondary level. Most people I spoke with recommended Dunraven Secondary School and Hitherfield Junior mixed school, both within walking distance from home.

On the first day of term, at the end of the school day, I went down to the Secondary School and stood by the railings outside the large impressive building and watched. The behaviour of the children leaving was as impressive as the building itself. I decided to speak with someone but could not find a black boy or girl among the steady sea of faces. I stood there thinking, thinking long and deep, when a black girl aged about thirteen walked out towards me but not looking in my direction. I quickly walked towards her and greeted her with a smile. I asked her if she was happy at the school and if she thought she was learning well. She replied, "O I like it here, it is a good school", nodding her head as she hurried away. I sensed that she was contented at the school.

I arrived with my daughter the following morning to see the Headmaster, the children were all filing into the large hall for assembly. Asked by the Secretary to await the availability of the Headmaster, we took our seats. I had already prepared her for an interview and went through some passages to familiarise her with comprehension exercises, should he decide to test her ability. The music coming from the assembly was joyful and the ambience was captivating. I sensed that he was not really keen to admit this immigrant child to his school. He asked a number of questions that I answered to the best of my ability and I had him explain the curriculum she would be following.

It was now her turn to sell herself. He did not attempt the comprehension exercises I had envisioned but he wanted to know about any extra-curricular activities that she undertook at her former school. She informed him that she played the clarinet in the school's orchestra; a raised eyebrow followed.

She then went on to emphasise her love for sports and that Silverthorne Girls School was the champion in the South London Cross Country Races for three years in succession and that she held the gold medal for one of the races. His eyes beamed as he adjusted himself and moved back in his large upholstered chair to a relaxed pose. "OK", he said, "I will offer her a place. She can start as soon as possible; tomorrow if you like". Thanking him, I breathed a sigh of relief.

We then made our way to the school's outfitters. On the following morning all decked out in her new uniform she became a pupil of the Dunraven Secondary School, settling in without any undue difficulties. The following year she was asked to join the athletic team and it so happened that Dunraven won the much-coveted trophy from her former school.

Having missed out on continuing tutorship from the school's music teacher and the inevitable set back to the bright promise she showed in playing the clarinet, she competed and was awarded a Bursary from the Inner London Education Authority to study on Saturday mornings at the Royal Academy of Music, undertaking graded examinations.

The younger children were offered places at the Hitherfield Junior Mixed School, two in the infants and one in the juniors. Christopher, who was a pupil in the juniors was already quite advanced and skilled at playing the piano with a good command of reading music. He displayed a manner that endeared him to everyone. This art form, stimulated by his father, who read music and later played the accordion for his pleasure, was effectively nurtured. He left no stones unturned in providing all the necessary support and equipment (the piano being his pride and joy) to encourage the development of a talent which showed promise. Fortunately, the headmistress, Miss Collicott, recognised his passion for music. Not only did she allow him to play for the school assembly but she often invited him to recitals given by accomplished pianists. By his eleventh birthday, he was awarded a Bursary by the Inner London Education Authority to study the piano and cello at the Royal College of Music on Saturday mornings. He also gained a place at the Bec Grammar School in the Borough of Wandsworth.

By the autumn of 1968, he started to travel further afield to continue his education. We were very happy and proud of his development, happening at a time when the crisis in education loomed. The plan for the establishment of Comprehensive Schools and the abolition of Grammar Schools came at a time when a tiny trickle of black children, like Christopher, were beginning to gain entry to prestigious Grammar Schools.

There were talks about merging the Bec Grammar School with a nearby secondary school and when that eventually happened, creating the Bec-Hillcroft School in 1971, my son faced an interesting conundrum – how to blend in with the secondary and comprehensive school ambience and culture without shedding too much of the Grammar School codes and practices. Christopher could not face going to school wearing his school tie nor using his briefcase to carry his books. We soon learnt that he had been hiding the briefcase under the Hydrangea tree in the front garden, substituting it with a plastic shopping bag. He was so anxious to be identified as one of the new breed of boys, to fit in, to belong. It must have been tremendously difficult for him to adjust to the rapid changes but then children are such resilient beings.

As time went by I sometimes visited the Hitherfield School to help children with reading, telling stories or doing playground supervision in the afternoons. At the end of the school day I used to walk up the hill with the children. I missed them so much that I would have them come home for lunch. That was not exactly the only reason; in fact, we could not afford the lunch money for five children and although the school pointed out my entitlement to free lunches, there was no way that my pride could allow me to subject my children to that form of torture by them having to stand in the free dinner queue. Therefore, I would prepare a cooked lunch for them every day, winter or summer.

Frank, my second son had, in the meantime, arrived from Jamaica aged 12 years and began his secondary education at Dunraven, as did his sister.

With the children all settled in school, except for Richard, the youngest, I decided to commence fostering children of all ages from the London Borough of Lambeth. There was then the growing crisis between the first generation parents and their teenaged children, most having arrived from the Caribbean to join their parents, many of whom they knew only by photographs. There was a lot of work to be done with the sometimes aggrieved parents and the challenging attitudes many young persons displayed. This was further aggravated by the emotional response to the culture shock they were experiencing and the strong feeling that their parents or step-parents did not love them. If there were siblings born in the UK, this new encounter could breed enormous rivalry. Again the Social Services intervention soared.

My task was to help to prevent some children being institutionalised in local authority homes and to minimise the damage to their personalities in the future. My door was open to these young people for over twelve years, deriving a small maintenance fee for each child through the local authority.

Life at our Barcombe Avenue home was a happy one. The Caribbean Folk Group met there for rehearsals on Friday nights. There were parties and literary evenings to give or attend. The children, all six of them, were usually engrossed in some form of music making - Christopher, who we called 'Wren' in homage to Sir Christopher Wren, playing his classical pieces on the piano; Valarie playing the clarinet, sometimes accompanied by Chris (Wren); Jenny playing the violin and Frank working very hard to get a tune out of the cornet. Christine would display her acrobatic prowess and Richard would sing songs from the old time music hall TV programmes.

There were regular 'at home' events with friends, family and colleagues as audiences. Midweek evenings were set aside for schoolwork and Herb would be seated close by to make sure that the homework and revision were carried out fully. Herb could be quite moody and difficult at the best of time and would, unfortunately, try to stifle conversation unless, of course, he was the one wanting to converse - he even forbade any talking at meal times!

As time went by, his attempts were scuppered. Body blows can be dealt to family life and a family seemed to reel and recover but not for long. The next soft tap can bring things tumbling down but while Barcombe Avenue stood, how well it stood!

We were afforded the opportunity to purchase the house from the Council through the Right to Buy Scheme. No time was wasted and the transfer of the freehold was executed without any delay. We very much welcomed the security of being an owner-occupier again. Houses have heydays just as people do and that of Barcombe Avenue ran for fifteen years.

CHAPTER 5

THE TURNING POINTS IN MY LIFE

There are times when I can look back and say for good or evil a turning point in my life had come.

In the spring of 1969, I made a conscious decision to discontinue my fostering arrangement with the Local Authority. All of my children were at school, except for the youngest who had celebrated his fourth birthday. A Nursery School placement was made available and once he was happily settled I applied for and was offered a position as Secretary to the Engineering Manager at Remington's Office Equipment. The journey was quite a tedious one but I was prepared to make the best of the situation for as long as I possible could. My husband predicted that I would not be able to continue in the post for more than three weeks. I was determined to prove him wrong. Two years later, I was happily settled in my job.

Another turning point was May 1971. Just as I was about to leave for work I recognised Lambeth's logo on one of the letters delivered in the morning post. I placed the letters in my bag intending to read them at a more convenient time. I walked briskly along Barcombe Avenue, SW2 and across Streatham Hill to get to the bus stop outside the Cat's Whiskers, Mecca's Dance Hall in South London. I peered nervously for an oncoming bus destined for Brixton Underground Station where I would join the newly opened Victoria Line to Finsbury

Park Station, North London. A tedious journey, coupled with my already tired and frayed nerves.

Having prepared and seen off my six children to school, my weary body usually experienced relief followed by a sense of freedom borne out of my determination to break out of the shackles of the typical servility of Caribbean women. I boarded the number 159 bus that was soon careering down Brixton Hill at such a speed that the driver omitted a request stop where an angry lady punched the air with her right hand in disgust. I held onto the rails for dear life while the bus rolled and tossed me around as the strong wind blew my carefully combed hair into disarray. I was so pleased when a seat, known as the 'beauty seat' nearest to the exit, became vacant and suddenly I remembered that the postman had brought the mail that I had tucked into my bag.

The bus was now near Jebb Avenue with HM Prison Brixton in its shadows, I quickly opened the letters. One was immediately evident as coming from the London Borough of Lambeth.

It read:

Dear Mrs Cameron
I am pleased to inform you that Lambeth Council has through a Home Office Bursary asked me to offer you a one year Community Liaison Officer's Course. This will take place in the Autumn of this year".

A sudden wave of heat rushed through my body with electrifying intensity, thrusting a tingling sensation through my stomach, cheeks and legs. The tears rolled up in my eyes, as I tried to dry my wet face. I muttered, "Thank you, Lord". I repeated the old proverbial adage, 'The darkest time of the night is just before dawn'.

I was enveloped with a sense of relief; the bus had now got to the intersection of Acre Lane with Coldharbour Lane on the right, the traffic lights indicating 'stop'. The Lambeth Town Hall stood out on the left, a bastion, that seat of Local Government that could, through its chosen Government, determine the future aspirations of its black inhabitants.

The bus was soon to stop outside Morley's Department Store where I alighted and crossed over to the Brixton Underground Station. My heart was humming and buzzing with restrained joy and as soon as I was settled in my seat for the forty-minute journey to Finsbury Park, I re-read the letter. Smiled. Yes! I became more convinced that the dawn was peeping through! Years of failure and frustration fell away. At that instant, I took my dreams off the shelf and dusted them.

Arriving at the Remington Office Equipment National Parts store outside Finsbury Park Station, I went directly to my office. John Tarling, who was transferred to London from Birmingham to set up this National Store, was now due to return to his former post. He was responsible for engaging me a year earlier.

Andy Anasi took up the position as store-man three weeks prior to John leaving; he was quite petrified as to who John's successor would be. For nearly six weeks, I was plunged in at the deep end, responding to the deluge of orders and enquiries from commercial concerns, individuals and of course Remington's own technical department.

We were informed that a successor to John had been appointed. I wondered what kind of person he or she would be. Although I was confident that the standard of my work was good and that I had proved to be a reliable conscientious worker, I could not help feeling unsettled. What if the new manager preferred a dolly bird for his secretary? After all, I was 38 years old, a mother of six children and black!

On the day that Leslie Scott, the newly appointed manager, was expected, I arrived at the office about half an hour earlier than usual. Surprisingly, Andy Anasi was already there. He was as apprehensive as I was. Andy was anxious to keep his job with an added concern. Andy's employment was a direct lifeline to his family in Eastern Nigeria. He was still reeling from the bloody experience he had had in the Biafran War and had a strong commitment to support his family who were left behind.

For me, holding on to my job was very important. It was also my lifeline for liquidity of cash and, more importantly, for the boosting of my mental and psychological wellbeing. My husband was determined to prove that he was right in believing that I could not be successful at any job but my housework. Such success, he feared, would result in my acquiring independent status within the home. Holding down this job was thus a major challenge.

Les Scott arrived on schedule. He was a quiet and experienced typewriter engineer/technician in his late 50s who had given nearly thirty years' service to Remington. He soon became reliant on my newly acquired expertise – and we were soon to become a formidable team in dealing with and supplying components throughout the United Kingdom.

My dream was fast becoming real. Working outside of the home for the first time in twelve years was extremely stimulating and in some cases liberating. However, there existed this constant inexplicable wish to work in the field of social welfare, aroused soon after my arrival from Jamaica in 1957. Two years later, I became a member of the St John's Interracial Club where I came into contact with a number of people who, like myself, were trying to put down roots in a strange and sometimes hostile environment. There was much to be done but I wondered where to start? It was like paddling in a pool not knowing in which direction to swim.

My first tentative steps in finding a direction was putting in motion, with the blessing of the St John's Interracial Club, a variety of activities – all aimed at the preservation of our Caribbean Family Life - to provide pre-school activities to aid children for whom intellectual and social stimulation were not available in their homes.

So the offer of a one year Home Office Bursary to undertake the Community Liaison Officer's Course was indeed a welcome one.

Following an interview in June 1971, conducted by the Principal of Hillcroft Women's College, Mrs Janet Cotterel, I was offered a place on the course to begin in the autumn of the following year.

At that time, I was the Vice-Chairperson of the Council for Community Relations in Lambeth (CCRL), a voluntary organisation set up in accordance with the 1965 Race Relations Act. The Caribbean Folk Culture Company, formed in 1963, to preserve and project the cultural heritage of the Caribbean and the West Indian Parents Action Group (WIPAG), initiated by parents to tackle educational under-achievement remained an active and important parts of my voluntary contributions.

Therefore, after spending three years in the post as Secretary to the Remington's Engineering Manager, the time had come for me to tender my resignation, to begin a new era. This was not only in terms of embarking on an academic course but also to acquire the inner-strength to be able to over-ride the intensity of the resistance that I would most certainly face from my husband.

To cope with Herb's resistance, I had to put into operation a strategy and plans so that the children could continue to enjoy a full stable home life to which they had been accustomed.

During the period, I was quite gratified by my children's absolute grasp of my situation. They demonstrated a positive understanding of the quality of life and the philosophy that I had strenuously fostered and our once per week meetings grew into a fountain of knowledge and humour. Prayer brought us closer together. My efforts in attempting to row against the rapids and my husband became a long upward struggle but my determination to succeed was by no means abated. My sense of accomplishment helped me to put the gloom and frustration on the back burner and allow laughter to get us through the hurts; such humour certainly helped to make life more palatable.

So the year 1972 began with high hopes, with a silver lining on the horizon. I was due to join the Liaison Officer's Course at Hillcroft Women's College in Surbiton, Surrey. All my expenses would be paid by the Home office through the London Borough of Lambeth's sponsorship.

As this bursary was nearing completion, I was informed that Lambeth Council had agreed to 'second' me to the Council for Community Relations in Lambeth as Assistant Community Relations Officer with special responsibility for Community Development with Women. The opportunity to study full-time for a year had certainly whetted my appetite and I would have preferred to continue in full-time education at University, perhaps to a degree level in Social Administration. But that was not to be. I was already aged forty-one, with six children of varying ages at school and my eldest daughter following her training in nursing. The time was definitely not right.

The disappointment that I felt in not being able to equip myself for the opportunities that were becoming available to me prompted me to run away from my situation, to flee from the daily reminder that I had become dependent on a husband who would do anything in his power to prevent any attempt that I may make to acquire the tools for my independence. I thought about my children's future. I recognised that without my constant presence they could become locked in a situation that might fall short of anything my dreams could have accomplished. I agonised over my dilemma, blew it all out of proportion and nearly drove myself crazy with fear, remorse and doubts. In the end common sense prevailed!

I accepted the offer of the secondment to the Council for Community Relations in Lambeth and convinced myself that the opportunity could lead me along the road to realising my ambition in life. Of equal importance was being around to continue with promoting my children's welfare. But at the back of my mind was how the radical left-wing and black groups within the community would view my appointment, suspecting me of hitching my wagon to the enemy and I could be labelled an Uncle Tom; or to be more specific, Aunt Jemima.

Jamaica Re-Visited

Visiting Jamaica fifteen years after leaving, I felt the need to retrace my steps in the neighbourhood where, as a child, I spent countless happy, idyllic times. But mother tried to put the idea out of my mind, "You must not go there", she whispered, "that area is not what it used to be. I will not be the one to take you there". The words slipped from her lips erratically, followed by that all familiar stare that I recognised from my early childhood to mean, do not expect me to change my mind. "But why?" I questioned, feeling somewhat indignant.

I soon realised that my questioning of her attitude resulted in an impasse and there was no point pursuing it. My first visit home since leaving to settle in the UK should be a celebratory occasion; I must try to be as agreeable as far as I possibly can. There was in fact a lot of talk about the remarkable changes that had taken place in the social, cultural and political life of the island and I soon came across examples of how real they were. I thought to myself, how odd, after all these years why do I want to retrace those steps which should have been long forgotten but then there was a deep rooted feeling, nostalgia I suppose, something one treasures and somehow essential for a feeling of belonging.

A week later my school mate, who was a lecturer, telephoned to invite me to accompany her to the downtown area of Kingston where she was due to attend a consultation meeting on the restoration of historical monuments. I readily agreed to go with the hope I might just be able to persuade her to drive through my old neighbourhood so I could feast my eyes. I replaced the telephone on its cradle, glowing with happiness. So it was on that bright sunny September afternoon she parked her car around the corner of the road where I had lived as a child. As I walked up to Chestnut Lane, towards my old house, the nostalgic feelings became stronger. I fought against the lump that was steadily rising in my throat and an unusual thumping in my chest was ever present.

I wondered what had become of the boys and girls with whom I played many a game of hopscotch and skipping and the many talented extroverts who readily participated in the cultural life of the community. We used to rehearse songs, plays, folk dancing and sharing of Anancy stories during the long hot evenings in preparation for our regular 'Yard Concerts', which I was overly keen to promote.

They too have probably got married, moved far away and now playing their respective roles on the world's stage. People were passing up and down the lane but I did not recognise any of the faces. The elders, I knew had probably all gone. No wonder, it was almost 21 years since I had been to the area and yet it seemed as though it was yesterday.

There in front of my house, I had expected to see the Tamarind tree, spreading majestically in the front garden but alas, there was nothing quite so spectacular. The fruit from that tree had quenched many thirsts during the humidly long summers. A picket fence was now in place and the Azalea and lovely bushes which once adorned the original fence, together with the flowers and shrubs Papa tended so lovingly, were gone. I gazed at the house in utter amazement, the white painted exterior had been changed to an olive green colour and the vented windows of the same colour had replaced the glass sash corded windows which could be pushed up and down to let in the sunlight and floral aroma from the garden. I murmured, "What have they done to my lovely house?".

The neighbourhood buzzed with a variety of sounds coming from radios, hi-fi systems and loud chatter. During my childhood, there was one radio station called ZQI and only a few people had a windup gramophone – loud chatter was very much frowned upon. I noticed the other houses; they too were not at all as I remembered them. They were so in need of some tender loving care. I turned away sadly. The memories of my early years flowed before me like a steady stream but I did not want to stem that flow.

It was natural that I would have wanted to see my elementary school that was about two blocks away. Off we went, having been warned that the area had become notorious. We stopped a little way from the school, opposite the Coronation Municipal Market. The sight of the immediate environment brought back memories so vivid that they jostled with what my eyes were seeing. My recollections transported me to those early childhood years when I was a pupil of the Ebenezer School. The wrought iron fencing and the wide gate were still the same, straddled between the dark grey stone pillars.

The gate was open, there was no sign of the heavy chain link and padlock which was always systematically placed and removed at appropriate times by Mr Morgan, the caretaker. Our Headmaster, Mr E J Hendricks, a fearlessly strict disciplinarian, nick named 'squire wid de baldhead', would not tolerate anyone using the school grounds as a public thoroughfare. I took a few steps through the gate and noticed the lawn and most of the trees were no longer there. Further along, adjacent to the now sun drenched, parched remnants of the once well-kept lawn, was the Ebenezer Church and Cemetery.

The cottage which housed the caretaker and his family was no longer there. The whole place seemed rather deserted, so still, I could hear the pods on the sturdy gungo trees rustling in the wind. I pondered about the visual changes, as my memories took me back to those childhood days when together with other children we roamed around those vast parcels of land situated beyond the cemetery, nicknamed 'back a wall', that was exclusively populated by people of East Indian descent.

Today elements of Indian dress styles and jewellery, particularly bangles, have been incorporated and adopted into African dance forms in Jonkunoo dances and during Christmas festivities. The East Indian population has now been replaced by a more deprived group who have captured the 'crown land' for their own use and it is said that lawlessness abounds in this once idyllic area. The church and cemetery have now become redundant and the school now serves as a Health Centre.

The muted sounds of the increased traffic along the Spanish Town Road merged with the rustling of the dry pods on the sturdy gungo tree as we walked back in silence, taking in the scene, all around us. A couple of men, taking advantage of the thoroughfare, as a short cut to what had now become 'no man's land', were walking towards us. They were bearded, locks men, whom most people shied away from in fear and horror, carrying what appeared to be long broomsticks in their right hands, their shoulder length locks bobbing around their faces, almost in tune with the evening breeze. Their puzzled gaze reached ours.

As we came closer, one of the men lifted his left hand and hailed, "Peace and Love, Sisters". We immediately acknowledged his salutation by saying, "Jah Rastafari". We smiled; my cousin, a bit shaken, led the way towards the school gate.

I could not pass the school building again without peeping into the lunch centre – the smell of school dinners and the musical lilt in the voices of the dinner ladies were no more. I looked with fondness at the areas to the left side of the school building where the outdoor lessons took place during the hot afternoons and recalled the stature of the headmaster taking poetry and English literature lessons, my favourite subjects. I remembered him saying to those who were not giving full attention, "You'll never miss the water until the brook is dry". We used to mouth this phrase to each other accompanied by laughter but seriously, the meaning rings through even in our adult lives.

It was time to leave the area, to detach myself from the past and look to the future, my eyes immediately focused on the triangular space, left of the fence in Ebenezer Lane, and my eyes fired with recollection upon recollection. Gone are the people who made their livelihood selling foods at the school gate – Chinaman, with his snowball cart. His cart was labelled on both sides, 'In God I trust' and his snow ball (shaved ice) was served with strawberry or lemon syrup. If anyone fancied his homemade ice cream, then the combination is called, 'Back an Front'. Mr Myrie who made 'frisco', a kind of malted milk, whisked together with milk, vanilla flavouring and yeast. Miss Stella, a very large lady with her appetising patties and plantain tart. I used to watch her stoking the fire coal under the specially designed tin to keep her patties hot to our satisfaction. There was also the candy woman, Miss Gracie, and Madda Dear with her ready to eat ripe fruits. She used to give bratta (this is extra fruit) to only those children who were well behaved and polite to adults. They all had their own vernacular and style and liked to be called by pet names which we used as a term of endearment.

Many had served generations of children outside the school gate in that very triangle but this too was empty. I looked across the main road for the thriving commercial businesses and the structured municipal market that provided the backdrop for the vitality of the setting that had attracted the country folks and townies alike. Papa's textile and haberdashery store, where I was introduced to the habits, customs beliefs and more of my island people, were now all but memories.

CHAPTER 6

COMMUNITY DEVELOPMENT

The Challenges

Returning to London, I joined the staff of the Community Relations Council in Lambeth in July 1973 at a time when the climate of race relations was complex and constantly evolving. The key features of this evolution were the obsession of politicians and the media with the presence and continued arrival of people from what was called, the New Commonwealth – Africa, Asia and the Caribbean; heightened tensions between the black community and the police with young black males being targeted by frequent stops and searches under the 1824 vagrancy laws and the emphasis by the Government on restrictions on immigration.

My area of speciality was outreach and development work with women. This invariably encompassed the family as a whole. Pressures were caused on account of housing stress, lack of recreational facilities, discrimination in employment and a social service directorate with its gross misunderstanding of Caribbean family life and their child rearing practices. This meant an intervention process which was one of the main factors in aiding the disintegration of the family units. The limited access and opportunity for children to benefit from pre-school education, further subjected a disproportionate number to be classified as Educationally Subnormal (ESN).

By being regarded as so disadvantaged, all the misconceived assumptions boxed many into a particular category, thus contributing to their inability to fulfil their true potential.

By December 1977, the reception of West Indian children into the care of the Social Services had reached an alarming proportion. Area Offices, particularly those serving the central sections of Lambeth, became overwhelmed by the steady stream of youngsters who were referring themselves for reception into care and a marked number of parents allegedly blaming the Social Workers for using strategies to snatch their children away from them. Not surprisingly, Senior Practitioners sought to broker partnership working with the Council for Community Relations in Lambeth and the West Indian Parents Action Group, with a view to improving the services given to West Indian families who were experiencing 'difficulties'.

For the Social workers, these 'difficulties' stemmed from young adolescents being rejected by their parents or who were rejecting the values of their families. The problem took two forms. Firstly, there were the children who were left in the West Indies during the early years of their lives with a relative. When the children came to London to join their parent(s) it was often the case that there was a new 'father' or 'mother' to become accustomed to. Things remain under control until the child reached adolescence. At that point, the interests of the child naturally go beyond the family and the normal conflicts of adolescence are exacerbated by the tensions generated because the child does not regard the people with whom he or she lives as their parents.

Secondly, there are children who have lived in England for all or most of their lives but who, upon attaining adolescence, embraces values that are the opposite to those of their parents. This is a variation of the generation conflicts that affect all ethnic groups. This particular form of conflict results from the experience of young black people who have grown up in the system to expect all the opportunities that are open to their white peers. When it becomes clear that in the labour market and in other aspects of life this is not so, they turn for support to an emerging black sub-culture whose values are opposed to those of their family.

It was thought that the incidence of the first type of problems would decrease as fewer children were brought over from the West Indies. Though this has undoubtedly been the case, there are still a sizeable number of children, not born in this country, coming to the notice of Social Services.

Neither of these problematic situations were amenable to help from the traditional support systems. The extended family and friends or relatives living in England had their own problems in getting by and were not able to accommodate children who had fallen out with their parents. Because of this, alienation from one's nuclear family tended to become alienation from the black community in general.

The response of Social Services was usually based on a conventional 'casework' approach with the Social Worker trying to 'mediate' between the child and the parents. This goes on for a few days and in some cases for weeks until the Social Worker finally relents to pressure from the parents and/ or the child and the reception into care takes place, usually against his/her professional judgement.

Social Workers tend to feel that black parents often find their approach difficult to understand, as they cannot see the point of trying to get past 'the presenting problem' to the cause of the difficulty. For many black parents, the solution to both the presenting problem and the cause of the difficulty is obvious - .Have the child removed to a Local authority Home where there will be 'discipline' and a regime to teach the child the error of his or her ways.

If the Social Worker does not accept this view of things, the parent tends to see this as evidence of prevarication rather than good intentions.

At the core of this phenomenon of broken attachments and traumatic reunions, we began to identify how loss and separation influenced family life in our community. We were all witnessing how the symptoms resulting from these fractured experiences were affecting families and individuals, listened to the solutions being proposed by community activists and professionals and seen examples of the impact on individuals. I was thus heartened to come upon the work of Elaine Arnold it provided me with a conceptual tool to focus my work with families. She said: "Unsatisfactory reconstituting of many, and the seeming trans generational trauma, have impacted adversely upon the lives of many children and impeded progress in their development, educationally, socially and economically." We recognised this and committed ourselves to campaigning for the eradication of all the obstacles that made it difficult for our young to live comfortable lives and be successful in several areas of society.

In my capacity as CCRL's Development Officer, together with the WIPAG counselling services, we carried out a review of Social Workers' interventions in several case studies involving West Indian families. We found that, at the outset, social workers were at a disadvantage. They had very little feelings for what is 'normal' within a West Indian family, so they quite often mistook a show of pride on the parents part for a final answer and took the child into care, where a more persistent and long term approach with the parents might have saved the situation. Also their inability to make much of an impression on the parents often left the social worker to over identify with the adolescent and accept, unquestioning, their view of the situation. This led to further estrangement of the young person from their family.

Pressure for reception into care did not, of course, always come from parents. Children who for one reason or another are experiencing difficulty at home, especially those who are subjected to a more 'traditional' regime, may well think that life will be easier in care. They may well perform delinquent acts or run away from home in order to ensure that they are taken into care. The younger the child is, of course, the more concern this causes. Parents often react to this by saying that, "it is all of the child's making" and if the Social Services intervene, they say that "the problem is nothing to do with them". Even if Social Services are not involved at this point, the parents may employ the final sanction of giving the child 'notice'. This extreme sanction, as a traditional solution, may well be the preferred option for many, accustomed to its use but it acquires a different significance when the child is given notice to leave the family home in a country where there is no extended family network to fall back on.

During the course of our dialogue with social workers in trying to find solutions to these problems, they solicited our help. We were apprehensive about what this joint working would mean for us as a voluntary organisation.

Having discussed the Social Services' approach to secure our help, we examined a number of constraints that we felt would, over time, mitigate against the difference in our styles of working. Our operational framework cannot be glibly merged with that of a Statutory Government regulated system, unless, of course, adjustments were made to certain policies. In many instances, the contacts between social workers, children and parents often happen within a milieu of conflict and crisis and where a high level of mistrust already exists between both parties. Many of the decisions taken in relation to the children are taken in crisis situations during the day. For example, a child runs away from home and is completely unwilling to go back or the parents are unwilling to have the child back. Once a decision is made in a situation like this, the tone is set for the rest of the contact.

Quite often the home situation has deteriorated to such an extent that there is no way in which the child and parents will get together. Consequently some kind of residential provision is often needed. The initial work that was carried out by Ansel Wong, Anthony Ottey and Gerlin Bean at the Gresham Youth Project, provided valuable information about the plight of many parents and their estrangement from their children. This led the Council for Community Relations in Lambeth to set up a much needed provision known as the Brixton Overnight Accommodation and Counselling Services (BOACS), used only at times of emergency. It was envisaged that this provision would be used as a 'cooling off' period but the result was that once a child had been accommodated, even overnight, it was likely that he/she would be taken into care for a longer period. This strategy did not seem to produce the desired effect, that is to have the child and his family reunited.

In view of the aforementioned constraints, in addition to our limited financial and human resources, it was incumbent on us to choose a less precarious way to involve ourselves in this very important emotional issue.

With the full support of George Greaves, my Principal Officer, I joined the Social Services Training Unit in devising induction and training programmes to sensitise workers to the key issues. One such course, on Cultural issues, was aimed at sensitising social workers and front line staff to the needs, hopes and difficulties in bringing up a family within an unfamiliar system. This course became a regular component of the Social Services Training Programme that included contributions from other West Indian workers in the field of youth and community work.

Our educational institutions faced the same dilemma. For a variety of reasons, parents did not get involved in the life of their children's school. As a member of the Caribbean Education and Community Workers Association, I was quite alarmed to learn about the extent to which West Indian children were going through the education system and leaving without being educated and without any qualifications.

During my times at school in Jamaica, I recall my teachers saying that if I wanted to reach the top of the mountain I must aim for the stars. Our children, it seemed, were made to feel that to aim for the stars was trying to be overly ambitious. Many soon became disinterested in the school environment to the point of becoming disruptive in the classroom. Truanting, particularly among the boys, became a growing problem. The gap between the children and teachers grew wider and wider as each child was viewed as a West Indian bearing stereo-typical labels, rather than an individual who was in need of motivation.

Forging links with the junior schools was another important element of my work. I commenced my involvement by first sensitising teachers about the cultural issues involved when working with the parents and their children and undertook reading and storytelling sessions with groups of children. For those who were constantly getting into trouble, many of them avidly seeking attention from any figure that represented authority. I tried to stimulate them through the introduction of creative pursuits. Out of this effort the Lambeth Youth Steel Band was formed in which initially ten children, aged nine years old, from three schools within the Borough, participated. The Inner London Education Authority provided a music teacher.

Before long their twice weekly, after school rehearsals had equipped them for public performances in the parks on Sunday afternoons, television programmes and school concerts. These occasions were joyful ones for the families and for the community. It also brought a sense of achievement to the young performers and pride in being musical ambassadors for the culture of their parents. Pride also in the use of the steel band, the only acoustic instrument to have been invented in the 20th century and that originated in a country from where their parents came – Trinidad and Tobago.

I received support and assistance to promote Caribbean culture, specifically the Folk Culture Company during 1960 – 1970 from the Library and Recreation Services of the London Borough of Lambeth.

This led me to collaborate with Manley Young, a past student of Guildhall School of Music and Drama, to write and stage the first Caribbean Pantomime - 'Anancy and Brer Englishman' - in 1971. It was commissioned by Frank Cousins, the Artistic Director of the Dark and Light Theatre in the Myatts Field area of Brixton. The plot for this 'Christmas Send Up' depicted the process of the attempted assimilation and integration of the West Indian migrant community into the host community's life style.

We projected some of the migrant's rejection of parts of a foreign culture mingled with the colour, wit, sarcasm, hypocrisy and the humour of the rhythmic Jamaican music and speech, garnished with the Anancy de Spiderman characteristic. The presentation was hilariously received by an appreciative multi-racial audience. Its popularity was marked by requests for us to extend the date originally scheduled for the performances. Again it was staged the following year, 1972, when the renowned theatre producer, Yvonne Brewster, came to our aid, making our effort a most outstanding fusion of professional actors and actresses, working successfully alongside amateurs. Later it was made into a film, under the direction of Brian Taylor, as part of the World History Curriculum Programme for the Inner

London Education Authority Schools Television Programme.

The Effra Creative Arts Centre, based at Brockwell Hall, Effra Road, owed its existence to the concerns expressed to me by Mr Reg Collins, the then Principal for the South Lambeth Adult Education Institute. He was particularly concerned about the lack of out of school provisions for the growing number of children in the area who were engaged in damaging properties, defacing objects, rowdy behaviour and menacing the elderly living on the estate. In short, this group of seven to fourteen year olds were regarded as 'out of control'.

My help was sought to spearhead some form of activities to utilise the children's energies in a more positive way. Brockwell Hall, on the edge of the estate, was offered as a venue and sessional fees from the Inner London Educational Authority could be made available. I took on the challenge.

My main help came from Jennifer Bean, Rose Lake and Jennifer Cameron, a team of students from Philippa Fawcett Teacher Training College and Clifford Adams, a Steel Band tutor. At first, the young people were reluctant to enter the building. Instead, they sometimes resorted to smashing the windows and displayed abusive behaviour. However, our door to door visits to speak with parents in the area won over their support and soon the hall was buzzing on Saturday afternoons with at least fifty children. Of course, we occasionally experience smashed windows by those who preferred to remain outside. The activities were based around creative pursuits – steel band playing, drama, singing, folk dancing, reading and writing. On a whole the three and a half years existence of the project served as a positive rehabilitative experience for the children who participated and a satisfactory and enjoyable pastime for those of us who gave our services to the venture.

After the dedication service of the Richmond Park Moravian Church, Jamaica, 1956.

Outside our first home in the United Kingdom in Myatts Road, Brixton, Lambeth, March 1957.

At farewell service, Kingston Moravian Church, with Bishop S. U. Hastings and the choristers, February 1957.

At Barry Road, East Dulwich visiting the Eddie family house, 1960.

Celebrating Jamaica's attainment of Independence in 1962.

Caribbean Folk Group first performance at Lambeth Town Hall, 1963.

Left to right: Courtney Laws, Gloria Cameron, Barbara Hicks, Mazie Spencer Stanley Dawkins, Marcia Davis, Carol Gordon, Herbert Cameron.

Family photograph at the St. John's Interracial Club, 1966.
Left to right Gloria, Chris, Valerie, Jenny, Herbert, Christine.

Family picture at Danes Road, Camberwell, 1966.

Caribbean Folk Group at Jefferys Road Methodist Church, Stockwell.
Left to right: Gloria Cameron, Stanley Dawkins, Elma Pitkins, Chris Cameron
Henry Davis, Mazie Spencer, Herbert Cameron, Valerie Cameron
Len Garrison, Gwen Byfield, 1967.

Gloria – 1967

Chris accompanying Valerie on clarinet at a house concert.
Barcombe Avenue, Streatham Hill, 1968.

Caribbean Folk Group performing the "quadrille dance", 1974.

Photograph courtesy of The Gleaner Co. Ltd

Presenting Clarence Thompson to the Honourable Michael Manley, Prime Minister of Jamaica, following his poetry rendition. Chris Cameron looks on from the right. 1974.

Photograph courtesy of The Gleaner Co. Ltd

Story telling session – School programme in Northern Ireland, 1975.

With Lambeth Youth Steel Band during performance in Brockwell Park, 1975.

Story telling session at Brixton Library, 1977.

Honourable Mrs. Louise Bennett-Coverley and the Cameron family on her visit to London in 1978.

Encouraging a group of women in the setting up of day care provision for under five year olds. 1979.

Outside the gate at Buckingham Palace after the investiture on that cold February afternoon -1980.

With Queen Mother Moore – the African–American political activist for Black Womans rights in USA and Amelda Inyang on her visit to London to inaugurate the Queen Mother Moore School and the Black Cultural Archive - 1982.

Caribbean Folk Group, in 1982
Left to right: Jennifer Bean, Gloria Cameron, Paula Tapper,
Joyce James, Jenny Cameron, Loilyn Thompson.

"Balancie"

Surprised by Eamonn Andrews during a Caribbean Folk Group performance in Brixton for "This Is Your Life" 1983.

With Mummy on "This Is Your Life" 1983.

George Greaves during "This Is Your Life" 1983.

With three senior members of the Nursery Staff, 1984.
Left to right: Pat Dunne, Jenny Cameron, Linford Anderson.

Attending the Honourable Alexander Bustamante Memorable Service at Westminster Abbey, London. - Left to right: Jenny Cameron, Susan Walker and Mrs Eva Walker (the wife and daughter of the then High Commissioner of Jamaica), Doris Thomas (Mummy), Gloria Cameron - 1984.

Being congratulated by Honourable Edward Seaga, Prime Minister of Jamaica
after being presented with the Medal of Appreciation for my contribution to
Cultural Awareness and Community Development in the United Kingdom, 1987.

Photograph courtesy of The Gleaner Co. Ltd.

Receiving congratulations from Judy Welleminsky-Smith on 60th Birthday. - 1992

Mummy – Doris Thomas with grandchildren, great grandchildren and family friends, 1992.

Caribbean Folk Group – Commonwealth Institute performance, 1996.

On board ship on the occasion of a cruise of the Eastern Caribbean Islands, 2001.
Left to right Craig, Richard, Chris, Shadid, Kumar.

With Grandchildren and Great-grandchildren, 2007.
Left to right Kristian, Ayanna, Nathanel, Vickie, Shadid, Unwray, Francesca,
Wrayell, Lamiyah, Gareth, Martina, Samaaya, Safron, Craig, Neo.

CHAPTER 7

MY KEY MILESTONES

Gloria Cameron JP

The appointment to serve as one of Her Majesty's Justice of the Peace was not without its unfair share of confusion. In 1973 soon after I commenced work with the Council for Community Relations in Lambeth, a prominent member of the community, Rudy Narayan, a Barrister, nominated me to the Lord Chancellor's Advisory Committee to be considered for an appointment as a Justice of the Peace. He shared with me the contents of the letter he submitted and I was quite happy with the language he used in describing my character and capabilities. The penultimate paragraph of the letter expressed the assurance that in his estimation my appointment as a Justice of the Peace would bring to the Bench a most desirable presence.

My agreement for the nomination to go forward was fired by the unfavourable set of circumstances we, the African-Caribbean people, were facing. At that time, few people within the black community of the Borough of Lambeth were regarded as having a reputable standing. I therefore viewed this move as a forward step to rise above this negative thinking by assuming the much needed and important role of signing declarations and witnessing signatories. Furthermore, with the Nationality and Citizenship Act making its way on to the Statute Book, this appointment would equip me to serve the community at large. I also became aware that one of the main functions of the position was that I would be required to undertake Court sittings on a regular basis.

My knowledge of the disproportionate number of African-Caribbean youngsters, especially boys, who were going through the Court system was sharply aroused on a daily basis whilst carrying out my duties in the Community Relations Office. The traumas faced by parents whose children had re-joined them from the Caribbean after years of separation was manifesting itself in ways alien to all concerned. My awareness of how cultural factors could be seen by the host community as a form of delinquency and dysfunctional behaviour when dealing with the new comers, certainly helped me to understand some of the situations. Since our community did not, at that time, have the experiences or liaison with the establishment I felt ready to give my service.

Within a few weeks I was invited to an interview at which I dealt with the searching questions asked of me to my honest and best ability. Soon afterwards, I was informed that my name had been placed on the waiting list. One year elapsed, two years went by and the whole idea of this appointment became a distant memory. There was a twist in this nomination which afterwards, on reflection, made me smile. In the Spring of 1975 a decision to appoint me was made by the Lord Chancellor's Advisory committee. Unfortunately I was away in Scotland with a group of children who were taken on an Educational Retreat Project by the Education officer and Project Officer for CCRL.

On my return to London, two weeks later, there were two letters from the Lord Chancellor's Office awaiting my attention. One carried the good news that I had been appointed a Justice of the Peace for the Inner London Commission and asked that the information be kept in the strictest confidence until it had been gazetted and the swearing in ceremony had taken place. The second letter greatly alarmed me. It asked me to explain why the confidentiality as set out in the previous letter had been breached. A South London Press reporter had sought confirmation of my appointment. I felt awful about what the second letter had conveyed because I had no idea as to how the information could have become public knowledge.

Faced with a situation that required careful handling, I shared my dilemma with CCRL's Principal Officer, George Greaves and the Education Officer, Miranda Hislop, the latter being one of whom I had accompanied to Scotland. Together we formulated a response to the Commission for the appointment of Justices of the Peace. We explained in detail the facts of the matter. I later learnt that my nominee who as a Barrister, worked within the Court system, mentioned the appointment in a 'Brixton Pub', hence the South London Press reporter's interest in having the news confirmed. This also brought to the surface emotional problems for me because my husband was at a reception held for a visiting Jamaican public figure and heard the public announcement of my appointment, which made him feel that he was the last to know of the appointment.

Tried as I did, he could not be convinced that I was not to be blamed for the blunder. However, the Commission wrote to accept that the leak was not of my doing and went ahead to have the appointment published. I was quite pleased about the outcome of the blunder and more so when the date for my Swearing-in-Ceremony was communicated to me. My husband indicated that he did not wish to attend the ceremony but I thought he would have changed his mind as time went by. On that morning, his behaviour had not changed despite the fact that I made every effort to accommodate his ill feelings.

As one who does not thrive on solitude I found a friend of the family to accompany me, composed myself and soon began to think of the afternoon's event.

It was a beautiful day in July, backing up the weather forecast of temperature reaching nearly seventy degrees by noon. The sky was azure blue in colour without a cloud in sight and the sun shone brightly. I was quite pleased about the dress and matching turban I had chosen to wear, glazed cotton with a gorgeous pink and peach pattern. I could feel my spirit soaring as I began the journey to the Newington Crown court, Borough High Street. By the time I got there, together with my friend, my mind was clear of the worry and I had let go of the pressures that had been weighing me down.

I will get into the mood of the afternoon, I kept reassuring myself. As we approached the door through which we were instructed to enter the Court, the doorman without attempting to look at the identification card, refused us entry. He used a nearby window to communicate with us, his stereo-typical belief appeared to have come into play, he could not work out why these two black people were insisting to enter the Court via the Magistrates' entrance rather than the defendant's door, so he continued to make signs to us pointing to the defendant's public entrance. It became embarrassing to say the least; we stood there for a considerably long time. Reluctantly he swung the heavy door ajar, in a confrontational mood and I quickly pushed the identification card before his eyes. His reaction was immediate, with a sweep of his right hand he directed us to the area where a Clerk was awaiting our arrival. Though he apologised profusely when he realised the stupidity of his action to us I nonetheless was left with a strange feeling.

The ceremony was performed by the Lord Chief Justice with precision and judicial style, followed by a social gathering where we met senior members of the Bar and the Judiciary and shared the refreshment of wine and cheese. A pleasant and enjoyable afternoon had ended, so we made our way to the Council for Community Relations Office where colleagues had gathered to congratulate me. For me this was truly the end of a perfect day that began with despair but turned out as one that I will always remember with an abundance of pride.

Gloria Cameron MBE

The New Year's Eve party at the Lyceum Ballroom in the Strand was an ecstatically happy occasion. We wined and danced as though there was no tomorrow! The favourite touring band from Jamaica, The Jubilee Stompers, played some old tunes, reminiscent of home, especially for the many forty-something age group who could identify with the 'rumba', 'ska and, of course, the 'lover's rock'. Thunderous applause greeted the midnight chimes of Big Ben - the historic clock on the Parliament building in Whitehall, Westminster - as it ushered in the New Year.

Jeff Crawford and Joseph Hunte, officers of the West Indian Standing Conference, took their places on the dais. We were reminded about the collapse of the Federation of independent states in the West Indies that was established, among other things, to jointly tackle political, cultural and economic development issues peculiar to small nation states and to reap the benefits of a greater united positon on the global stage.

The leaders of the ten countries worked ceaselessly to reach a common ground in their approach to Federation but there were many obstacles and challenges that, in the end, proved insurmountable.

The vision was eventually abandoned in two years. The disappointment of losing out on a formula for region development left many in despair. For the Caribbean communities in the UK, this was keenly felt and led to the creation of a pan-Caribbean forum, the West Indian Standing Conference – that which spoke with an all-embracing voice for Caribbean peoples, highlighting issues relating to education, health, economic development, immigration crises and its effect.

So on this New Year's Eve, there we were enjoying ourselves together, creating our own amusement. As the early hours of New Year's day dawned, I climbed into bed, tired, but brimming with happiness and deep in thought about my resolutions for the New Year. I fell asleep, only to be jarred from my sleep by a ringing phone.

"Is that Mrs Cameron?"

"Yes"

"So you are in the New Year's Honours List?"

"What do you mean, whom am I speaking with?".

The male voice at the end of the line did not respond but continued:

"Do not accept these people's honour. Don't you know that Jamaica has a honours system and do confer honours to Jamaicans at home and abroad? Don't accept it".

I then said, "But I have spent all of my working life in this country so ..."

"Let them keep their honour", he concluded sternly.

I was left with a shocking headache and, of course, curious as to whether it was true that I was in the Honour's List. I then recalled that earlier in the year I was informed by the Prime Minister's Office that it was minded to put my name forward for recognition for my services to the community. But having acknowledged the communication, I did not receive any more information of the time scale and thought no more of it. This call aroused my curiosity but my husband, having listened on the telephone extension, decided to drive to Trafalgar Square, perhaps the only place one might get national papers at that time of the morning.

He was back in a relatively short time armed with three national newspapers. We lost no time in perusing the Civil Sections of the Honour's List and low and behold my name was very much there, Florence G. Cameron – awarded the MBE for services in Community Development for the furtherance of better Social Community and Race Relations. I returned to bed but was not relaxed enough to sleep. The first of January 1980 dawned on a happy note as my children, on hearing the good news, staged something more like a stampede. I could hear them scampering down the stairs towards my room, rushing in wildly, hugging and patting me all over and beaming with admiration for their mom's achievement.

Well it had been a very exciting week with the national and local press giving the good news. A solitary letter arrived within hours of the announcement, "Let me be the first to congratulate you...". This was from my boss, the Principal Community Relations Officer for the London Borough of Lambeth, Mr George Greaves. The buzz began there and then, huge sacks of letters, cards and numerous phone calls followed conveying some of the most heart-warming congratulatory messages and thoughts anyone could have expected to receive.

Colleagues from all walks of life registered their happiness and pleasure. The British Association of Social Workers and The Community Relations Commission hailed the achievement as a splendid recognition for those in the field of Community Development. Directorates of the London Borough of Lambeth sent their individual congratulations, the Inner London Education Authority's Inspectorate and head teachers, staff and several children from schools within and outside of the Borough added their sweet thoughts. The Commonwealth Institute's Education and Arts Department, the Inner London Magistrates Association, Caribbean organisations within and outside of the Borough, individual well-wishers and, last but no means least, my bank manager sent greetings.

I was alive to the buzz around me and felt humbled and loved. Tell me of anyone who does not experience a sense of belonging when their efforts are rewarded with illuminations! I could not, however, ignore the 'mist' that seemed forever present around me. My sensitive nature did not help because the Honour, though appreciated and overwhelming, brought with it, particularly as a black female community worker, an embarrassment of being identified by some of our more political, radical, hostile brothers and sisters as one who have 'sold out' and become an establishment figure, otherwise an Uncle Tom; this being one of the most popular thinking which stifled our progress in those early years. At that time, as the first black woman in the Borough and the third in London to be so awarded, it sometimes felt as a mark of shame rather than a mark of appreciation.

Then came the historic day in February 1980! I arrived at Buckingham Palace for the Investiture to be performed by Her Majesty, Queen Elizabeth the Second. Restriction of guests was limited to two per award but I successfully negotiated for an extra place. My husband and two younger children accompanied me. I so wanted both children to share with me the special occasion. We alighted from the hired Daimler with driver in attendance, outside the Palace and walked out in the hazy mid-morning sunshine. The chilly wind blew against me, my body made warm and comfortable with a sable mink coat enwrapped around me, courtesy of Robin Foxley's, the Furrier, my eldest son's employer.

Savouring the ceremony - the ambience of the room and the melodious music coming from the band on the balcony - it was my turn to walk up to Her Majesty to receive my decoration. She congratulated me while appending the medal to the left lapel of my coat. At that high point of my emotional satisfaction, I could feel the presence of Papa in our midst - he had always wanted me to serve my people. I knew that his spirit was well pleased!

There followed an office based reception, organised by my colleagues in Community Relations, to which many workers from other projects attended. I accepted the tribute as a mark of true friendship and appreciation for my achievement.

With the investiture thrills over, I was left with a lovely, satisfactory feeling that my career in Community Development, and the actual benefits brought to the country, which I adopted as home for over forty years, had been regarded as important enough to merit such praise. I pledged to remain my own modest self and carry on my everyday life as usual. I have my medal in its cosy case all tucked away but I also have a miniature which I sometimes wear when attending civic receptions or functions where decorations are worn.

I remember attending a 'Women of the Year' luncheon in 1982 at the Savoy Hotel in London on a somewhat windy bleak day. On my way home I stopped at a stall outside London Bridge Railway Station to purchase some fruits and my favourite bunch of longiflorum lilies. While in the process of shifting my handbag and the newly acquired items, my unbuttoned jacket revealed my miniature medal. Before realising that this had happened, the young male attendant pounced on me with startling attention. Staring at the medal, now slightly visible through the opening of my jacket, he moved closer towards me, gasped and asked, "What is that?"

My reaction to this sudden explicit attention was equally immediate. "Oh", I said concealing my fright, "so you like my car boot bargain as well?". Moving quickly from his intimidating shadow, I glanced at my watch and quickened my steps to give the impression that the train's departure was very imminent. I stood on the platform shaken, promising myself to be more discreet when wearing my treasured gift.

The West Indian Parents Action Group

The West Indian Parents Action Group (WIPAG) and the Caribbean Folk Group are the two projects that I am particularly proud of having been involved in their creation.

WIPAG started as a group of like-minded individuals meeting regularly in 1971, following a most stimulating talk by Bernard Coard. We decided to take seriously the exhortations he made to us to participate, as parents, in the education of our children. We were about forty parents, mostly women. The group did not at any time attract a wild enthusiastic following compared to other community groups - not that the matter we sought to address was regarded as less than important but rather that the approach we adopted was less dramatic and aggressive. We had set out to build a foundation with patience and determination. However, the group continued to look at and discuss the problems of the black community and, in particular, black children's under achievement in the school system.

The whole-hearted support of both Miranda Hislop, Education Officer at the Council for Community Relations in Lambeth and Judy Welleminsky, Community Relations Officer, specialising in Housing and Policy issues, helped steer the group away from becoming a talk shop by keeping us informed of current policies in childcare. They collated statistical and factual information about the Borough's provision of services for the under-fives, so that we could ascertain how the black families fitted in the pattern of the Social Services allocation of nursery places. This was no easy task, even for those of us who worked in the Community Relations Head Office where it was possible to find policy documents or reports from the Home Office, Directorate of Social Services or the Community Relations Commission.

Day Care up until the late sixties was administered by the Health Department and with the changes to Social Services, following the implementation of the Seebohm and Plowden Reports, priority areas were identified, focussing on Community Development, Health, Housing, Education and Social Welfare provision. These initiatives were followed by a major breakthrough: the Urban Programme that introduced an annual programme of Central Government Funding to Local Authorities to select statutory and voluntary schemes. The successful schemes were subsidised based on 75% Central Government to 25% Local Government funding over a three-year cycle.

The expressed needs of the black community, particularly the single unsupported mothers, presented adequate proof that a more flexible type of Day Care provision was urgently needed to cater to the special requirements of these mothers. Many had children and families left in the Caribbean and were motivated to hold down employment. These reasons for wanting nursery places, although admirable, did not fit into the Local Authority's criteria for being placed on the waiting list or be given a glimmer of hope to be allocated a place in any such facility.

As we set out to consolidate the development of the group, we sought help from the Pentecostal Church movement that had begun to establish itself in the Borough of Lambeth. I recognised the important roles that community-led churches have played in the survival and development of disadvantaged communities. In fact, upper most in my mind was the Moravian Church missionaries that started their work in Jamaica in 1754 joining in the campaign for the abolition of slavery. Their efforts and that of those who followed led to the founding of the Bethlehem College, one of the earlier Teacher's Training institution in Jamaica. I wondered whether the Pentecostal Church in Brixton could eventually embrace this pioneering role of setting up a nursery provision in Lambeth. My approach to a number of Pastors was greeted with much enthusiasm. Discussions on the subject were held over a long period but in the end we were unable to marry the secular with the religious in the pursuit of community empowerment.

The focus of our group to establish a Day Care Centre for Under-Fives remained strong. We decided to take the final step and constitute ourselves as an organisation with a constitution. The West Indian Parent Action Group (WIPAG) was born and became formally constituted in February 1974. Its first Management Committee included a Solicitor as Chairman, a Health Visitor, Accountant, Nursery School teacher, two Community workers and Four Founding members.

The main thrust of the organisation was to provide a Centre that would offer a stable and stimulating environment for the under-fives, aimed at redressing disadvantage before their entry to compulsory schooling. We agreed that one of our main tasks was to identify a building suitable for the setting up of a Day Care Centre and take active steps to secure it and the necessary resources for its use.

The Secretary of State for Environment announcement about the new initiative to regenerate the inner city areas and the White Paper that embodied the initiative, Policy for the Inner Cities, kindled a ray of light for the newly established organisation.

We sent letters to the Director for Social Services, Principal Officers, Housing and Development Directorates and to the Community Relations Commission outlining our aspirations, detailing the expressed need of the community for Day Care provision and listing our aims and objectives. We received responses applauding the organisation's vision but very few offers of help or support.

We decided to focus our efforts on targeting the London Borough of Lambeth to allocate a building for our use. We did not sit around for a response but took the initiative to find a suitable building to house a nursery in the Borough. We were aware of the number of Council properties that were boarded up and we started with those, focusing on properties that were in close proximity to the main rail and underground stations, major bus stops, the market and shopping centre to ensure easy access for those parents who, we envisaged, would be rushing from work or college to the nursery.

Our attention was drawn to a row of empty terraced houses on Canterbury Crescent, located behind the Brixton Police Station and the disused St John's Church of England Primary School. We approached the Housing and Development Directorate of Lambeth about the possibility of a lease for any building we may find. They replied positively.

We chose No.7 Canterbury Crescent. Although the basement was already blocked off, indicating that the building had already been deemed unfit for habitation, the rest of the building on three floors could be used with some renovation and modification; enough for us to successfully register it under the Nurseries and Child Minders Act 1948.

In August 1976, WIPAG was allocated a five-year lease, at a peppercorn rent, to 7 Canterbury Crescent to use as a Nursery. The Directorates who had responsibility for the Borough's property maintenance would not agree to undertake any of the renovation. This did not deter us. But when we received a letter from the Director for Social Services, Mr Johnson, stating that he could not support any initiative which sought to be exclusive to black children, we felt that we had lost the battle.

But our members were not willing to give up that easily. A group of parents started to clear out all the debris from the premises and tried to make good as many areas as possible. In the end, a grant from the Community Relations Commission, together with voluntary efforts from members and supporters, we transformed the building into a temporary Day Nursery. The Senior Day Care Officer for the Social Services Directorate, Iris Oliver-Smith, proved to be one of the most helpful and encouraging officers within the Directorate. She inspected the facility and made positive comments and suggestions for improvements. We were then given a Registration Certificate for the premises to accommodate 24 children, aged 2-5 years.

You can imagine our joy and our feelings of accomplishment and on the day when Cannon Sebastian Charles from Westminster Abbey came to dedicate that building to the parents and children of Brixton, we all stood tall! All the electrical equipment for the kitchen and domestic use was donated by the well-known philanthropist, Anthony Rampton O.B.E., of Freeman's Catalogue and Author of the Rampton Report on Education in Primary Schools.

We needed more equipment and funds for employing staff. Applications were made to the Manpower Services Commission (MSC) Job Creation Scheme and to the 1977 Urban Programme. The latter was unsuccessful and it was not until the autumn of 1977 that the MSC decided to fund the salaries of six workers for twelve months.

During the months of waiting for funds and equipment, the premises housed a Community Relations project which myself and Judy Welleminsky initiated, called Care Assistants Project (CAP). CAP encouraged unemployed youngsters to get trained to work with the under-fives and to register for the NNEB Course at Brixton College.

WIPAG Day Nursery finally opened its doors to nine children in January 1978 under the guiding hands of a qualified Nursery School Teacher, Mrs Joyce Haynes.

WIPAG's activities grew from strength to strength. We reached our registered number of children – 24 children aged 2 to 5 years - in a matter of three months and added four older brothers and sisters who came to the Centre after school to await collection by their mothers. Our waiting list soon rose to eighty two children, many of whom would not have the opportunity to attend a Day Nursery. Obviously, the Management Committee of WIPAG did not lose sight of the fact that revenue funding and better premises were to remain a high priority and all efforts had to be concentrated in achieving these aims.

By April 1979, I was invited to join the Under-Fives Sub-Group of the Inner City Partnership Unit that comprised representatives from Statutory Agencies and Voluntary Organisations. Its tasks were to bring together those who were providing services, to discuss the needs and problems of the client groups, to prepare schemes for submission under the Urban Programme 1978/1979, and to give consideration to the Inner City Programme 1979/1982.

We were able to look at schemes put forward in the Final Traditional Urban Programme before the Sub-Group was disbanded.

The recommendations of our Sub-Group were accepted thus ensuring that the Inner City Partnership gave priority to six Under-Fives Schemes in that funding cycle.

WIPAG's application to the Urban Programme in 1977 was now re-submitted to the Inner City Partnership and was approved with revenue funding to cover salaries and a Capital Grant of £52,000 for the conversion of new premises. This approval came at a very crucial time in that we had come to the end of the Manpower Services Commission's twelve months grant. The grant approved was not, however, due for immediate payment - but in a year's time, which left us without any funding for salaries.

Three founding members of WIPAG to whom thanks are due - Mabel Carter, Gerlin Bean and myself - decided to pool our personal resources in order to supplement the child care fees paid by parents so that we could pay the wages due to the six members of staff on the MSC grant. In addition, all three of us volunteered to come in each morning, for up to two hours, to open the nursery and receive the children.

During this time, we appealed to the Inner City Partnership Unit to bring forward our revenue payment. They did so eight months later but not in time to prevent a turnover of staff because we were unable to pay the going rate, fifty pounds per week, for staff wages.

Approximately two months after the receipt of the revenue funding, a community activist and parent of a child at the nursery organised a few parents and two members of staff to protest against us for operating the Nursery in premises that they felt were substandard. They gained the support of other parents to remove five children from the nursery to hold a demonstration and sit-in at the Social Services office for two weeks. The protestors sent letters to the Greater London Fire Regulations Inspectors and Structural Maintenance Engineers about structural conditions and accused staff of not showing enough love to one of the protesting parent's mixed race son.

These interruptions from our main tasks left us reeling but we had to apply ourselves to the tasks ahead. Officers from the GLC Fire Inspectorate and Structural Engineers inspected the premises and presented their reports on the state of the building with recommendations. Lambeth Council and, particularly, the Officers in Social Services Directorate, acted professionally in their approach to the conflict.

The complaints made by the protesting parents were thoroughly investigated and the Council decided to undertake all the necessary repairs and suggested that the operation of the Nursery be suspended temporarily so that the repair work could be carried out. This did not satisfy the protestors and they applied considerable pressure on the Council by lobbying elected members for premises and grant-aid in order to set up their own nursery. They were encouraged to apply to the Inner City Partnership and Manpower Services Commission for funding. However, in the interim whilst they operated their nursery in a local church hall, the group split amidst recrimination and did not stay together long enough to achieve their goals.

We were determined not to be defeated by these setbacks and, instead, to fight to offer continuity of childcare services to our parents. We arranged to use the lower floor of the Abeng Centre to continue offering nursery care to our children whilst repairs were being made to Canterbury Crescent. At the end of the six weeks, WIPAG's Day Care Centre was eventually re-established in a more attractive and renovated premises. With the disturbance behind us, we threw our energies into identifying a building to house our growth and to meet the growing demands from our community.

Growing Nursery Care

One day Gerlin Bean and myself walked past two large houses with four floors that had seen better days. Walking outside these houses, it felt so still, it seemed forgotten. The gloomy days passed over the space in a timeless procession and at nights the nearest approach to its doors was the passing footsteps on the pavement and the rumbling sound of the numbers 35 and 45 red double-decker buses on their way to Clapham Common or towards Camberwell Green.

As we walked past, we turned our heads to each other and immediately acknowledged the potential of these two adjacent houses and with a heartbeat of excitement, we there and then resolved that this was worth battling for.

WIPAG approached the Housing and Development Directorate to make further enquiries but they would not engage in any dialogue with us. In desperation, we approached the Leader of Lambeth Council, Councillor Ted Knight, who listened sympathetically to our request and without much delay, 3 to 5 Gresham Road, obliquely opposite to the Police Station, were allocated to WIPAG under a thirty years lease at a peppercorn rent. We owe our successes to Ted's vision and unqualified support that allowed us to accommodate a fifty place Day Care/Family Centre for the children of Lambeth.

Planning permission for the conversion of the Gresham Road properties was granted in 1979. Architects were appointed and Charitable Status attained in 1981. WIPAG steeled itself for a long and rocky ride but the determination of its members to achieve the goal never wavered.

The complexity of the negotiations and the time involved in servicing the various meetings with several different officers across many Directorates could no longer be undertaken, on its current voluntary basis, by myself, Gerlin Bean and David Bryan.

With Gerlin Bean's imminent departure for Zimbabwe, David Bryan in full-time employment, WIPAG decided to use the Department for the Environment Inner City Partnership funding to employ a full-time co-ordinator to liaise with the Directorates within the authority and to manage all aspects of the Capital Funding and building works. Mr Hasset Auguste was appointed.

The relief that this appointment brought was soon tempered with growing anxieties as more and more problems surfaced.

However, the Quantity Surveyor, Bryan Cullum, was able to guide the organisation through the maze of procedures.

We suspected that our first Architect was over-charging for the drawings and not preparing the specific designs asked for. There began a dispute between the Architect and the Quantity Surveyor with threats of legal action. WIPAG had to prepare signed affidavits and seek help from the Borough's Legal Department to keep the matter out of Court. This problem came about because the Council Officers were not in a position to give the guidance that was needed. We ended up paying out £6,000 to the Architects for just the drawings. It was very frightening and frustrating.

The Council's Quantity Surveyor helped us find an alternative Architect and tenders and contracts were supervised and managed from his office. WIPAG had to seek further funding to complete the work and the Department of Environment and the Greater London Council came to our rescue with a grant to complete all works and make the building safe and legally compliant. Councillor Leslie Hammond gave invaluable support during those troubled times.

WIPAG's appeal to Jeremy Brown, Head of the Lambeth Inner City Partnership Unit, for the initial approved staff salary payments to be brought forward fell on fertile ground. We found him to be unfailingly courteous, never self-seeking or overtly assertive but this masked a spirit and a capacity for quiet persistence that repeatedly overcame obstacles. The negotiation through to the handover of the premises took five years to be completed.

I had moved from being a Community Relations Officer to being the Director at the Abeng Centre, 7 Gresham Road, next to the Nursery building. I felt it was time for me to become engaged in a practical developmental role within the community. George Greaves, the Principal Community

Relations Officer at CCRL, agreed that the Abeng, which was set up to rehabilitate young people, the majority male, needed a more meaningful leadership. He, however, felt that, "I would be good for the Abeng, but that the Abeng would not be good for me" - those were his exact words.

It did not take very long, once I arrived there, to realise that precisely what he feared was coming home to roost. Most of the boys attending the Centre were living and some barely surviving in impoverished and disadvantaged environments, many headed by single mothers, iterant male figures and often in trouble with the police. The Abeng Centre was inadequately staffed and resourced to make any meaningful interventions with these young men. Lack of adequate funding from the Local Council and the Youth Service, coupled with the lack of vision as to how to provide a meaningful facility to aid the young person's development, meant that all we offered was a glorified baby-sitting service and, like a rudderless vessel, these young men would continue to drift aimlessly seeking respite from time to time in the Centre.

All the agencies had abdicated their responsibility to work towards supporting these young people, mainly males. The three workers who started the work at the Abeng Centre had positive visions of its success. They saw the significance of the name – Abeng, a cow's horn blown from a hole on the concave side - and the work they had proposed to undertake as a positive outlet for the young people.

Gloria Cameron, Director of WIPAG
By 1983, with the nursery building near completion and the volume of the work at the Day Nursery/Family Centre greatly increased, the Management Committee decided to appoint a Director to develop the work with the under-fives to include an after school provision for the primary school child, a nursery

class for the rising five year olds and a parent education programme.

Following a successful interviewing process I was offered the position as Director for WIPAG. I took up the appointment in July 1983 in time for the handing over of the newly renovated premises at Gresham Road. The transfer of services from Canterbury Crescent went very smoothly. Everyone was happy and I could feel that sense of achievement with such contented staff and parents around. The transformation was spectacular! We organised the spacious areas at Gresham Road with a feeling of high hopes and expectation. It was a big thrill for me to see the rising five years old going off to school and when the opportunity came for us to develop links with some of the schools our children moved to, it guaranteed our continued interest in their educational achievements.

It was the desire of the Management Committee to have a public Official Opening of the Centre. We wanted to whole-heartedly thank the many people whom in their own way contributed to the realisation of our dream. One of the organisation's Patron, the Honourable David Sief of Marks & Spencer's, afforded us the opportunity to gain the guidance of their Public Relations personnel who gave us invaluable help and support in the planning and execution of an Official Opening which I look back at today, with enormous pride.

Diana, Princess of Wales, was eagerly suggested, being a young mother herself, to be the special guest for the occasion. I felt this would have been completely out of our league to even contemplate such an action. However, at that time there were a number of liberal minded influential men and women with links within the Borough who reached out beyond the dividing line of race and class and having decided on a date for the event a letter of invitation was sent off to ask the Princess of Wales to officially declare the Family Centre open.

Before long a positive response was received and all the necessary arrangements were put into gear. There were a few telephone conversations with the Princess's representative regarding details prior to the visit but on a whole we were able to make the visit a pleasurable one. A plaque, which was designed by the Architect, was erected in the reception area of the building and a large life size photograph of her, before her marriage, was donated to the organisation and artistically framed by one of our past parents that she duly signed. The warmth of the Princess, meeting parents, Council Officers and friends of WIPAG, while the children put on a musical display of singing and dances in the Caribbean idiom radiated throughout the time she spent in the building. Everyone was happily enjoying a wonderful day. The large crowd of onlookers were now dispersing after their resounding cheers as she exited the building. The Police cordon, together with the mounted Police troop, was in the process of leaving.

I walked on to the pavement and there were a number of multi-coloured leaflets on the ground. I reached out and picked up a few. It read, in bold capitals, "Grass Skirt cannot fight the Revolution". I then realised why it was necessary to have such Police presence!

Is this a portent of things to come?

CHAPTER 8

THIS IS YOUR LIFE

The BBC's invitation requesting the Caribbean Folk Group to participate in an International Programme of cultural expressions scheduled for early January 1984 was gratefully received. The Folk Group had already begun its Christmas break and my reluctance to reassemble all the members, in such a short space of time, had to be considered. However, the members had no hesitation when I communicated the reason for the recall, so we agreed to meet on the evening when the BBC Outside Broadcast Unit arranged for the recording. The day, December 1983, turned out to be a very busy action packed one.

I had already agreed to attend two Christmas parties to do the usual storytelling and sing-song entertainment with the children. The Outside Broadcast Unit came earlier than I had expected to set up their equipment and we were experiencing staff shortage on that same day. On my way to one of the nurseries, a young man stopped me for a talk. I told him I was in a hurry to an appointment but he could call in to see me the following day. He was not at all pleased. Then he said, "Just because you are going to be on the Hughie Green Show, you don't feel that you can speak with me".

I thought, what does he mean, anyway Hughie Green's 'Opportunity Knocks' programme has been off the air a long time ago. That statement left me thinking for a while.

In the midst of the preparation, Herb arrived saying that he had suspicion that a break-in had taken place at home. He seemed quite upset because he was missing one of his suits and a pair of shoes from his wardrobe. He was now insisting that I return home to deal with what he felt was urgent. I thought about what he said and reasoned with myself as to how someone would break in only to remove two items from his wardrobe and nothing else. I therefore decided not to leave at such a crucial time.

The afternoon went quite quickly and members of Folk Group began to arrive; some of the parents stayed on with their children to listen to the Group. Soon we were all in our Bandanna costumes. The plan was that the BBC crew would televise the rehearsal for the International Programme. Suddenly, at the point of completing the recording of the second song, my expectation of the evening's event took on a new dimension. I could hear thunderous applause and wild excitement coming from the corner where the parents were. I looked in their direction, held my hands out to stop the interruption and there was Eamonn Andrews, the Thames Television presenter of the This is Your Life programme, walking towards me with a large red book clutched under his arm! Recognising him as someone usually seen on television, now facing me in person, I stopped in my track and with my hands covering my face to disguise the surprise grin underneath, I was immobilised by the profound realisation that this was real.

"Hello everyone", he said as he moved closer to me. "Gloria Cameron, This is Your Life".

I remember stepping away, moving my head from left to right in utter confusion. Frank, my son hugged me and whispered in my ear, "Take it, Mom. Please take it, even for our sake". Everyone around me was in a very happy mood. Euphoria was high.

We were asked to accompany the crew to the theatre. I recalled saying I can't. I will need to change but it was explained that I needed to arrive in costume. We were all transported to the Theatre Royal in Drury Lane in Central London.

A limousine drove me quivering with fear to the stage door from where I was ushered to a room. There I was introduced to a young lady who would be my dresser and companion for the evening. Nervously I sat, wondering where the others were and feeling quite uncomfortable attending a theatre in my costume. My eyes roamed around the room, looking at the lovely pictures and decorative artefacts when, by chance, I noticed a dress hanging on the far end of the room which looked familiar. On closer scrutiny I recognised another dress which I knew as mine. The dresser then put my mind at ease. She informed me that I would be required to change and that there were two of my dresses there for me to choose from. I was still numb from the experience I had and wondered what was coming next.

Having dressed, it was time for me to enter the stage and a large stage it was! The entire Folk Group was there looking radiant and happy in their Jamaican National Costume – 'The Bandanna'. Seated on one side of the stage, opposite me, were a number of chairs laid out. I was ushered to a seat close to this section. I looked around in trepidation and wondered who would be seated on the many laid out chairs. I was struck by the large audience seated in the auditorium and felt alone, but for the life size photograph of myself peering at me from the left side of the stage. Eamonn Andrews, in his usual gracious manner, took to the stage and for the first time in my life I experienced being one of the players in an unrehearsed dramatic performance.

I heard Eamonn's voice coming from a large screen and noticed a BBC film of the Day Nursery building with Her

Royal Highness, the Princess of Wales, opening the newly converted building in Gresham Road.

> *"This is Your Life and that piece of news film showed the world's most celebrated young mum, here in London's Brixton only weeks ago opening that modest building over there, two houses knocked together which has become the nerve centre of life for so many young mums here… and it's where I am headed now with six members of the nursery staff, where I am hoping to surprise the lady whose drive and personality led to its creation, and by the way, to many more heart felt and indeed heart-touching achievements right here in a community with more than its share of upset and upheaval – I hope to be smuggled inside".*

I sat spellbound and completely flattered to hear and see flashed on the screen tit-bits of activities I had been involved in. A steady stream of colleagues was called to attest to the contributions I had made to good causes over my working life.

Closing my eyes, I let Eamonn Andrews' words caress me, listening to the tributes to my work being expounded was truly humbling. Everyone, especially those who knew me well, could identify with something which created a light of its own. My elation was further heightened when His Excellency, Herbert Walker, High Commissioner for Jamaica in the UK, and one of the Day Nursery's Patrons walked on to the stage to bring greetings and congratulations from the Government and people of Jamaica. For me it was both moving and amazing.

My husband, dressed in the suit which he thought had disappeared in a break-in; my three scheming daughters who provided 'Thames' with the information to construct the programme all unknown to me and my two sons were introduced as they took their seats. We were told earlier that one of my sons, Chris, would not be with us as he was touring with the popular music ensemble, Errol Brown and Hot Chocolate.

Chris, as Musical Director in Poole, Dorset, in front of an audience of two thousand people, would be brought to us by sound and vision, via the live link. He, along with Errol Brown and the Hot Chocolate, appeared on screen. The audience applauded – they knew they were in for a real treat. The audience from the Arts Centre in Pool and the audience at the Theatre Royal were linked to hear the amazing Errol Brown and Hot Chocolate, with Chris leading the ensemble on the piano, and Errol singing "It started with a Kiss", which he dedicated to Herbert, my husband. We were all thrilled and excited.

The applause was prolonged and overwhelming. Before the audience could recover from the rendition from Errol Brown, there entered my 83 years old, silver haired, mother who was flown over from Jamaica. I almost fell off my chair. The family rushed towards Momie, hugging and embracing her. I hugged her, my trembling hands too weak to grasp her properly. The ovation on stage and in the auditorium was deafening; the audience roared their appreciation. Eamonn Andrews eventually quelled the pandemonium in order to present the Red Book, with his famous phrase, "Gloria Cameron, This is Your Life".

I bowed, applause engulfing me. I was dumbfounded by the audience reactions to what was presented. The fundamental principle of my work was all about fostering identity and cultural awareness. What it meant to struggle against multiple oppression, how to carry one self, how to interact with others of unlike minds and how to remain silent when it is best to do so.

I was deeply happy and humbled to receive several congratulations, cards and phone calls. It was a pleasure to join the crew and all the participants afterwards for cocktails, many of whom I had not seen for some time. This occasion will go down as one of the most beautiful memories of my life.

Oh what sheer joy to have mother with us over the festive season. When we eventually learnt that she had been given a three months stay in the UK with us, we were overwhelmed.

Thames Television informed us that the programme was due to be aired on the 26th December. Long before the allotted time, the family was glued to the television, not wanting to miss anything. In our recollection, it seemed the only episode to extend beyond the News item. Added to this it was peak-time viewing during the Christmas period, which served to exaggerate the elation we felt. We had much appreciation for the diligence and professional pride that was displayed by the researchers and programme planners to have amassed such a factual and entertaining programme for viewing in the joyous yuletide. Mother's presence surely cemented that closeness that had existed within the family. The happiness which abounded within the three generation household was one we maintained with an abundance of pride.

Mother was soon exposed to a variety of social and cultural outings which she enjoyed, as much as meeting and making new friends who came to love being in her company. Her pleasant and outgoing disposition endeared her to many, indeed a group of sisters from the Jehovah's Witness Church befriended her. This afforded her day time company and outings, a sisterhood which she enjoyed and valued immensely.

We eventually negotiated for mother's long term stay in the UK and with making such a decision it became imperative for us to purchase a larger accommodation. On coming across a large family house with amenities conducive to accommodating such a large family as mine, my married daughter and her husband sold their property and together with the sale of the family home, 'Plough' was purchased on mortgage. The three generation family settled in happily sharing the everyday upkeep of the property and maintaining a balanced life style for near on two and a half years.

CHAPTER 9

MORE GROWTH - 90 KELLET ROAD

I was happily immersed in the development of the fifty places Day Nursery in Gresham Road in the eight years of its existence when, in February 1985, the chairperson for the Social Services Committee mentioned that the Council had decided to make 90 Kellet Road, the Brixton Cares for Kids' Nursery building, available to the community. We viewed the idea as an excellent one. At that time, a greater part of Lambeth's redevelopment programme had taken place in Central Brixton while a reduced patchy programme existed in the Kellet Road section known as the "Frontline".

The 1981 census indicated that Lambeth's population was relatively young, working class, transient and elderly. Estimates suggested that twenty percent came from non-white groups, with people of Caribbean origin being the largest group (twelve point five percent) of that number concentrated in Central Brixton. While a few skilled and managerial middle-income groups found employment outside of the Borough, the semi-skilled category relied on local employment opportunities that were rapidly declining - a decline which accelerated since the 1981 disturbances.

One family in six, according to the 1977/78 estimate (London Borough of Lambeth), nearly twice the national average, many with children in the Local Authority Care, were living in poor council and privately rented housing. The inadequate education and recreational services, the low morale displayed by some residents, high level of vandalism and crime, made this much talked about area of social need overdue for intervention from the Local Authority.

Lord Scarman in his report, following the 1981 Brixton disturbance, highlighted the strengths of Lambeth's life by recognising the persistence and creativity of Lambeth's parents and interesting citizens. With this fact in mind, in addition to our overall interest to see the authority tackle the existing inadequacy in the area, WIPAG's Committee welcomed the proposed development.

It was suggested that we forward an application to manage the proposed facility but having discussed it at a committee level; the opinion was that the bidding should be left to other organisations that might want to get into the field of Day Care.

We later learnt from the Chief Co-ordinator Community and Voluntary Services (CCCVS), in his letter of the 18 April 1985, that the bidders were unsuccessful. He urged us to apply, intimating that we would be in a more favourable position for the directorate's funding when the current Inner City Partnership grant expired. This was the situation we knew would arise in March 1987.

Our grant had been renewed for three cycles and in accordance with partnership guidelines, it would then be for the sponsoring authority to provide for our project under their 'Main Programme Budget'. The reality of our situation jolted the Committee, albeit with some reluctance, to agree to put an application forward. The CCCVS letter of 18 April 1985 also stated that the Brixton Cares for Kids facility had ceased operation in September 1984 and because it was considered to be a vital provision in child care for that particular 'Frontline' area of Brixton, the Director of Social Services was keen to ensure that the provision continued as a voluntary one.

The CCCVS letter also clearly stated, *"We are therefore inviting your organisation to bid for the management and running of the project".*

The Management Committee at a meeting held on 10 May 1985 considered a detailed questionnaire that was attached to the letter. There was much discussion of this, some members expressing concern in relation to dealing with the Local Authority, particularly where such a large portion of funding for salaries would be expected. High levels of scepticism were expressed over the unreliability of short-term funding, the challenge of coping with the insensitivity of local authority officers, the danger of compromising the organisation's independence, the danger of dependency and the potential of political interference.

One of the very concerned members had been influenced by the National Council for Voluntary organisation's discussion paper on Government Influence on Voluntary Organisation (1983) which she later shared with me.

Despite those misgivings, an agreement was reached for us to go ahead. I was therefore instructed to proceed with a proposal. As one who possessed no inhibition when it comes to initiating things, I soon put my innovative powers into gear. A comprehensive proposal was prepared, dealing in detail with all aspects of managerial requirements as was requested. All relevant correspondence was sent to the Social Services by 30th April 1985.

We were invited to an interview scheduled for 12th June 1985. WIPAG was represented by the Chairman, Treasurer, a Trustee and Founder Member, one Nursery Officer and myself, the Director of the nursery. The Social Services panel consisted of the Chair of the Social Services Committee, the

Principal Day Care Officer, the Race Relations Advisor, Senior Finance Officer and the Chief Co-ordinator Community and Voluntary Services (CCCVS). During the interview, WIPAG representatives spoke individually to the sections of the proposal, and gave additional information about the administration of the nursery, the ethos and its aims and objectives for the future. In addition, we asked questions that were relevant to the take up of the project that was on offer.

A few weeks later, a letter, signed by the CCCVS was received with information that the Social Services Committee had approved officers' recommendations that the resource, known as 'Brixton Care for Kids', be offered to WIPAG. The penultimate paragraph of his letter heightened the organisation belief that the Social Services Directorate was committed to the reinstatement of the provision. It read: *"As I stated in the invitation letter, the Directorate will be happy to encourage a quick take up of the resource, in this respect the Principal Day Care Officer and myself hope to meet with you and/or your representatives at the earliest convenience"*.

A copy of the report that was presented to the Social Services Committee of the 19th of June was attached for our information. We noted that the CCCVS had requested the Committee to delegate him to negotiate acceptable arrangements with WIPAG for the efficient management of the project. We were particularly pleased to note the following comments: *"The Directorate is impressed by the quality of service and the organisation and running of the WIPAG Nursery. WIPAG has demonstrated in a clear way the ability to manage the resource effectively"*.

The Management Committee was very pleased to receive such an outstanding compliment and felt that their eight years provision of day care in the Borough was suitably noticed. These compliments were especially welcomed since they were made by Social Services, a Local Authority Directorate which was highly regarded as the Government's strategic arm. It carried responsibility under the 1948 Children and Young Persons Act, to inspect, police and supervise, and to see to the implementation of excellent Day Care practices.

About three weeks later, a questionnaire arrived from the Assistant Director of Social Services Children and Young Persons seeking an opinion on the notion of Social Services offering 'free Day Care' to all parents. Our response was to applaud the efforts of those who were sympathetic to the idea of free Day Care, although our concern was that this might be interpreted as encouraging a system of dependency among parents. The Officer, soon after the receipt of our comments, communicated our reservation to the parents, who as a result regarded me as one who did not want them to have free Day Care. At this stage, the Officer requested that we send him a budget estimate for the operation of the Kellet Road site, hereafter called "The Annex".

I submitted this in July 1985.

Some parents who were employees of the Council said that the Council was in the process of offering free Day Care to them in all nurseries in the Borough, including those that were privately run. In view of what had been communicated to the parents, I did not know for sure whether any charges to Council employees, using the Annex, were being proposed by Social Services. This would, of course, have a financial bearing on the estimate that had been requested. There was no response to my enquiry in this regard.

The prepared estimate was sent with all aspects of costings and projected income from parents' fees and earmarked for running cost. Days later the Officer telephoned to ask for a revised budget estimate and indicated that he was unlikely to agree to top up the salary of the part-time development and creative workers who were at the Gresham Road site. We thought that if the services were to be integrated, although operating on separate sites, the programmed activities offered would have to be extended to the Annex. The Officer, however, thought otherwise.

For the revised estimate sent on 4th December 1985, the Management Committee decided to include a column headed 'Directorship, Administration and Management Cost'. Each item was clearly costed totalling £14,500. In fact, none of the submitted budgets was ever formally approved. We next heard from the CCCVS in February 1986 giving his permission for us to advertise and employ five care staff for the Annex. The job descriptions and dates were sent to him for his approval, together with advertisement, invoices from the newspapers and dates for the interviews. The five staff members were appointed in March 1986 and grant aid for the salaries of staff appointed in April 1986 arrived.

The Challenges at 90 Kellet Road

The men from the Lambeth Direct Workforce had removed a huge built-in climbing frame that occupied about ninety percent of the only activities room on the ground floor and had painted the walls and doors. The premises was then handed over as ready for occupation. On inspection, the Management Committee was dissatisfied with the shoddy workmanship; in fact, the walls on which the climbing frame structure was secured had a large gaping fracture through which masonry could be seen. The team responsible for carrying out the work was called in and decisions were made to demolish and reconstruct the wall, put in order and complete the unfinished work, in readiness for the Registration Officer's visit.

Initially I had requested a visit from the Assistant Director, Children and Young Persons whose responsibility it was to assess the layout within the premises prior to its use as a Day Nursery for the under 5s. I hastened to do this because I was unable to ascertain any information regarding previous registration for the use of the premises. I wanted reassurances from a responsible officer of Social Services as to the safety of the environment. I cannot now recall that she did ever visit! I am however positive that the Registration Officer inspected up to the time of closure. She did not issue a Registration Certificate for that building despite promises to do so.

On 4th February 1987, I was asked to receive some equipment which was being stored by the Council and that would be delivered to Kellet Road (the Annex). The following afternoon I arrived there to find that the items included urine soaked soiled beddings, sleeping mats and grime covered utensils. I reported the unacceptable condition of the items that the outgoing Chair of the Social Services Committee inspected and also found unacceptable. All of these items were put out for garbage collection.

Sometime in mid-March, I was encouraged to apply for an equipment grant not exceeding £30,000. This had to be done in a matter of days before the end of the financial year. In view of the short time available to prepare an accurate application and costings, we were encouraged by the Officer to submit pro-forma invoices. I immediately summoned the help of the Senior Nursery Nurses to select and compile items appropriate for the varying age groups and abilities of the children. They conversed with the suppliers and obtained pro-forma invoices from three of our main suppliers. The total cost was £25,758.89. All invoices were sent to the CCCVS. We later learnt that the Social Service Committee had agreed the equipment grant for £30,000 to be spent on both nurseries.

On 2nd July 1986, a cheque for £25,758.89 arrived in an envelope. There was no letter nor was there a complimentary slip attached. I immediately telephoned the CCCVS to ascertain if the cheque had come from his Department. He confirmed that it had and that he had held the balance of £4,242.11 in case we needed further funds in the future.

The Handover of Kellet Road

Despite all the preparation there were a number of unexplained delays either by the CCCVS's unavailability for consultation or the Lambeth Council Labour Force Team's delay in the handing over process.

The nursery at Kellet Road was due to become operational in March 1986, then delayed to September 1986, then January 1987, finally opening on 23rd March 1987. The team of five care staff who were appointed in April 1986 had been deployed at Gresham Road for nearly twelve months. After all the extensive preparation and agonisingly long wait, the time had come to commence the operation at the Annex.

The waiting list of 15 children had now dwindled to seven because parents got impatient and made other arrangements for their children. The Management Committee got frustrated because of having to make excuses that left them with the feeling of being regarded as irresponsible.

Three children came on the opening day. There were five care staff, a nursery officer, cleaner and a handyman/driver from the Gresham Road nursery who was deployed to supplement the daily operations. Even at this stage, we were unable to get an appointment with the CCCVS, neither did he visit the Annex to see what was happening. The Registration Certificate had not been issued nor did the Assistant Director for Children and Young Persons given us the benefit of her professional advice as to the layout of the premises. We were literally left in limbo to carry on the best we could. By the end of April, the number of children increased to eleven, aged two to three years old.

Over the period March 1987 to the beginning of May 1987, the toilets were constantly "out of order"; one permanently. Plumbers came on several occasions but were unable to resolve the problem. Some of the newly recruited parents' information on the application forms led us to believe that their children were potty trained but this proved to be not so. This meant that the children needed extra staff supervision, which we had but nevertheless the nursery floor was constantly wet.

On 27th April 1987 a progress report detailing the situation was put before the Management Committee. It was agreed that no further intake of children should be undertaken until the toilets were in good working order. Because of the safety and hygiene considerations regarding children and staff working in a constantly wet environment a final decision was made to transfer the two and three year olds to Gresham Road where facilities were larger and where we were better equipped to deal with the situation.

A full staff meeting was called on 29th April 1987. The matter was fully discussed and although there were no real objections from most staff, a minority was concerned that the one to two ratio, to which they had become accustomed, was likely to change. They were not entirely happy.

We met with the parents on the 5th May 1987 and informed them of the situation and the Committee's decision to deal with it. There were no objections nor arguments against the children's move to Gresham Road. The move was agreed to take place on 15th May and the children began on Monday 18th May. Soon after the move, the numbers increased and in no time, we were operating at full capacity.

The Kellet Road Annex was therefore used to accommodate the rising five year olds who were already being introduced to a nursery class programme with links already established with the schools that they would attend in the autumn. One of the Senior Nursery Nurses who had the experience of working in an Education Authority Nursery School supervised the programme.

With all this crisis settled, I breathed a sigh of relief and began to think of a way forward out of the uncertainties which were forever looming. Over this period an opportunity to meet with the CCCVS and the Assistant Director for Children and Young Persons, presented itself when in response to my many requests they agreed to convene a meeting for the 30th April.

Two members of the Management Committee of WIPAG, a representative of the parents of children registered with the nursery, the Senior Nursery Nurse, a Trustee/Founder Member and myself attended this meeting. We were very keen to discuss:

the progress made during the integration period;

the delay in the receipt of the first quarter grant;

a letter we had received from the Lambeth Inner City Partnership Unit, dated 7th April 1987. This informed us that funding for both projects had ceased on 31st March 1987.

I quote,

"In these circumstances the Policy and Resources Committee of Lambeth Council has indicated a commitment to provide main programme funding to replace the Urban Programme funding. The Council Committee which sponsors your project will now consider the grant payment. Please contact your Liaison Officer in this regard".

Despite assurances from Council officers that, *"there is nothing to worry about"*, we still felt anxious, uncertain of our position and helpless. So the 30th April meeting, we thought, would be a golden opportunity for us to obtain some answers and confirmation that there is indeed nothing to worry about.

At the meeting on the 30th April, we presented the areas of concern that we wanted to discuss. The CCCVS looked disdainfully at the list of concerns we presented, held it up to the Assistant Director's eyes for a minute and returned it to me saying, *"This will be dealt with at some other time"*.

His dismissive tone was as sharp as the edge of a gilded knife! He seemed quite angry. This was evident as he inhaled and exhaled, breathing like an athlete who had just passed the finishing line!

He was not prepared to discuss any aspect of the difficulties and disappointments we had encountered during our attempt to get the building fit for purpose and ready for operation. His colleague remained mute throughout all this time. It was like having to engage with a schoolboy who was in the throes of dragging his satchel unwillingly to school. Nevertheless, one of my colleagues expressed concern that continued prevarication by the Council would put WIPAG in an unenviable position whereby it would not be able to pay salary cheques to staff in sufficient time to guarantee such payments are cleared by the 15th of the month. She explained that this would force WIPAG to delay its remittance to the Inland Revenue in order to have sufficient cash to make the staff salary payments.

The CCCVS listened but made no comment on our dilemma. *"Let's move on to the question of staff"*, he said.

There was an audible rustling of papers. This summary dismissal of our concerns and the sudden shift of focus from the substantive matter under discussion surprised us. He continued, *"There are a number of concerns that I wish to raise with you when next we meet. There are the collection of fees from parents which has been done without my permission and the non-payment of the Inland Revenue contributions"*.

He then looked at everyone seated around him, looked at his watch and declared the meeting closed. Their exit from the room was silent and swift, conjuring a picture of two saints fleeing from an unholy place. These blatant assumptions sent a chilling sensation through my body like a sudden bolt of thunder on a fair day in spring. This way of conducting a meeting was quite unreal to me, a clear deviation from what we had expected. He appeared very dissatisfied with something that I could not identify.

On 15th May 1987, a three paged letter was received from Social Services signed by the CCCVS, copied to the newly elected Chair of the Social Services Committee, the Assistant Director for Children and Young Persons and the Senior Finance Officer for Social Services. The contents of this letter appear to address the outcomes of the meeting on 30th April.

In view of the complexity and tone of its contents, the misrepresentation of the issues we discussed on the 30th April and the inclusion of matters he was purporting to have discussed and agreed with us then, it was imperative to seek the Management Committee's collective response to the issues raised.

I immediately acknowledged receipt of the communication, informing him that the Management Committee would send a response to the Council in due course.

At the time, we viewed this letter as typical evidence of the impersonal nature of local authority bureaucracy and a failure to have ready access to all the facts. But in hindsight, it was the turning point in our relationship with the Council that was being led by the Chief Co-ordinator Community & Voluntary Services (CCCVS). It was a drawing of the line in the sand at high noon!

Incitement, Manipulation, Interference and Power

The expressed concerns of the CCCVS are thus important to outline here in some detail. Not just to set the scene for our battles ahead but to highlight the contested areas that became the actual battlefields and to trail evidence of a very personal tone in the CCCVS's pursuit of us.

The CCCVS charged us with deviating from agreements in four areas: Staffing, Director's Salary, Nursery Fee and Finance.

Staffing

He wrote:

"Matters pertaining to the staffing of 90 Kellet Road element of the project were first raised in your letter and budget estimate to me on 4 December 1985. I agreed to the appointment of three Nursery Assistants and two NNEB's. I also agreed it was reasonable to fill the post of Nursery Officer by the transfer of an existing senior member of staff from Gresham Road. I note from our meeting of 30 April that the following staff are in post and include one Nursery Officer, two NNEBs, four Nursery Assistants and one cleaner".

The CCCVS blatantly misquoted the number of staff that were deployed at the Annex in Kellet Road. The budget estimate was dated 4 December 1985, a follow up from the first estimate submitted in July detailing the number of care and ancillary staff that was never approved. Over the period, the grant aid covered the salaries for only six Care Staff and no ancillary, i.e. cook/cleaner. Despite the suggestion that the part-time ancillary staff be deployed for further sessions to carry out the work, he had never addressed that issue. The opening hours of the nursery were 8am to 6pm and with great difficulty, we had to manage by deploying part-time ancillary workers from Gresham Road to cover Kellet Road. At no time, however, was the Kellet Road Nursery being covered by eight members of staff as he had implied.

Director's Salary

In this same communication of 12 May, he stated.

> "We also agreed that the salary of the post of Director should be £14,350 as proposed in your budget estimate of 4 December 1985. I agreed that your salary should take effect from 1 February 1986, the date on which the first member of staff started work. With regards to the outstanding matters on other salaries we have agreed that they will be looked at in the very near future".

My appointment by the Management Committee of WIPAG to the post of Director started in July 1983. I had no knowledge that any changes in the administration of the project had occurred. My Contract of Employment, including the expected salary, was agreed prior to my taking up my appointment. The CCCVS's assertion that he had agreed my salary to take effect on 1st February 1986 further alerted me to his misunderstanding of the issues involved. Try as we did to establish a dialogue, he was unprepared to respond to our plea for a meeting to address the issues about salaries.

Finance

He further stated:

> "I was very concerned to learn that the project had incurred a deficit. A consequence of this has been the project's inability to meet the Inland Revenue's obligation. As you know, the grants towards staff include provision for Inland Revenue payments. The Council is keen to impress on organisations it funds the inadvisability of incurring deficits, as such a situation could have a direct bearing on the Council's willingness to continue funding. I shall therefore be grateful if you can let me have very detailed information on the deficit, and your

Committee's proposals for clearing them. The Principal Day Care Officer, Assistant Director for Children and Young Persons and myself will be discussing this matter shortly and will contact you to arrange a review".

At the meeting of 30th April, the WIPAG's representative merely mentioned the difficulty we experienced when the salary grant for April 1987 did not arrive. She said this caused a delay in sending off the Inland Revenue contributions, as we feared experiencing a cash flow problem.

Here is a typical example of how a slight statement to the CCCVS was transformed from an expressed concern to a prohibited action. The CCCVS's misinterpretation of our ability to manage the organisation proved in a matter of weeks to be a passing dark omen that set the project on an irretrievable collision course with the Council in the person of the CCCVS.

Nursery Fees

Under this heading he stated: *"There seem to be some doubt as to whether the Council has approved the current charges of fees to parents. Both the Assistant Director and I are concerned about any increases in fees, and we are specifically requesting that no further increases should be implemented".*

The charging of fees had been a standard requirement since the inception of the Nursery in 1977. Indeed a projected sum under heading "Income" of the Urban Aid Programme Circular 17 Application in 1976 was regarded as a plus for those projects that had a built in plan to generate a portion of its running costs. All of WIPAG's Annual Reports and audited accounts since then had always been submitted to the Directorate of Social Services. They did carry this important information. In fact, the collection of fees was the organisation's only means of payment of utility bills. Part-time fees were for ancillary staff and the additional five staff needed to upgrade the operation when it moved into the new premises at Gresham Road in 1983. The staff compliment that we had for the twenty-four place, Canterbury Crescent Building could not possibly suffice for a fifty place larger building including a baby section with eight places.

The organisation's appeal to the Social Service Directorate, its subsequent letter to the then Minister Sir George Young at the Department of Environment and his visit to the Nursery in December 1983 perhaps helped to secure funding in the 1984-1987 budget, for exactly the same compliment of staff – but did not address our plight for additional staff.

By 1987, and without any discussion whatsoever with Social Services, or any other body regarding the charging of fees, the CCCVS decided to inform parents against the payment of fees and in his letter of 12th May expressed his doubts that the Council had given permission for the charging of fees.

It had by then become clear to me that the CCCVS was at cross purposes with the real and factual differences between voluntary organisation and the Local Authority Social Service Directorate. His letter concluded with the following statement: *"We are agreed that the best way forward is to undertake a review of the project and we will be eager to complete this exercise as soon as possible. The Assistant Director and I will be in contact with you shortly".*

The Management Committee sent their promised response to the CCCVS on 18th June. During this period between the receipt of the CCCVS's letter of 12th May and the Management Committee's response on the 18th June, a series of incidents occurred. They included complaints from some staff and a small percentage of parents that followed with painful rapidity, getting more and more intense daily. Staff were signing the attendance book but leaving the premises for hours; meals were being boycotted and meals supervision for the children disrupted.

The daily collection of children from their respective schools, for the after school project, was carried out on an irregular or haphazard basis because the mini bus driver abdicated his job responsibility to collect the children. Instead, he decided to keep the organisation's vehicle for his own use. The children were not collected on several occasions, much to the frustration and inconvenience of the teachers. The husband of my part-time secretary was appointed as the part-time mini bus driver to collect the children from their schools during term time. He now started to make demands for a full-time position within the organisation. There was no vacant post to accommodate him, so he devised extortionate activities that grew to a disproportionate and intolerable level.

This included not collecting the children requiring us to send taxies to collect children from four separate schools in the Borough.

The quarterly grant due to cover the salaries for the month of July did not arrive. My call to the Finance Officer of Social Service Directorate revealed that the CCCVS had not authorised any payment for the organisation. It was suggested that I should call the CCCVS to find out what our situation was. In conversation with him, he informed me that my secretary had told him that I had no intention to respond to his letter of 12th May, hence his reason for withholding the grant cheque.

I immediately assured him that that was not the case and reminded him that I had acknowledged his letter in which I stated that in view of the seriousness of its contents the Management Committee would collectively send their response in due course. I assured him that their letter was sent off to him on 18th June and expressed my dismay that he had not yet received same. He eventually agreed to instruct the Finance Officer to release the cheque.

In view of the delay, a letter of authorisation from the Finance Officer was sent to the Bank asking for an overdraft facility to ensure that the staff salary cheques could be honoured. All attempts to establish dialogue with the CCCVS remained muted. The Management Committee was at pains to have a review of the overall function of the provision undertaken but that was not to be.

CHAPTER 10

LAMBETH COUNCIL

Lambeth Council had been a Labour led council for many years. During the turbulent 70s and 80s it was led by councilor Ted Knight. In the wake of the Council's reluctance to set a rate, thirty-two councillors, including the leader, were issued with Disqualification Notices by Central Government. As a result, an election of prospective Councillors ensued. There is no doubt that the months of election campaigning, the departure of the outgoing much experienced community spirited Councillors and the uncertainties of whether there were other sanctions the Government might take against the administration could have created a great deal of upheaval. In particular, the drastic reduction in the rate support grant could have had implications for the Council's main programme funding,

Incidentally, amidst all these changes and prior to the departure of the Chairperson for the Social Services Committee, the Chief Co-ordinator Community and Voluntary Services (CCCVS) was made the Council's Grants Liaison Officer to WIPAG. This was both unusual and a clear departure from the norm. The Council's Social Work Area Co-ordinator and Senior Day Care Officers were delegated to the other under 5 schemes. WIPAG therefore became the solitary under 5's scheme with the CCCVS as its Grant Liaison Officer.

The CCCVS had no knowledge of working within the social work framework or indeed had any experience and perception of the ethos which under-pinned the work of WIPAG and his fierce refusal to recognise the importance of those skills lay at the heart of the community's loss of a Day Care facility.

WIPAG's experience of working with the CCCVS in the initial months, prior to taking up the Brixton Cares for Kid's offer, was amicable. His predecessor had, since the organisation's admission to the Inner City Partnership in 1979 and even prior to the acquisition of 3-5 Gresham Road, supported and guided us through the modification and renovation process, dealt with the architect, helped us to secure top-up capital funding from the Greater London Council (GLC) and continued revenue funding for salaries. This support and guidance saw us through to the official opening of the nursery. He ensured that the appropriate financial and legal requirements were met. He discussed and agreed with the Management Committee's Officers the implementation of the project, in particular the accounting and budgeting aspects.

Finance became one of WIPAG's strongest areas of administration. This was due, in a significant part, on the unshakeable loyalty of a young student of economics who managed the accounts in a voluntary capacity for over six years.

In fact, this former Grant Liaison Officer assisted, assessed and advised WIPAG in developing a clear knowledge of the Council's procedures and expectations thereby helping us to plan and develop the project. He was able to mediate on the organisation's behalf with the Directorate of Social Services by using factual information obtained by his monitoring process and professional ethics which were laid down by the Directorates "Condition of Grant Aid".

Therefore, our anxieties became heightened when we were confronted with a new Grant Liaison Officer whose demeanour was officious, unnecessarily bureaucratic and unsympathetic.

Our anxieties became reinforced when we received a written notice to attend a meeting on 20th July in Room 2, Mary Secole House, Clapham High Street and have the meeting cancelled on the same day. I therefore telephoned the CCCVS who was out of his office. I then called another Officer, Assistant Director Children and Young Persons and the Finance Officer who were both listed on the Notice to Attend but they claimed they knew nothing about a meeting scheduled for 20th July. I suggested that we meet on 23rd July, to which both officers agreed, with the hope that the CCCVS would be available to attend but they rang me the following day to cancel, saying that this arrangement had displeased the CCCVS.

On the morning of the 23rd July, an obviously upset CCCVS rang and asked me not to arrange any meeting with Social Services Officers as he was the senior and would take care of what happens in his department. So the meeting for 23rd July did not take place.

Our regular monthly parents and staff meetings continued as a feature of our communication with the parents but it became noticeable that some parents had become less communicative, anxious and often displayed contentious and confrontational behaviour. The Management Committee decided to devise and circulate a questionnaire to the parents in an attempt to discover their thoughts about the services offered to them by the organisation.

Following the response to the questionnaire, we started to hold a series of small group meetings, because a considerable number of the parents were with us for a relatively short time. This exercise was aimed at giving the new parents and the staff an opportunity to get to know each other better and to get an understanding of any difficulties that either party might be experiencing. After several of those small group meetings where no particular complaints were aired, I was taken by surprise when on the 16th July 1987 at a full and well attended parents meeting some parents began to complain bitterly about the lack of care and the poor food their children were given.

The Chairman, Headley Johnson, assured all the parents that the matter they had highlighted would be seriously examined by the Management and he would report back to the next parents' meeting. Moving on to the next agenda item, Fundraising, the Chairman informed the meeting that a problem of continued funding for staff salaries had arisen. With the expiry of the Inner City Partnership funding on 31st March 1987, four months into the new financial year had elapsed and the Management Committee still awaited a decision from Social Services as to WIPAG's acceptance to the Main Programme Funding.

"It was crucial", he continued, *"that we considered making appeals to other funding bodies and organised events to help raise funds for the purpose of keeping the project afloat"*. He appealed to all the parents for suggestions as to how this could be achieved.

One parent of two children who attended the nursery offered to get a group of parents together to discuss ways of generating funds. Suddenly a few parents became agitated and in one outburst, a parent shouted, *"But the Council gives a lot of money to this nursery, why fundraising"*?

Another, in a progressively angry, confrontational manner asked, *"Why are these two white parents given nursery places for their children here and why was the last Chair of Social Services given nursery places for her children?"*

She continued angrily, *"This nursery was set up exclusively for black children of working parents"* . She shook her head vigorously as she passionately repeated, *"No. They shouldn't be here. It is unfair, it is unfair".*

Abuses were hurled at the two white mothers who were present in the room, transforming the meeting into a verbal battleground.

Parents whom I had credited with a wealth of understanding about the nature of community development and race relations waded into the affray with venom. The uncomfortable mood of the majority gave the Chairman no alternative but to adjourn the meeting. I left that room, my head bowed, I could feel the perspiration trickling down my body, and my mind accepting failure.

The following afternoon, when I had a chance, I shared what had happened at the meeting with my secretary and informed her of the parent's offer to get those parents who showed an interest to join in fundraising efforts. She had already done so. I could not believe that she had passed on the names and addresses of parents, including past parents, to this parent prior to speaking with me! All letters and circulars should be issued from the office and I was alarmed to find that my secretary would take unilateral action to set up a grouping of parents without due consideration of terms of reference and membership.

The focus for the future development of the nursery seemed to have changed from 'fundraising by collective action' to the launch of a Parent and Staff Action Group that appeared to undermine and oppose the Management Committee and Senior Staff. This was confirmed when this Action Group presented themselves to the Council's officers and members of the Social Services Directorate, Members of Parliament for the Borough, Directors for other Directorates, NALGO Union Branch Secretary and the Lambeth Black Workers Forum.

It did not take long for us to discover that this was not a sudden action but was part of a strategy arising out of clandestine meetings with the Leader of the Council, the Complainants and the CCCVS.

During the course of these meetings, some of which were held in the Town Hall, a series of complaints, allegations and concerns were presented to the Council's officers. Most of these were hair-raising and serious enough to merit immediate investigations that these officers had a right and duty to undertake. But no one communicated any of these with me or the Management Committee of WIPAG.

On reflection, the majority of the new intake of children during that period was from black parents who were employees of Lambeth Council and or who had connections with local activists.

In hindsight, I now recognise the importance of a number of incidents and developments that were precursors to what finally happened. The visiting patterns of these new parents with regular attendance during the day and frequent conversations with certain staff members ought to have indicated a trend worth noting. But two incidents stand above all others.

One afternoon, as customary, I went on a walk about around the building just to observe some of the children's activities and to communicate with the staff. Suddenly I saw a figure of a woman moving quickly across the hallway on the lower ground floor. I continued down the stairs as a member of staff met me at the bottom and engaged me in conversation.

I dealt with her quickly. Then I looked into the rooms adjacent to the hallway and there I saw this woman looking around, examining the displays on the wall. I introduced myself to her and offered to help. The woman described herself as a student from Goldsmiths College in the Borough of Lewisham who just wanted to look around. She spoke in a drawling tone, as if mimicking a North American accent.

I asked her kindly to leave but gave her the assurance that if she cared to make an appointment for a later date, outside of the children's lunch and rest period, she would be welcomed. The appointment being made, she left promptly.

Suffice to say the appointment was not kept. Her name was not familiar to me so I thought nothing more about the incident.

My suspicion was, however, aroused as to how the visitor could have entered the building and got to the lower ground floor without anyone's knowledge. So I asked my Secretary, who was at the time engaged on reception duties covering lunch period for the receptionist, as to how the visitor gained entry to the building. An intercom system, with a device to release the door lock, formed part of our safety procedure to keep intruders out.

She told me that the visitor had asked to see me and she directed her to my office on the second floor. However, she did not alert me that a visitor was on her way to see me as was the usual procedure.

Alarm bells began to ring! About a fortnight later, a female with a similar accent telephoned to say she was the CCCVS's Assistant and that she was instructed to request a listing of staff, together with the salary they received. The reason, she said, was that they had been informed that there was a significant gap between the Director's salary and that of other members of the staff group, so they needed to check this information.

In the absence of a written request, I thought of not complying but having grown accustomed to that departments' reluctance to conduct their affairs professionally by putting the request in writing, I sent the items to the CCCVS. After all, I reasoned, I had nothing to hide.

The second incident related to a parent with whom I had never had a dialogue. She did not accompany the child's father for the formal interview prior to the offering of a nursery place for her daughter neither had she ever attended any of the monthly parent/staff meetings. My first meeting with this parent was a scheduled individual parent meeting that was designed to give parents an opportunity to discuss their children's development.

The report we presented to her included observations recorded in the reports of the Paediatrician, Dentist, Audiologist and Speech Therapist. The nursery's support system also included professional services by visiting specialists from the Camberwell District Health Authority and WIPAG's Child Care Consultant. The report highlighted in a clear way the progress that her three-year-old daughter had made.

We, the staff, were altogether happy with the child's progress and harboured no complacency regarding her ongoing development. The meeting proved quite disappointing in that this parent expressed total dissatisfaction with all our efforts, claiming that the child had mastered the age appropriate skills she presently displayed long before attending the nursery. She went into a long lecture about the advisability and desirability of caring for black children in a monochromatic environment.

Realising that I was confronted by a person who seemed entrenched in the art of belittling others, I avoided her angry glaring eyes by looking at the objects on my desk, giving each a kind of special attention. I wanted the scrutiny of the objects to convey the non-verbal message, *"Your problem, racist bitch"*.

Her ranting having abated, I said, *"You are obviously unhappy with what we are able to offer your daughter here"*.

"Yes", she snapped.

"OK", I said, *"Perhaps we will need to discuss your dissatisfaction further. I am sure we should be able to find a common ground on which we can agree."*

The influence and respect I have in the community are important factors in understanding why some people would spend so much time and energy to undermine my work. I was not expecting blind uncritical acceptance of what we were trying to do. As an embattled community, we needed to develop and manage our own intervention and developmental initiatives. WIPAG choose to intervene in childcare and we were always open to different views, criticisms and support from within our community. The decisions that I made at certain times or those which I had to oppose, in pursuit of what I believed to be reasonable, fair and just, were not always seen in that light.

Being a black woman, placed in the position of administering a growing Day Care facility and catering for the majority of African-Caribbean children, in my view, added to the problem. The community in which I had lived and worked for over thirty years had become entrenched in harbouring mistrust in others. It felt like a kind of pathology; crabs in a barrel.

Areas of conflict concerned the amalgamation of the Brixton Cares for Kids' nursery building in Kellet Road with WIPAG's ongoing facility. Initially staff and parents seemed happy with the development, then I noticed that a mixed reaction began to emerge. A few were hostile but we got on. I accepted the conflict and disagreement as part and parcel of my professional life. However, as we shall see from the emerging facts, some of these conflicts were soon exploited by others who were armed with their own specific agenda that contributed further to the demise of the day nursery provision.

In exploiting these conflicts, concerns and incidences, they made each one to assume critical importance.

Another particular area of conflict concerned the use of the organisation's mini-bus.

The bus was purchased to be used for carrying out various nursery activities such as servicing the after-school project, collecting the children from their schools at the end of the school day; transporting children and staff on visits and undertaking errands that staff had to undertake for the organisation's benefit.

However, the full-time driver left suddenly for health reasons but later claimed that he was harassed. A young man, who was at the time unemployed, was offered the position on a part-time basis, specifically to service the after-school project and facilitate shopping activities during term times, commencing September 1986.

Within nine months, a number of incidents occurred that worried us. Children were, on several occasions, left at their school, uncollected. We had to hire taxies to collect the children.

On several of these occasions, we found it impossible to contact the driver.

However, when I approached him and pointed out that his personal activities should not interfere with the smooth functioning of the organisation's activities, he became quite aggressive and threatening. His defiance of the rules and regulations of the organisation soon reached astonishing proportions.

He began to demand money over and above the agreed amount for petrol grew whilst his tasks completed for the nursery decreased considerably. He came in only to sign the attendance book, then left the building. His behaviour became threatening as he shouted abuses at me and made demands to be paid, although for days on end he had not carried out any of the duties for which he was employed. The minibus was eventually smashed!

On seeing the damage, I asked him for a report which he blatantly refused to produce. More damage was then noticed when he eventually parked the minibus outside the premises and put the keys through the letterbox.

The school leaver who was on placement, awaiting the commencement of a Nursery Nurse training course at Brixton College of Further Education and who usually accompanied the driver as an escort for the children, produced a written report about the accident.

Sadly he was threatened by the driver who scared him away. He did not even take up the offer for training at the college.

The school term ended on 23rd July and with it the driver's position. However, he would not accept that he was no longer entitled to a weekly wage. On 29th July, he decided to stage a sit-in at my desk until his demand for wages was met. He paced about the room, muttering to himself, then shouted agitatedly. *"You think this place belong to you? This nursery is not yours, it belongs to all of wi, you think wi going to allow you to teck it way from us, you must be mad"*.

I asked God to give me the patience to ignore all his ranting and raving as long as he did not abuse me physically.

I kept saying, *"God, are you still there for me? You promised to give your divine protection to your children when they are in need. Where are you Lord? I do need your help, please help me"*.

I fought to keep the tears from streaming down my cheeks, I must not give him such satisfaction but my heart was throbbing with fear. I could not believe what I was hearing from a young man who not too long previously was introduced to me by a church based youth initiative as one in need of support, guidance and help in acquiring the basic skills that could help to secure employment. There he was, about three years later, no better equipped to move on into the world of work, despite all the courses offered to him and the practical help given to him over the period.

Two hours passed by. I tried to reason with him. I asked my secretary to encourage him to leave but he would not budge. Eventually I felt that something had to be done, so I telephoned the Police Station that was situated across the road from the building. When he realised that the police were called he left the office. As they met in the reception area, he continued to walk past the police officers towards the front door where he was apprehended. The officers told him to leave the premises and warned him not to return in the future.

In an aggressive tone he said,

"Gloria Cameron you have bitten off more than you can chew.... This nursery does not belong to you and your family..... you call the police, this is the second time you call the police on me. You are black and a magistrate, always sending people to prison. Alright the same system that you serve... I will get them to sort you out".

At this point, the officers firmly moved him towards the door, closing it behind him. I was advised to report it if he came anywhere near the building but I prayed to God that our paths would never cross in the foreseeable future.

However, I learnt something from his last tirade, "This is the second time you have called police on me". I realised then that this was someone from my past. What was this young man trying to tell me? The mind boggles!

CHAPTER 11

UNDERSTANDING THE CONFLICT

Each year, staff, management committee members and a consultant meet to assess the nursery's work, redefine its strategies, plan relevant approaches to the delivery of services and critically review what had been achieved over the year. This particular year, 1987, with its emerging uncertainties, posed an enormous challenge for the nursery's survival. Some staff showed little interest in the forthcoming annual seminar but the Management Committee considered it even more important for the event to take place.

The parent who expressed her dissatisfaction with children other than African Caribbean children being allowed a place at the nursery suggested that someone from the National Council for Voluntary Organisation be asked to chair the conference. This we were able to arrange. The annual seminar was set for Friday 31st July.

On 27th July, the CCCVS telephoned my office to inform me that the nursery driver had reported to him that he had been dismissed from his post at the nursery and that several members of my staff had lodged complaints against me to officers of Lambeth Council.

I offered to send him a copy of the duties of the driver showing that he was employed on a part-time basis, during term time to collect children from four schools and to attend the after school project which is housed on our premises. The Officer paid scant regard to my offer and insisted that the driver should be put on suspension with pay. I told him that that would have to be a decision made by the Management Committee and that his request would be conveyed accordingly to the Committee.

This period also coincided with the period when I served, a day each week, in the Inner London Juvenile Court. On the 28th July, my court rota was completed early and so I telephoned my secretary to say that I would be back at the office earlier and proposed to collect the weekly wages and petty cash from the bank. I asked her for the calculation and exact figures of the amount to be withdrawn. She told me that she had a very busy day and was not able to prepare the figures. She went on to inform me that the NALGO Union Secretary would like to meet with me at 5pm on that day in my office.

I wondered what that was all about. I had never had any dealings with the Union, had never thought of it, had never received any complaint or mention of anything to do with dissatisfaction regarding conditions of service or wages from any member of staff. I asked her what this was all about?

She replied, "I feel that I am underpaid, so I have asked him to come to see you".

I immediately called the nursery's Chairman and Treasurer but neither of them could be contacted. Reluctantly, I rang the CCCVS and told him what I learnt from my Secretary. I did not know how helpful he would have been but it was imperative that I had someone else with me at the meeting. In the throes of conversing with the CCCVS I was overtaken with a horrible feeling of being caught between the devil and the deep blue sea; such was the enormity of my fear and mistrust. Without my asking for his presence, he exclaimed in a no-nonsense tone, *"I want to be at that meeting"*, placing much emphasis on every word in the sentence.

"OK", I said, "See you at 5pm".

I arrived in my office at about 4pm and started to prepare myself for yet another gruelling ordeal. I did not feel that this would be a positive or pleasant encounter but the situation had to be faced. At about 4.56pm my Secretary, the NALGO Union Secretary and a representative of the Lambeth Black Workers Forum who later turned out to be the sister of the parent who wanted only black children to attend the nursery, arrived and following closely on their heels, the CCCVS.

The steam from the coffee that I made them rose like a curtain as we sat looking at each other across the conference table. My troubled spirit must have spread around the room, even the chief protagonists of the plot seemed overwhelmingly uncomfortable but certainly determined.

The NALGO Union Secretary outlined his concerns about the low weekly wages that the Secretary had been paid for the part-time post she held. He compared the Council's rate of pay with ours and demanded that she be paid an equal sum – completely dismissing the fact that the Council did not give salary grant-aid to voluntary organisation at the same level and grading as its Council's employees. He then accused me of not paying the staff London Weighting and demanded that this be rectified by the next salary pay date.

The CCCVS, however, hastened to correct him, by drawing to his attention the fact that London Weighting is paid only to employees of a local authority, central government and perhaps by large business conglomerates. WIPAG grant–aid, he continued, did not provide for London Weighting.

Alas the CCVSO had served a purpose being there! He certainly did dispel the myth that the Union Secretary had been circulating to staff, that I had been cheating them out of London Weighting benefits. Nevertheless, they all agreed that both Secretary and driver were due pay increases in line with the Council's level and that this should be given to them by the next pay date. My Secretary's salary was not paid from the Local Authority Subsidised Grant-aid but through WIPAG's own resources.

I left the meeting under no illusion whatever about the strength of a conspiracy which had been growing in proportion by the minute, with each day adding yet another thread to what had begun to look like an intricate tapestry.

The demands for increase in salaries, free day care and London Weighting got uglier, wilder and has been increasing by the minute. What started as a defiance of the Nursery's regulations soon became an organised collective discontent.

The following day, 28th July, had almost come to an end and a number of parents were arriving to collect their children. Walking around the building I went to the lower ground floor activities room to speak with a newly appointed member of staff when I found her reading what seemed to be a letter, held up before her eyes by the parent who wanted the nursery to cater to African and African-Caribbean children exclusively. She was reading aloud the contents of a letter. They were so engrossed that I left the room without either of them raising their heads.

I continued my walk about and on my return to the office, I noticed that a letter addressed to me was placed on my writing pad. The letter stated:

I am presently extremely concerned and disturbed about the way in which my daughter is showing great admiration for white, half-caste and mixed race people while being negative about herself and black people generally. I am particularly alarmed about this as I specifically chose the nursery because it catered for the needs of African and African-Caribbean children. I recognise that we live in an inherently racist society which makes the contribution black people have made to the development of human kind invisible. Studies after studies have concluded that black children suffer racial confusion to the point of denying their identification with the black race. The school of thought on this is quite overwhelming and so advanced that nurseries run by white people have for some time adopted policies and practices aimed at promoting positive identification in black children with some successes.

My experience of working in community development since the 1970s teaches me that there is an argument to be made, with some justification, about how the presence of black people is viewed and the impact of racism on identity, self-worth and ambitions. However, encasing this argument with an allegation that I was colluding with the reinforcement of racist practices in the delivery of services at the nursery hurt me greatly.

Unfortunately, I was never able to address these concerns and misguided claims because the boycott of the staff seminar on 31st July happened in quick succession to the receipt of the letter. At that time, I had far too many distractions to deal with. Suffice it to say, I was distressed to learn that the ethos of the nursery, which dictated the kind of activities we undertook with the children, had been grossly misunderstood.

African Jamaicans have come too far and we have too far yet to go to take a detour into the swamp of hatred. I simply refuse to let the acid of race hatred and false accusations destroy my humanity.

29th July came and with it in the first post of the day, a notice headed 'Parent Committee', signed by a group of eight parents. An invitation to a meeting scheduled for the 5th August was extended to me. It was planned to be held at the Brixton Recreation Centre, 'a neutral territory' - the description they gave to the venue. The aim of the meeting to which they required my presence was to help them to decide whether they should support me or work against me. Unfortunately, due to a previous commitment I could not attend the meeting. I replied, declining the invitation but asked for an alternative date to be agreed. Nothing further was heard from this Parent Committee.

At our annual seminar held at St Mathews Meeting Place. Brixton Hill, on Friday 31st July, the independent person from the National Council for Voluntary Organisations took the Chair. Twenty-two members of staff, ten Management Committee members and the Consultant attended. My Secretary, who was given the responsibility to minute the day's event, did not arrive. Instead, her husband, the former driver, attended in her place, introduced himself as a member of staff who would be the note taker for the day. There were objections but he insisted that no one could prevent him from taking notes.

The state of unease became so intense that each item on the agenda was met with stony silence and tight-lipped reaction. His intimidating strategy was left bare for everyone to see. It was clear that he had dared the staff to participate in the discussions.

The wall of silence continued throughout the morning sessions. After the lunch break, only twelve of the twenty-two members of staff returned. So there was no alternative left to us but to suspend the activities for the rest of the day. The Chairperson suggested that we reconvene the seminar at a later date. It was therefore agreed that 1st September 1987 would be appropriate as it would be the day we returned from the summer recess. The children were expected back on the following day, 2nd September.

Saturday, 1st August dawned, it was a bleak morning, but according to the weather forecast a bright sunny day would follow. I was not feeling particularly well, the experience of the failed staff seminar made me acutely uneasy, the churning inside of my stomach was ever present. However, I began to think of the historical importance of 1st August, that glorious day when in 1834 the emancipation of slavery was declared in Jamaica. I reflected on the variety of celebratory activities in which I had participated since childhood and because Jamaica's attainment of independence within the Commonwealth of Nations happened on 6th August 1962, the reflection resurrected in me an unexplained mood.

The connection of my thoughts with the humiliation that my ancestors endured as enslaved people, lifted me in a state of mind which focused on my sense of historical continuity of identity and roots. I thought about the remarkable history which had been built into our heritage, that deep reserve of loyalty, passion for justice and equality, love and liberty and a rich national culture that retained a sense of spiritual value. All those thoughts were a gentle reminder of who I am and whence I came. I began to feel uplifted; it was as though a spark was kindled within me that sent my spirit soaring high. However, a glimpse of my sad eyes and drawn features reflecting from the wardrobe mirror prompted me to move away quickly; that figure to me, was that of a stranger. The Thanksgiving service, to celebrate Jamaica's 25th Anniversary of Independence, was scheduled to take place at St Martins in the Field Church, London, later in the day. I had never missed a service over the last 24 years and despite my broken spirit and disappointments I did not wish to be absent from this most important event.

My contemplative and peaceful state was suddenly interrupted by the piercing ring of the telephone. In an upbeat and cheerful voice, I answered, *"Hello, Good Morning"*.

"Is me, Ms Cam".

Immediately I recognised the voice as that of the caretaker of the building next door that housed the Abeng Centre. Mr Grace was a member of my staff for the three years of my employment there as Director for that project and that excellent working relationship continued when I left and became Director for the WIPAG Day Nursery. I knew him very well and trusted him unreservedly.

In a tone tinged with sadness and urgency, he said, *"The nursery. Dey pon fire you know, you better come quick"*.

My heart skipped a beat as I tried to think of a question to ask, then I asked, *"What do you mean?"*.

He replied, *"Ms Cam, mi sey dem a try fi bun down the place, mi call the fire brigade already, come quick"*.

I promised him that I would be on my way, replaced the receiver onto its cradle, cogitated for a minute then announced the news to the rest of the family. Shock, horror and disbelief registered on their faces. As we tried to come to terms with the unexpected news, I telephoned the Chairman and two other management committee members who were equally shocked. They promised to meet with me at the building. On that journey from home in the company of one of my daughters, we were as solemn as anyone who was on the way to a scene of death. We were both silent in our thoughts, not exchanging any words during the thirty-five minutes ride.

The fire fighters were still on the premises when we arrived but thankfully, the fire was already brought under control.

We entered the still smoky lower ground floor area where the blaze was confined. Looking in wide-eyed amazement, I ran over to the opposite wall and turned the light on, for a split second the sudden glare of the light blinded me, then I became aware that something was terribly wrong. I saw the small heaps of debris on the floor, laid out around the large room, sitting in its charred embers. I was struck with the realisation that after four years in the WIPAG Day Nursery Centre, I had been revisited.

The whole pattern of the attack on the building and its contents were identical to the style of the plundering and damages to the Abeng Centre on almost a weekly basis during the late 1970s. I viewed the burnt educational artefacts that were sent to us from Zimbabwe by Gerlin Bean, a founder member of the organisation, newly purchased play equipment, children's art displays and broken burnt nursery furniture. There were splashes of glue everywhere.

I looked nervously through the broken windowpanes of glass into the garden. I could see the fire extinguishers on their sides among an array of torn books, heaps of sugar paper, crayons, broken easels and paint pots. The garden play equipment were removed from the shed and scattered around.

The Police visited the scene and promised to carry out an investigation. After spending over three hours surveying the damages and satisfying ourselves that the remaining areas in the building were untouched, we left. The image of the water soaked objects, lying around, coupled with the strong burning smell of the place remains etched in my memory for good.

For two weeks, between the dates of the failed staff seminar and the eventual closure of the nursery on 11th September, the incidences of intimidation, sabotage, harassment, extortionate activities and defamation of my character continued unabated.

I was left in utter despair, I struggled to determine why these things were happening to me, the injustice of it all made me angry and confused.

I would walk into the building and notice little groupings of staff, away from their work post in deep and agitated discussions, which would stop abruptly, followed by dispersal. This became a regular occurrence. Some parents became regular visitors to the Nursery outside of the collection times.

The whole behaviour affected my relationship and affected my ability to concentrate on my daily tasks. I became less confident as I tried to work out why this was happening. Who were the people involved? Why? But I just could not work this out in any coherent way.

I felt the antagonism of most staff and parents, whom I believe had the full encouragement and support from Council Officers and politicians. I just wanted to retreat from the place.

On Monday, 3rd August, I went into a building that felt so strange, so alien, the dark burning smell hovered over the premises – there were lots of clearing up, cleaning and repairs to be carried out on the lower ground floor where the blaze occurred. The once vibrant atmosphere with sounds of children playing happily had been overtaken by muffled, unclear sounds, sad faces and unpleasant behaviour.

Amidst all this, the ex-driver reported to work, signed the attendance book and sat in the reception area. I asked him to come and see me on the following day, 4th August. He kept the appointment that gave me the opportunity to remind him that he should not have been at work the previous day – he started to shout angrily saying that he had reported to the CCCVS that I had given him the sack. He demanded his day's pay for Monday 3rd August. When this was not given to him, he sat in the reception area complaining to parents who came in to collect their children. On the 5th August, he was again distributing leaflets to parents and passers-by, aimed at defaming the profile of the nursery.

I searched for an explanation, as to the reason, the logic behind all these actions, because I could not comprehend the growing attacks on my character and on my work. Those actions brought home to me the true wonder and complexity of the human mind. It brought me closer to understand the phrase that was used by one of Jamaica's visionaries during the period of the revolutionary ferment of the 1930s when the emergence of racial and national consciousness was at its height. He observed that. "The depressed and dispossessed when politically aroused often displayed a mood not a mind".

Destabilising our Work

The summer's day sunlight shone its yellow-gold colours in the room as though it was high noon but it was almost the end of the working day. I tried to put out of my mind the unusual spate of negative behaviour that I had been experiencing from some people around me. I felt at peace with myself as I admired the glow of the evening light that had settled on the conference table.

As I attempted to clear away the documents lying around, the telephone rang. A voice which I recognised as that of our CCCVS and Grant Liaison Officer asked, *"Can I come to see you? I must speak with you"*.

I asked, *"When?"*

He replied, *"Straight away, say in about fifteen minutes?"*

"OK. *I will wait"*, was my response.

I replaced the receiver on its cradle and continued to clear the table. A feeling of relief washed over me. I thanked God. He is coming. At least I will be able to unravel some of these strange happenings. I then sat back in anticipation of the visit.

The doorbell rang and the caretaker advised me, by intercom, who it was. I instructed him to release the latch. The CCCVS and Grant Liaison Officer came up the stairs and stood in the doorway. I greeted him. He then walked briskly into the room. His entry was as though a sudden gust of wind had blown him involuntarily towards the conference table where I was seated. I offered him a seat, but he declined, he remained standing and asked if I know a young man by name.

I nodded in the affirmative.

"Well", he said, *"He has complained to the Leader of the Borough Council about you and she has instructed me to do what I have to do".*

His faltering voice, repeated, *"I must do what I have to do".*

Now he was confusing me because he had said nothing of consequence. Was he trying to tell me something in particular or trying to find out how much of his pot-pouri of intrigue had come to my attention? In fact, I knew no more about the reason for the destabilisation of the day-to-day operation of the nursery, except that some staff and some parents were quietly transmitting a negative form of behaviour whenever I spoke to them. His face grew hard, as though it was carved out of stone, and his strange eyes conveyed an intention to scare me. In a tone low, but intense, he warned, *"You are in a lot of trouble, aren't you going to ask me not to go ahead"?*

Calmly I asked him, *"Go ahead with what"?*

I was quite puzzled, the atmosphere in the room vibrated with a certain tension. I could feel the blood curdling through my veins. At last, he walked towards the door, looked over his shoulder and said. *"My position would be at stake if I am seen to do otherwise".*

By the time he got to the end of what he was saying, his voice had modulated to an unbelievable whisper. *"But the leader has not spoken with me, how can… "* in mid-sentence I realise that he had already moved away from the door and was stomping his way down the wooden stairs.

On hearing the click of the latch, as the door closed behind him, I sat back in my chair. His words hung in the air like acrid smoke overshadowing everything in sight.

On the 13th August, I received a phone call from the National Association of Local Government (NALGO) office informing me that a member of my staff was at their offices. He wanted to know if his wages were ready for collection because the CCCVS and Grant Liaison Officer said that his pay should be backdated to the 3rd August. This, together with an increase in wages to the secretary, was eventually paid because of the interference and pressure exerted on me by the NALGO Secretary and the CCCVS and Grant Liaison Officer.

A visit from Lambeth's Assistant Director, Children and Young Persons was made on the 14th August that coincided with the day prior to the summer holiday recess. It was usual for the walls to be cleared of most of the artwork. Toys were sterilised and packed away and a general clearance done – ready for new materials to begin the autumn session in September.

The report of her visit did not, however, take into consideration the reason for the sparse displays and the general clearing away of most of the equipment. Instead, her report highlighted that there was a lack of African-Caribbean artwork in the activity rooms, lack of displays on the walls and very few equipment around. The overly cleanliness of the premises and the staff wearing identical overalls suggested that they were being regimented by the management. With equipment and toys not scattered around the room, it was interpreted as a lack of equipment hence the rumour that the equipment grant was not used for the envisaged purpose.

The Assistant Director for Social Services with special responsibility for Children and Young Persons had a statutory responsibility to visit the premises. She had not visited for more than a year, despite WIPAG's invitations. I was therefore surprised and saddened to read her most misleading report of that visit.

I left the nursery that evening to begin my two weeks annual leave, the nursery was to be closed for this period. A tentative date to meet with the CCCVS/Grant Liaison Officer on the 27th August was agreed. I returned earlier from my holiday in order to honour that date but unfortunately, he had cancelled the meeting.

As planned, I returned to work on 1st September to meet with the staff to reconvene the failed staff seminar of the 31st July. Of the twenty-two members of staff, only five reported for work, the Independent Chairperson from the National Council for Voluntary Organisation also attended. There were no apologies from the absent members of staff.

On the same day, I was overtaken with shock and disbelief when I noticed that my office was ransacked. There were sheets of A4 paper strew around, some crushed up and lying on the floor and both typewriters were bereft of their covers.

There was also an eight-page compilation of allegations against me arranged in fifty-three sections signed by a parent. A parent claimed that the staff and parents had mandated her to produce the documents setting out fifty-three allegations against me that she circulated to all the Directorates within Lambeth Council, Members of Parliament, Local Councillors, the Charity Commissioners and copied to the Management Committee of WIPAG. Letters were also sent to the Social Services Committee and officers of the Council containing allegations of a personal nature, with threats to the Council that should her demand for an enquiry remained unmet, she intended to take the matter to the Ombudsman or ask for a judicial review.

These 53 allegations included personal charges against me, poor nutrition of the children, inadequate supervision and accusations of racism.

There then followed a letter of invitation, addressed to me, to attend a public meeting which was due to take place at the Town Hall on 14th September. Having endured such adverse publicity, false allegations and humiliation, I was left to wonder and wonder deeply as to why in God's name these people had thought it necessary to invite me to participate in a discussion about the administration of the nursery in such a contrived and emotionally charged environment. What did they expect to achieve from my presence? What could I expect to achieve from being in their midst?

I decided to decline the invitation. I did not feel that there was any respect left between myself, parents, staff or community activists. I had already reached the point of feeling irritable and angry. I felt as though I had moved into the path of a cloud of insects, worst were the leeches who managed to get through my clothing, then under my skin, biting the flesh and bloating themselves on my blood.

The 2nd September dawned and the children were expected to return from the summer recess. The atmosphere on the premises was dismal. Twenty-five of the seventy children attended the two nurseries. The staff all signed in as reporting for work but more than half of them left the premises.

Later during the day, the Clerk to the CCCVS rang to request a copy of WIPAG's Constitution and a bound copy that included the embossed registered lease document was delivered to him by hand. This was never returned. The

CCCVS indicated his willingness to meet with WIPAG's Management Committee and, in this regard, he offered the dates of 4th, 9th and 10th September. We agreed on 4th September, such was the level of our anxiety to establish dialogue with him. During the period of chasing him for a meeting, three reports were sent to him, none of these was ever acknowledged. These were:-

A report on the damages to the Organisation's mini bus.

Damage by fire to the lower ground floor activity rooms.

Destruction and theft of equipment.

A report was also sent to the Assistant Director, Children and Young Persons, Social Services Directorate regarding the disruption to the day-to-day services and the disregard for the standards as laid down by the Nurseries Regulations. We anticipated that the Director for Social Services would have acceded to our wish to be present at this meeting.

We therefore expressed to him, by letter, our anxiety to discuss among other things the destabilisation of the nursery by a number of the staff who had joined with parents who were employees of the Council. Both groups, we felt, were encouraged in their disruptive behaviour by the CCCVS.

We further informed him that staff were being given incorrect information that the salary they were paid was far less than the grant-aid provided by the Inner City Partnership - Social Services and that they were posting notices around the building demanding payment of London Weighting which they claimed that the Branch Secretary for NALGO had advised as their entitlement. We did not receive any response from the Director to this letter but we felt that the matter was serious enough for him to make an effort to dispel the confusion that had arisen and help all concerned to reach an amicable understanding of the true situation.

A Defining Meeting

The long awaited day of 4th September arrived. Five Management Committee Members and I attended the meeting at the scheduled time at the Mary Seacole House, the Borough of Lambeth's main Social Services Directorate's building in Clapham, South London. We waited in the room designated for the meeting for over 30 minutes before the CCCVS and two others entered. A female was introduced as his assistant. I immediately recognised her as the person I found wandering around the nursery premises a few weeks earlier, posing as a student from Goldsmith's College. The other colleague was the Department's Finance Officer with whom we had had a good working relationship ever since our receipt of the Partnership Funding. There was no apology for the Social Services Director's absence.

The CCCVS/Grant Liaison Officer was in a foul mood from the outset of the proceedings. This was made visible by his facial expression and body language. I wondered if we should have risen to attention when they entered the room. Did we not receive the CCCVS and his colleagues in the manner he wished? I can assure you that no disrespect was meant, to do otherwise just did not seem appropriate. His displeasure was made clear when we noticed that his nostrils flared in the middle of a face that had hardened into a scowl, revealing a wildness in his dark eyes and a sound of deep breathing. Those expressions communicated to me a degree of anger.

We began by introducing ourselves by name and positions in WIPAG. The CCCVS immediately took control and would not allow us to deal with any of the items on our agenda. We noticed that they had no written agenda with which ours could be merged; when we asked for clarification as to the items to be discussed, he brushed our concerns aside, treating them as irrelevant. He launched into a criticism of all our efforts. He accused me of malpractice, mismanagement and all the ills that could be blamed on officers of a disrespected organisation.

I sat there aghast! The sighs from committee members were audible, the weary muted shuffles from his colleagues were laid bare for everyone to see. Any stranger looking on would have been led to believe that his accusations were founded on truth; instead, they were based on information that he claimed was given to him by my Secretary. As he spoke, I felt that hurt and rebuke jostled for prominence in his voice. Hurt because of the degree of loyalty and zeal he was prepared to display to protect the Council from fraudsters within the community; rebuke to emphasise the authority that was vested in him by the Leader of the Council.

In an overwhelming projected voice, revealing the expanding veins in his throat – he paused to extract sheets of A4 paper from a folder, looked at them briefly and cautioned, *"And don't you dare carry out any plan to increase the nursery fees, dismiss staff nor reduce the numbers of nursery places before consulting me".*

My entire body went rigid. I thought, how on earth he got that document. He was referring to a document that must have been removed from the organisation's confidential files headed, 'Forward Planning'.

There we were at this long awaited meeting trying to salvage a semblance of what could have gone so radically wrong with the good working relationship we had built up with Lambeth Social Services and its officers. His reprimand, scornfully delivered, was received by us like a ton of bricks. He then remarked that he was aware that the organisation was classified as within the 'voluntary section' but that would not prevent the Council from doing what it liked. Pausing for a second, he continued in a most threatening tone, *"as a matter of fact, your quarterly grant will be suspended forthwith and be replaced with a monthly grant until a review and public enquiry of the organisation's employment practices, allocation of resources and financial management are investigated".*

At this point, I assured the officer that WIPAG's management and I would co-operate fully with whoever wished to lead an enquiry or review. One of the organisation's trustees pointed out that difficulties were bound to arise with a monthly grant arrangement. Having administered the project for eight years on a quarterly payment, this sudden change could create a serious cash flow problem. For example, the partnership salary grant, of which seventy-five percent was being paid by Central Government and twenty five percent by Social Services, covered the salary for thirteen of the twenty two staff who were required to maintain the statutory ratio of staff to the seventy children who attended the nurseries.

The organisation had a responsibility to pay the remaining nine members of staff from the fees paid by the parents. This decision would certainly create a cash flow situation. With a jerk of his left shoulder he said, *"Nothing can be done about this decision, it has been already made".*

The meeting was concluded by his statement that the Director for Social Services would send us the information in respect of the Public Enquiry. He then made eye contact with his two colleagues who remained mute throughout the meeting and walked out of the room with the latter following in his trail. I must say, he did seem to look much taller than his usual height as he left the room. We remained seated for some time bemused and in fear from a most extraordinary encounter.

The numbness remained with me as I left from the place named in honour of the Jamaican lady of mercy, Mary Seacole, whose contribution in the Crimean War transcended the barrier of race, sex and political affiliation. The stifling atmosphere was in no way conducive to the memory of the dear lady who is known to represent the pleasant fragrance of flowers and who gave hope to the injured and afflicted. Sadly, I began to realise that there were elements within the building that had made it into an impenetrable jungle.

My confusion was heightened by the CCCVS's provocative behaviour towards me and the fact that he was reading and interpreting the Management Committee's plans, recorded in their 'Forward Planning' document, as inappropriate actions. Actions and options that any committee, faced with such serious uncertainties as they were experiencing, were duty bound to consider. This was, in fact, the Committee's draft proposal for the continuation of the nursery's operations in case the partnership funding was not renewed. It included ideas for the nursery's survival and was an honest attempt to plan ahead, to keep the doors open even if it meant that the operation had to be scaled down.

We were forced into this plan because towards the end of the partnership vetting process and the Department of Environment impending selection of the successful bids for grand-aid, we received a letter from the Inner City Partnership Unit in Lambeth. It informed us in February 1987 that the organisation's grant-aid was time expired to take effect as of 31st March 1987. It further advised that the Social Services Committee had agreed to place our integrated project on the Council's 'Main Programme Funding' and suggested that we contact the Social Services Liaison Officer, CCCVS, for further information. This was done as a matter of urgency.

He assured me that there was nothing for us to worry about but did not in any way confirm the Inner City Partnership Unit's information. At that particular time in February 1987, we were in the final stage of utilising the Kellet Road building which he and the outgoing Chairperson of the Social Services

Committee had coerced us into managing and integrating with the ongoing Gresham Road facility. The integrated operation began on 23rd March 1987. However, by this date the officer had made himself unavailable to us. He did not return calls, neither did he respond to letters we sent to him but maintained a form of distance. The Chairperson for the Social Services Committee with whom we had a short but promising working relationship, had left the Council a few months earlier as a result of Central Government's 'rate cap' and 'disbarment' which affected thirty two councillors all at once.

In the ensuing period, WIPAG's liaison with the Directorate was left solely in the hands of the CCCVS. It would appear that he was immediately promoted to a position of guiding and cultivating the newly elected councillors many of whom, unlike the outgoing councillors, had no knowledge or experience of the nature of community development work in the Borough at the time. Community workers who had worked in the Borough since the late 1960s were well aware of the acute need for day care provision. Many first generation African-Caribbean parents together with many professional workers from the host community campaigned for nursery centres in order to help stem the tide of children being received in the local authority care and to provide pre-school intellectual stimulation and care for children whose mothers were at work.

The Social Services Directorate in its response recognised that it had a vitally important role to play in embracing such preventive measures such as work with the under-fives residing in the Borough. However, the new administration that took up office in late 1986, in their deliberations, ruined the Directorate's plans and good intentions for the wellbeing of the working mothers by reneging on their early offer of salary grant.

In this way, they created enormous confusion, conflict and mistrust among people who had worked harmoniously together for several years. The new financial year began in April with much uncertainty and there seemed to be an unwillingness on the part of the CCCVS to communicate with us as to our status. This served to increase our fears and anxieties for the future of the project.

On the following day, our Treasurer came to the office to check the fees that were collected, the petty cash book and to look through the records in the Kalamazoo case which housed all the accounting documents. She drew my attention to the defacement of the petty cash book and the absence of certain accounting documents from the Kalamazoo case. These were the responsibilities of my Secretary. We were extremely surprised and angry to be faced with such an outright disloyal and undermining act from a secretary whom we trusted. The Treasurer sealed the petty cash book and together with the Kalamazoo case, we agreed to put them in the custody of the auditors.

On my arrival at the office the following day, I found my Secretary sat with arms stretching either side of her, across the desk, weeping inconsolably, her shoulder bobbed up and down and her face filled with tears. I asked her, "*What was the matter?*"

She replied, amidst broken sobs, "*You have taken away the Kalamazoo case and the petty cash book and I have not been able to do anything since morning*".

I responded, "*You have done enough, and there is nothing else left for you to do*".

I was overtaken with anger that grew while I listened to her hysterical sobbing. I sat reading the morning's post but concentration eluded me, I put the post away, sat back in my chair and closed my eyes trying to calm myself. I made an effort to focus on my personal business but emotions were crowding in. I was truly angry and hurt; my Secretary had cruelly betrayed me by conspiring with others to frame me as a thief. She had then realised that her deeds had been found out; hence the hysteria. She left the office about an hour later and, although the Nursery continued its operations for a further week, she did not report to work.

At a full Management Committee meeting held on the evening of 7th September, the implications arising from the CCCVS/Liaison Officer's behaviour and handling of a matter which we viewed as of vital importance at the meeting held on the 4th September was fully discussed. Members clearly recognised what was implied by the CCCVS's allegations of mismanagement. Two decisions were made:-

that WIPAG's financial records be sent to the Firm of Accountants for auditing. The previous audited account was submitted to the Council six months earlier. No adverse comment or query had been received to date. Nevertheless members thought that in view of the existing climate it would be a good idea to prepare an up to date information sheet on the financial state of the organisation;

that a letter be sent to the Director for Social Services, soliciting his intervention, and pointing out the serious effect the CCCVS's decision would have on the organisation's cash flow and financial management.

The letter was drafted by the Management Committee members present at the meeting. In its conclusion, the members expressed their doubts that they could continue to sustain the management of the nursery due to the escalating disruption to the services – boycotting of the meals, constant abuses to those staff who refused to join in the disruption, the absence of positive liaison input from Social Services and the disappearance of groups of staff from the premises, at intervals during the working hours, leaving the children unsupervised.

On the following day, 8th September, I received two visitors. They were known community workers whom I had not seen for some time. I tried to hide my distress, putting on a brave welcoming face and treating the whole upheaval as a passing phase. At that time my heart was thumping hard against my breast and strangely a poem written by Rudyard Kipling which I used to recite at school sprang to my mind, the words came back to me, loud and clear –

If you can keep your head when all about you
Are losing theirs and blaming it on you;
If you can trust yourself when all men doubt you,
But make allowance for their doubting too;
If you can wait and not be tired by waiting,
Or being lied about, don't deal in lies,
Or, being hated, don't give way to hating.
And yet don't look too good, nor talk too wise;

Incidentally, these visitors already knew that I was embroiled in a lot of trouble, far more than I had imagined. They asked me to sit, because they had come to deliver a message to me from a person who was positioned in the hierarchy of the Health Service. My natural reaction was to ask for the identity of the person. *"You do not know her"* was the reply, *"and she has never met you personally, but she had knowledge of the splendid contribution that you have continued to make to your community for many years".*

I nodded my head, weakly.

"Well", one of the messengers continued looking intently in the eyes of her colleague,

We are asked to tell you that there are many people who are distressed about the erroneous gossip and rumours

which are being circulated about you. There are many who could not bear to see you being escorted by the Police from the building in full view of the children, your staff, parents and possibly the Press. That is the plan of certain people in the community, and encouraged by a few within the Directorates of the Council. The implementation of this plan is eminent. Do not turn up for work next week. You must leave!

I looked at them in amazement. A lengthy silence followed, while I tried to decode what I was told. I must say that I was knocked speechless. These words permeated my confused state, splintered it into dark threatening fragments. I felt frightened, trapped and helpless.

In my confusion I said dismissively *"Oh what nonsense. I have not stolen anything from this organisation or anyone else for that matter. How could the Police come to remove me from the premises?"*

I rose impatiently from my seat asking them to excuse me. I faced the window looking out on to Gresham Road, the sight of the Brixton Police station opposite the premises, conjured up a deep feeling within me as though I was being pursued by a mighty army of soldiers.

I was overwhelmed by a feeling of grief. I thought, but this is possible, there might be some truth in what I have just heard. I mulled over in my mind the contents of the 53 points allegation that some parents had compiled and circulated against my work, family and my person. I had had no contact with the young woman who led this compilation for well over eleven years. Prior to this time, I knew her as a young volunteer community activist. I reasoned, yes anything is possible.

Despite being overtaken by the horrible feelings of being attacked from various angles, I did not immediately think for a moment that I would actually leave the job I loved so much, although I was experiencing a strong feeling of rejection from those with whom I had worked, helped and supported during times of crisis and times of plenty. All of this was becoming too much for me to comprehend. The messengers whom I had come to regard as "Sisters of Mercy" left the office, promising to keep in touch with me. They certainly did. Their shoulders and utterances of philosophical sayings provided solace and comfort for me during those gruelling times when my despair and pain caused uncontrollable weeping.

On the morning of 9th September, I took the organisation's financial records to the firm of accountants to be audited as directed by the Management Committee. On my way back to the office, I met a parent who gave me a letter that was addressed to all parents of WIPAG Day Nursery. This was an invitation from a *WIPAG Staff and Parents Action Committee* requesting parents to attend a meeting scheduled for the 14th September to discuss the eminent closure of the nursery. Later during that same day, I noticed the ex-driver, dressed in black hooded coat and black trousers, standing like a sentinel at the entrance to the premises. I watched him intently from the window. Soon he began to distribute notices to the parents.

There was a complete breakdown of the day-to-day activities in the nursery, demonstrated by the drastic non-attendance of a number of staff and children; meals were boycotted, so were local outings. A lack of supervision, both on the playground and in the activities room, was clearly obvious. Preparation of the children's development report was no longer being carried out. Their abdication of the responsibilities entrusted to them coupled with their non-communication weighted heavily on my mind and disrupted all areas of my day-to-day life. As a result of all this, I did not consider it wise to be away from the office one day per week to carry out my duties as a Justice of the Peace in the Inner London Juvenile Courts. I therefore asked to be relieved of the scheduled sittings for the remainder of the quarter. I did not realise that that would have been my final sitting as a magistrate.

There was some hesitation on the Chairman's part to sign the letter that was addressed to the Director for Social Services. He had strong feelings that it could be a waste of time, he had no faith in the absence of a conventional way in which certain situations were dealt with. There were also strong feelings among committee members that they were disregarded by the Social Services because in all the months of the conflict they, as a Management Committee, had not been approached or given an opportunity to have a voice in the deliberations over the crisis that had developed. It was felt that the offensive power of destruction was centralised in the CCCVS's office and that he could wage any crusade he wanted. His reports were accepted in full and acted upon. We wandered what was the role of the Director of Social Services in all this?

Feeling flattened by the CCCVS's might and fuelled by the information delivered to us by the "Sisters of Mercy", the Chairman signed the letter to the Director of Social Services and I set out together with a member of the Management Committee on the afternoon of 10th September to hand in the communication. On our arrival at his office, his Secretary looked at us with much disgust. The Director seemed to reveal a pale blank countenance and eyes filled with frustration which conveyed the question, *"Do I know you?"*.

This was the Director with whom I served on the Inner City Partnership for over one year looking at the needs for under-fives provision in the Borough. This was the Director who had supported our bid for grant-aid in the duration of the partnership's eight years funding cycle.

This was the Director who had visited the centre on several occasions including the official opening of the Gresham Road Centre, which was performed by HRH The Princess of Wales in October 1983. Two years later, accompanied by the chairperson of Social Services Committee, this Director escorted Zindzi Mandela, the daughter of Nelson Mandela, on her visit to the Centre.

We were very much aware of the positive interest he had shown to the work we were engaged in and appreciated his contribution greatly. Now amazingly, he saw me as a major inconvenience, neither his Secretary nor he would take the letter from my hand. Instead, his Secretary directed me to the CCCVS's room to face his hostility – with the words and gesture, *"Take it over there".*

In that instant, I felt my black skin was regarded as one of nature's more unsightly mistakes.

Humiliated and feeling bewildered, I obeyed his Secretary's command and made my way to the CCCVS's room where, having read the letter that was addressed to the Director, he shouted at me in the presence of his assistant, *"I will not agree to you having anymore quarterly grant and you will not close the nursery. Make sure you are there on Monday".*

The air in the confined space that represented his office had become stifling. I moved out backwards to stand by the door where the Committee member waited. In a very strong irate tone, he dismissed us with the words: *"You will keep the nursery open".*

I walked away from that building. Or did I float? My feet were certainly not firmly on the ground. I could have been blown over by the slightest gust of wind.

The Director simply assumed that to be accused is to be deemed guilty and was ready to deny me the right to approach him in his capacity as the Director, to sort out a problem in which an officer in his Directorate had been embroiled. On my way back to the office the whole experience took over my thinking, right before my very eyes, the two people whom I regarded as normal, unexpectedly changed. They shifted and came together into one unit, two bodies with one brain, their faces hardened and their decision to leave it to the blacks were clear to understand.

How could I explain the extent of a power driven black man's urge to scale the professional ladder of success, using any means necessary, to a grown man who was born white? How could his white Secretary understand a black woman's plight when she decided to block my attempt to explain my innocence to the Director? Even if I had an eternity and the courage of my ancestors, I could not make the Director of Social Services and his Secretary, sensitive to the pain I experienced when I tried to deliver that letter to him.

We arrived back at my office just as the Committee members began to assemble for yet another decision-making meeting. I was very distressed, confused and frightened. I reported to them what had happened when I tried to deliver the letter to the Director of Social Services. I expressed to them the way I was made to feel by their actions and that were it not for the pride that I had developed in my colour and culture, I would have been left believing that my colour was a cruel joke rather than of a healthy design. *"I don't know why I thought that as a black woman I would have been treated fairly"*. I wailed, as the tears of humiliation flowed down my cheeks.

The Chairman, Headley Johnson's eyes were clouded with concerns. The other members could not conceal their anger and disappointment at the way that the Social Services officers were handling the situation. We agreed to continue to monitor the developments and meet again at short notice, if it became necessary. The following day, 11th September, was unusually quiet. Very few children attended. An eerie atmosphere lingered in the premises, muted sounds were occasionally heard, even the telephone was silent and no visitors called.

On that particular day, with the "mole", my part-time Secretary out of the office, we engaged a temporary typist to prepare undated notices to the parents and staff regarding a possible suspension of the nursery's operation until some semblance of normality could be achieved. The tension that I felt on that day became more overwhelming as the day progressed. Icy stares, sneers from people who usually spoke with me, avoidance and the pointing of fingers made me realise that I was being treated with contempt. Some parents and staff, together with certain known activists, had congregated in the reception area of the premises shouting that they were informed by the CCCVS and the Secretary of NALGO Union that we intended to close the nursery because the parents had asked for an investigation and had recorded a vote of no confidence in me. Some parents wanted me to give them an assurance that the nursery would remain in operation.

The situation that evening became even more contentious when some people announced that they were staging a sit-in later. The ex mini bus driver came in with a bunch of keys dangling in his hands and announced that he could gain entry to the building whenever he liked. These were the spare keys, taken from the key cabinet in my office. I immediately called a locksmith and changed the lock on the entrance door. I was slowly beginning to realise that my position had become untenable, just as I had on that awful summer's day in early August 1987.

As I walked along Gresham Road I passed two members of my staff who were walking in the opposite direction, one of the two pointed at me. Smiling cheerfully, I waved to them and said "*Yes it is a lovely day, isn't it?*"

The other laughed and sneered at me, both gesticulated gleefully towards Brixton Hill. It was only when one shouted, "*Prison for you*", that I realised that I was being jeered at. It was only a few weeks previous to this encounter that a Senior Officer for Social Services met me along the same stretch of the road and remarked that people were talking about my family home, how large and beautiful it was and that many were wondering how I had managed to acquire it, implying that it must have been by dishonest means.

My reaction to this information that she volunteered was one of hurt and dismay. I had occupied this home for just over one year, had not invited anyone within the community there, except for herself and her husband on the occasion of the touring Jamaican Folk Singers' visit to London in 1986, when we hosted a barbeque party in their honour a few days before their return to Jamaica. The couple arrived at the barbeque with a Council Officer whom I hardly knew and most certainly had not invited! A lukewarm atmosphere at work and within the community began to become noticeable to me. At the same time, I could not explain the reasons for my fears and uneasiness that lurked in my sub-consciousness. The strange carrying on of people around me was often dispelled and I wondered if I was becoming neurotic.

My reflection on all the occurrences during the five months of crisis jolted me into action. Friday 11th September became so unbearable that I summoned the Management Committee to an extraordinary meeting scheduled for 6pm that very evening. The tension in the meantime rose to boiling point, when tempers between staff and parents flared and confusion and anger wrestled for understanding.

The Committee members arrived promptly. They spoke with parents and staff who were hovering around.

At the commencement of the meeting, I was so bewildered. My head pounded, my body shook, I leaned over my desk and wept; I did not know for whom, was it for the children? The parents? The black community? Or myself? I was not sure, but through a turn in fate, there I was, sitting at the conference room table feeling as though I had been blown by a crosswind into a distant place where only God could possible effect my release.

CHAPTER 12

POINTS OF NO RETURN

Stepping Down as Director

I expressed my unwillingness to continue as Director for the day nursery facility. I cited the CCCVS's insulting behaviour towards me, the allegations made against me by some parents and staff, the NALGO Union Secretary's unfair involvement, the Leader of the Council covert involvement and the Social Services Directorate's conspiracy and collusion, all of which had caused this sorry state of affairs to develop. I reminded the Committee members of the tenacity and staying power that I had always displayed since those early years of setting up the nursery provision, long before grant-aid was ever given for such an initiative.

I am not one for giving in easily but at this stage, it would have been foolish of me not to be frightened – having assessed the situation and noted what gave me peace of mind and what humiliated and stressed me - my disenchantment with continuing the struggle was truly completed. There were suggestions as to how we could continue and pledges of support to me for the continuation of the work we had started and developed. Someone mentioned the "cause" and I was forced to point out that the struggle to keep the nursery functioning was due to my devotion to humanity, this could easily be equated by some people to a devotion to a cause, but causes as we should know could lead to blood thirsty actions. The whole ordeal over the six months period had left me feeling totally drained, I truly wanted "out".

The Committee went through the sequence of events dated from 12th May when the CCCVS's letter implied that the nursery was mismanaged. The whole matter was looked at in a professional and analytical way. The debate brought with it a clarity unlike any I had ever experienced. Committee Members were stunned to be faced with the dilemma of closing the nursery; a thought that was the hardest thing to contemplate but being pushed into an irresolvable situation, the temporary closure of the nursery became an unavoidable option, at least until normality could be achieved. We could no longer provide a safe and secure environment for the children in our care. This we felt was a very serious deficiency of our services. Neither could we treat the whole episode with the casual neglect that the Social Services Officer expected.

Storming the Building

In the midst of our deliberation, at about 6.30pm, we were interrupted by a loud bang on the door of No.3 accompanied by voices shouting and chanting in a distance. It transpired that CCCVS had informed the NALGO Secretary and the Parents and Staff Action Committee that we were proposing to close the nursery. It now dawned on us that these series of events were all interrelated. They were current in one stream aimed with a clear sense of urgency to silence me, before their lies, deceit and greed were found out.

They attempted to enter the building but the lock was changed so they demonstrated from the pavement. A few of us rose and went to the window overlooking Gresham Road, with the Brixton Police Station in the background. We gazed out in silence as the voices permeated the building. I focused my eyes from the second floor window towards the sounds below in the street. There were some parents particularly those who were Lambeth Council employees, staff members as well as community activists. They shouted chants like, "*establishment bitch*", "*Uncle Tom* (sic)". They mocked and jeered as they waved pieces of paper in the air.

The scene was reminiscent of the late 1960's and early 1970's, the revolution all over again except that the pendulum had turned on one of their own race. The crowd was restive, surging expectantly towards the building. I could feel the collective energy bounding from person to person searching for some place to manifest itself as the ex-minibus driver pranced around with the organisation's keys to the building, threatening to enter. The crowd clapped and chanted in agreement. The energy on display was one of anger with a lust for revenge. It was a very powerful and frightening display.

"*Prison for you*", "*Prison for you*", a woman shouted, her words bounced forward onto the group as if in a church, they echoed her words in a call and response style – "*Prison for you, Prison for you*".

I trained my eyes through the fading daylight in the direction of the leading voice and could identify the person as a young member of staff whom we had recently employed. One participant tossed some papers upwards above her head. They glided slowly through the air, landing all around them on the pavement and in the street. The group roared approvingly, like modern day gladiators cheering as their enemy is being fed to the wolves. I stood there at the window numb. The sight and the performance was an embodiment of the punishment that would have been meted out to everyone who had ever offended African-Caribbean people throughout the world. I shook my head. I could recognise how as a people we are still heavily steeped in rhetoric and symbolism.

I was so transfixed by the energy that was being wasted, instead of being utilised to the good of their children's needs. This unwelcome and shameful display of antagonism forced the Committee to release the prepared letters to the parents and staff, stating that regrettably the organisation had no other option but to close the nursery temporarily and with it their position as employees of the organisation.

Of course, we were aware of the absence of the statutory notices that should have been given to all employees and parents, but equally we also had a responsibility to secure the safety of everyone who entered the premises. The noises and verbal abuses continued for quite a long time but we did not summon the Police. With our meeting concluded it was time for us to leave the premises.

The Chairman summoned the help of the Police, who soon dispersed the crowd, but they had to maintain a presence because those who had left the scene were determined to continue the disruption by way of constantly bombarding us with abusive telephone calls. The Police were obliged to monitor the calls and warn off the perpetrators until the calls subsided.

I packed all my personal possessions – books, cultural artefacts, musical instruments, the children's medical records and staff personal records – that were the property of the organisation. The building was made safe. The Police rechecked all three floors, room by room. We then activated the burglar alarm and finally we were escorted out of the building. They watched our vehicles leave and promised to patrol the area and keep a close watch, the same precautionary measure was taken at the Kellet Road premises.

I arrived home at about 11pm on that night of 11th September, a depressive feeling intensified, seeping into my bones, piercing deeply into my heart. But although I was faced with the pain and reality of the situation, there was a reluctance to move away from the journey. I was unable to entirely detach myself from an area of work that I believed in; and a solution that gave our under-fives a head start in the British school system. An inner panic, resulting from my deep fears, surged through my exhausted frame and unable to muster the energy to discuss the worsening situation at the nursery with my family, I refreshed myself and retired to bed.

After the Closure

On that night of 11th September, I went to bed, my head in a whirl. This was the worst situation I had ever experienced in my life. I must have slept very well because the next morning I felt as though a weight had been lifted from my shoulders. A sense of calm enveloped me, although I remained dumbstruck. Just as Gran-Gran used to say, "*Things always seem to look better in the morning*".

I loved my job and enjoyed my duties immensely but when part of my brain started to disengage itself emotionally from the people around me, I knew it was time to step aside. I believed that I had a duty to those children whose care and education were a challenge for the organisation, but the unremitting pressures over a six-month period forced me to leave the company of those wonderful children who gave me a purpose in life. That nursery was the only place where I was the happiest, because in the peaceful rich ambience that it created, all my passions were combined. Sadly, all this had undergone tremendous negative changes that had deprived me of fulfilment and with it my dream. All of us have a dream. Deep inside I am still that same little girl with a dream and I hope I will remain that way; bruised but magically untouched.

The weekend went very quickly in a wave of activities. I spent much time explaining the situation to family members and receiving visitors who came to see me as a result of the rumours and allegations that had been circulated about me. I had no detailed information about the origin of the conflict and exactly how the various strands of the allegations related, neither why such a disastrous development had come about. However, I reiterated the sequence of events leading up to the closure of the nursery as best as I could. Every time I went over the events I could sense a relationship between one and the other. I was soon struck by a grim realisation.

For the first time I perceived my own misinterpretation of the behaviour that was sometimes directed towards me, and my short sightedness in not recognising that they were strands of the same hideous weave.

CHAPTER 13

TAKING STOCK, TAKING ACTION, TAKING LIBERTIES

Reflections on Leaving the Nursery

In retrospect, it was a wise decision to step down – the majority of parents who were still in child-bearing age wanted to gamble the provision which catered to their needs – they were not inclined to listen to reason or communicate their fears. They were completely blown along in a mighty rush of the prevailing whirlwind.

There were also a number of telephone calls. Many people offered their commiserations, while others ridiculed and threatened me for causing them the loss of the day nursery provision. On the first working day after the closure, Monday 14th September, I kept an appointment with a well-known community activist/journalist at the 'Caribbean Times' – a black weekly publication based in North London.

I explained what had taken place and emphasised that the allegations were false and the actions of those involved were seemingly contrived. I asked him to use his position to engage in some dialogue with the Leader of the Council, with a view to addressing the issues raised, so that the uninvolved responsible people within the borough and further afield could begin to grasp what was going on. I also needed to have a clearer understanding of what the Council's intentions were. In the absence of a meeting or correspondence from the

Council, no follow up information about the proposed review and/or inquiry into the affairs of WIPAG, we were left in a state of confusion.

I did not for one moment believe that this request would have posed any difficulty for him. On occasions as a community worker, I had made myself available to avert my brothers and sisters predicaments, when approaches were made to me for help. This brother had been the recipient of my unwavering support when he needed my help. Now it seems that those days of helping each other have long past.

I was taken aback when he disclosed to me that the Leader of the Council was a friend of his from whom he derived favours and support for the publication he worked for. He feared that his intervention might affect the relationship. He, however, suggested that I contact a firm of Black Rights Lawyers who could advise me on my legal position. With a feeling of hopelessness, I left his office.

At the Management Committee meeting later that day, I reported the day's event to a fully attended meeting. The developing situation had taken its toll on everyone. This left us struggling to move forward with plans for the future. However, it was agreed that two committee members would be present at the nursery building on the following afternoon of 15th September to meet representatives from a professional firm of assessors who would be compiling a full inventory of the organisation's assets. After a very exhaustive day, I returned home.

There were several telephone messages to be dealt with. In fact, because of the telephone we could have no peace! A caller was on the line; I picked up the receiver and cautiously answered; the voice of the person conveyed how demoralised she felt.

"Girl", she said, "All hell break lose in Brixton today. Your name was rolled in the mud so vigorously that try as you may, some mud will stick. Right now I am far from feeling proud to be a black woman".
Oh, the torment of those waking hours bore heavily on me.

On the morning of 16 September, I learnt, via a telephone call, that there was a news item on the front page of the 'Caribbean Times'. I soon obtained a copy and much to my consternation here was a front page spread captioned, "Moms Storm Town Hall, Fury over Nursery Axe".

It read: *"Staff and parents called for an immediate enquiry and Council Leader, Linda Bellos, yesterday promised swift action to reopen the nursery".*

I was being accused of stealing the nursery's funds to subsidise the mortgage payments on my family home in upmarket Purley. The photographs of the protestors, especially the children, were not entirely those who attended the nursery, neither were the parents recent users. The three who were prominently placed in the picture were those who had disappeared earlier without settling fees due to the nursery. I must say that I was taken by surprise to see them posing there for the camera.

Other publications, The Voice, a leading black weekly, the Comet and the South London Press followed suit with the additional news that £10,000 of the organisation grant-aid for equipment had gone missing and Lambeth Council Officers were unable to locate the various pieces of nursery equipment when the premises was searched. On that day, some parents and staff, together with community activists, organised a protest march to the office of the Council's Leader – and, it is said, they staged a sit-in in her office.

At the meeting convened by the Leader to receive the protestors, the Chairperson of the Social Services Committee, officers from Finance and Management Services and the Chief

Solicitor represented the Council. The CCCVS/Grant Liaison Officer to WIPAG, joined the protestors in putting their case as victims of my dishonesty.

Two of WIPAG's trustees were summoned and attended. Mr Greaves and Mrs Carter were asked to give their permission to the Council to enter the premises at 3-5 Gresham Road, SW9 to enable it, the Council, to continue the service. In Mr Greaves report that he presented to the Management Committee, he recorded that he told the meeting he would not be prepared to give such permission because he did not know enough about the events leading up to the closure and until he had spoken with the Trustees and members of the Management Committee he could not make a decision. The Leader then remarked that whether the Trustees gave permission or not, it was her intention to enter the premises and take possession.

Contrary to the advice given by the professionals present, the Leader, in the confident tone of a woman with enormous influence, instructed her officers to disengage the security system, change the locks and allow the protestors into the premises. In essence, she had handed over the 30 years leased building to the rival group. Thus, the Imani Day Nursery was duly created on the whim of the Leader's wave of the hand; her absolute power on display for all to see.

The parents and staff moved into the premises triumphantly in a merry dance of victory. I sighed as I attempted to clear what I felt like a tight knot in my throat, *"one man's pain is another man's gain"*. What has been a disaster for me had proven to be a miraculous gain for them. Jubilant and full of great expectation they were assured that their actions had paid off handsomely.

They continued to disseminate false information about my family. Anyone whom they believed respected and supported us was harangued and isolated. Several memos were sent around to parents, seeking information about me. Many were to parents whose children had moved on to schools in previous years. They were informed that parents and staff of the nursery had recorded a vote of 'no confidence' against Gloria Cameron, her daughter who was one of the senior nursery nurses and the two white members of staff. Two employees of Lambeth Council were the senders of these missives that requested replies in writing, recording anything they knew about me – *"the more derogatory the better"*, some were told.

The legitimacy of their actions now being reinforced by the Social Services Directorate's secondment of one of their day care officers to supervise the day-to-day work of the new nursery on their behalf. This served to strengthen the confidence of the protesting group. They had magically become employees of the London Borough of Lambeth. The salary scale, London Weighting and Local Authority Conditions of Service, which they craved, were very much in their grasp. So like moths, they circled the bright flame, not realising that that flame was supplied by a very short wick! I could not have envisaged the headlines that appeared in The Voice, Caribbean Times, South London Press and the Comet.

Their reports were totally biased in favour of the Council. None of the information that the Management Committee sent to them was ever acknowledged or printed. The shock of this conspiratorial action set my body into a furious reaction, every normal emotion accelerated, my tears surfaced and clouded my vision as I stood aghast, watching my years of efforts rushing by like streaks of rain on the windscreen of a speeding car. I was absolutely reeling from the pain the news had brought.

The Assessors were denied entry to the premises, leaving us without an inventory of the nursery's assets.

The level of anxiety among the Management Committee members and more so myself, grew to an high pitched fever. There were reports in the Press that Lambeth Officers' search of the premises had failed to locate equipment to the value of £10,000. With the premises being occupied by the protesting group, we could not be confident that items left in the building were safe from pilfering. We were further confused when the organisation's bankers froze the accounts, resulting in the immediate revocation of all salary payment mandates that were due to the staff on the following day, 15th September.

This action, I felt, was a deliberate ploy to mislead the parents and staff into believing that the nursery funds had gone missing. Naturally, the staff became quite anxious, angry and revengeful to the extent that a report regarding their suspicion about me was lodged at the Brixton Police Station. I immediately approached the Treasurer for the organisation. Shaking all over, I asked, *"Why did you not inform me that there was a short fall of £10,000 in the nursery's accounts?"*

She must have noticed that I was in a state of near collapse because she quickly held my right hand, with a tenderness that was in no way short of pity and reassurance. Leading me away from the spot where we stood, she calmly said: *"I have seen the news items and had intended to give you a call".*

She paused and shook her head from side to side in dismay, addressing me she said, *"Mrs C, I am absolutely clear that no money has gone missing from…."*

In mid-sentence, I interrupted, *"But the Press reported that £10,000 is missing".* No, she replied. *"That was a cheque for the transfer of £10,000 from the deposit account to the current account which was made in the summer of 1985. The transfer of this amount was to facilitate the payment of staff salaries, including the five new staff appointed to finalise the integration of Gresham Road facility and the Annex, also the settling of the quarterly utility bills".*

Although I could not at the time remember the transaction, I believed what I was told implicitly. Immediately I felt shrouded in a sense of enormous relief. This young woman who had been Treasurer for the organisation long before our receipt of grant-aid, had served us over a period of nine years voluntarily. Her once per week visits, usually on Monday evenings, were spent examining the entries made in the books by the Secretary, checking the fees received from the parents, authorising payments to the Inland Revenue and PAYE system.

At appropriate times she prepared all the relevant books and accounts for the Firm of Auditors who carried out the examination and certification of the accounts. She also worked very closely with the paid Secretary for the nursery, training her in keeping of records and data – and monitoring all aspects of the organisation's financial affairs. During her time with us, even while she was in the throes of studying for an economics degree, through to her becoming a Chartered Accountant, she had never omitted to deliver the best service that any organisation could expect.

To clarify matters further, one of the Trustees, Mr G Greaves, sought information directly from the Bank. He met the Assistant Manager in order to ascertain the truth about the alleged missing funds. The records showed that a transfer, not a withdrawal, did take place in the summer of 1985.

At this stage, I felt it necessary to find out more about the relationship that I suspected had developed between the Social Services Directorate officers and the Parents and Staff Action Committee of WIPAG Day Nursery. These officers were supposed to be responsible officers representing our sponsoring agency yet they had failed to communicate with the organisation. Instead, these officers treated the whole crisis with casual cruelty and neglect that beggared belief. I then decided to reach out to individuals who held important positions within the community.

Firstly, I contacted the new Chair for the Social Services Committee who was indeed no stranger to our family. During her earlier days as a young teacher, and me a housewife, I had been a mother substitute to her child while she pursued further education in her chosen field. We also shared the enthusiasm to stage socio-dramas in order to highlight aspects of Caribbean culture. We both felt that these could bring about positive awareness to social workers when they intervened in the West Indian mother-child relationships.

At that time in the early seventies when a number of children from the West Indies were re-joining their parents in the UK such relationships were fraught with difficulties. I therefore sought help in finding out what the Social Services was holding against me and her advice as to what I could do to alleviate the worsening situation. I assured her that the allegations that were being circulated against me were false and therefore without tangible evidence. I felt confident that she would have treated me with sensitivity and honesty. However, she frightened the life out of me when cold bloodedly, she said: *"I don't really know what is going on but it seems that they have a lot of evidence against you."* As though confronting a child on the playground, she scolded: *"You really shouldn't have used up the Council's grant".*

I replied, *"But I did not".*

She then concluded, *"Well, you better get yourself a damn good lawyer; you will need one".*

I shook with fear. What evidence is she talking about, I muttered. Because of the coldness of that voice, I recognised the attitude that implied in a non-verbal form, please do not ever bother me again, told me that my audience had come to an end.

I was left feeling as though I was in the presence of a total stranger. The disappointment sent an intense chill all over my body and I could not hold back the warm tears that trickled down my cheeks. After a long while I arrived home, the tears were persistent and when the crying had stopped, loneliness began to fill the void that developed.

This experience did not put me off from meeting with the other person on my list.

About a week later, I made an appointment and met with the Member of Parliament for the constituency, a person whose judgement I had always respected. I related to him the whole sequence of events covering the six months period. He listened with an air of sympathy and showed surprise at some of the actions that had been taken against me by those involved. I told him that I was desperate to know what I was accused of, and as to why none of the Council's officers or elected members wanted to speak with me. He promised to find out what was going on.

He, however, expressed concern about my allocation of two nursery places to a former Councillor and the outgoing Chairperson of the Social Services Committee. He wanted me to clarify my reason for the allocation, considering, he said, *"She was not registered on the nursery's waiting list".*

On hearing what he said and the disdain conveyed in his tone of voice, my heart skipped a beat. In a soft tone of voice tinged with regret, he leant over the table and said, *"You have upset an awful lot of people. She would have moved on long before she did but you took her children into the nursery so that she could attend the daytime committees.*

I was immediately fired up to tell him what my position was at the nursery. I thought, here is my opportunity to tell him that the nursery was not an extension of the Social Services "means tested", "at risk provision" where everything is embodied in political intrigues. The nursery's objective, I told him, strongly emphasised that the provision was aimed at helping parents who were genuinely in need of a caring environment for their under-fives and, unlike Social Services, we had no regulations which prevented us from admitting children whose parents happened to be professionals or non-professionals. We operated a non-sectarian, non-political and non-monochromatic facility for the under-fives in the community.

In my professional judgement, I was under no illusion that I was dealing with a deserving case. Therefore, I offered the parents whom I interviewed, as I did to others, a part-time slot of two to three hours, three times per week for which a pro-ratio fee was charged. My assessment of the children led me to believe that they needed to experience meaningful play in a stimulating environment that we were qualified to provide – and it was my responsibility to "put the children first" above all other considerations.

I sensed from his body language that he still felt I had made the wrong decision. I was overtaken by a feeling of disappointment. I left the company of the Member of Parliament, thanking him for taking time out of his busy schedule to meet with me. It was illuminating to have conversed with him. I came away much wiser. I was wiser in the fact that the demise of the nursery had overwhelming political undertones.

The community response was even more damning! Race Today, a periodical, carried a most emotive article captioned, 'O How the Mighty has Fallen', with the following narrative:-

"Little did she know that she would end up in Court as a common criminal?"

They treated my misfortune with the utmost smug and malicious pleasure. This had the effect of a parent denouncing an unwanted daughter whom she failed to abort - and had hoped and cherished the thought that that child would one day be trampled out of existence. This did a great deal of damage to my self-esteem.

The experiences of this journey had in many ways taught me to take one day at a time and each day had so far brought with it disappointments, surprises, hope and despair, but I felt that I must keep on going. The old maxim my Gran-Gran used to chant is appropriate here: *"The race Is not for the swift, nor the battle for the strong, but for those who can endure"*.

I waited anxiously day by day, nervously hoping that the Council would invite me to a meeting to clarify what appeared to be a one-way information system about the problems facing the WIPAG Day Nursery. I knew that the absence of 'truth' had served to inflame the situation. I also knew that if dialogue was not established a worsening situation would result. Trying to put 'truth' where greed and ignorance abounded could not be hurried, but even if it took a thousand years, 'truth' could not be kept out, it will always come knocking at the door.

The crisis had now taken its toll on me! I was feeling drained, exhausted and physically frail. Being isolated from my day-to-day activities was a constant reminder of the enormity of my predicament. I had ceased to attend the Lambeth Area Health Authority meeting strictly because of the unease I felt sitting with Lambeth Councillors and enduring their sneers and subtle rejection.

The Chairman of the Health Authority on which I had served for nearly three years as an independent member, not representing any political party, requested that I pay him a visit. I acceded to his request. On a rather pleasant day in October, my daughter, Jenny, and I arrived at his office to a very warm welcome. With a stiff little bow from his waist, we shook hands and he guided us towards the chairs. His friendliness was as usual infectious and no hint of condescension showed in his manner.

John had visited the nursery on a few occasions and had always expressed his admiration for our work. I explained the sequence of events that had led to the closure of the nursery. His surprise was noticeable as he arched his eyebrows in a questioning manner. I continued by expressing to him how pressurised and worried I was about the whole situation.

I felt quite comfortable in his presence and was not at all ashamed to let go of my emotions because I knew how sympathetic he could be to all kinds of people regardless of their cultural backgrounds. He promised to send off a letter to the Chief Executive at the Bank's Headquarters stating the facts surrounding the crisis and to implore him to defreeze the organisation's accounts. He warned me about the consequences that extreme worry could have on my health and advised that I try to maintain a measure of calm at all cost.

A few days after our visit, I received a copy of the letter he had sent to the Chief Executive and soon a response was received that brought a ray of hope to my soul. In the meantime, the Management Committee was in communication with the Bank. We were close to finalising arrangements for the staff to be paid. The list of names and amounts due to each person were requested and forwarded to the Manager of the Bank. To our utter surprise, we were informed that the rival group of protestors had requested to withdraw funds from the WIPAG account and had provided the Bank with a list of names.

Unfortunately, the names on both our lists were not identical. It was therefore decided that the account remain frozen.

The tower of silence in the Social Service Department remained cold and impenetrable, enough to break anyone's spirit however strong it might be. I was overwhelmed by loneliness, pain and confusion. I experienced a feeling of being caught in a dark place not knowing how to get out or what to do. I can only describe the feelings on that day as a 'valley experience'. I realised that my faith had sunk to an all-time low when I found myself kneeling by the side of my bed, I opened up a channel of communication to God, I prayed:

"Out of the depths of the valley I cry to you oh Lord. In your mercy, grant me the great blessing of your unfailing love. Guide me so that I may learn how to surrender my will to yours".

My emotion gave way to tears of helplessness. I must have fallen asleep soon afterwards because I could hear a ringing sound in a distance and woke up to find that it was my telephone. The caller asked to speak with Mrs Cameron. He identified himself and in conversation he extended an invitation to myself and the Caribbean Folk Culture Company, which I formed in 1963, to give a performance of folk music. The event would take place on 7th November in honour of the Prime Minister of Jamaica, the Honourable Edward Seaga's visit to the United Kingdom. The reception would be hosted by Mr Courtney Laws OBE, Director of the Brixton Neighbourhood Community Association, at their centre in Railton Road, Brixton.

Under normal circumstances, I would have readily agreed but with the dark cloud of uncertainty overshadowing me, and my weight loss of nearly three stones, I did not care to venture too far from my home unless it was absolutely necessary. In fact, I had been keeping a low profile especially when it came to visiting Brixton. I, however, informed the folk group members and my family about the invitation, stating my reluctance to accept. They suggested that we accede to the request and encouraged me to attend. With the invitation gratefully accepted, I put on a brave face and did what was expected of me.

Respite: A Reception for the Prime Minister of Jamaica

The occasion turned out to be an enhancing and enriching one. The Folk Group's selection of musical items, which were familiar to the Prime Minster, a well know folk culture researcher, was thoroughly appreciated and enjoyed. Towards the end of the other presentations, one of the Jamaica High Commission's Welfare Counsellors announced that the Prime Minister's visit to the United Kingdom was not only planned to strengthen diplomatic relationships and boast trade opportunities. It was also to meet Jamaican nationals and to convey the Government's appreciation to those nationals who were known to be making their contributions to this country in the field of music, sports, politics, social and cultural advancement.

There followed a short but eloquent address in which the Prime Minister expressed great pleasure in being among us here in Brixton, South London. The audience was euphoric in seeing and hearing the Prime Minister's message. Moving to the next phase of the evening's deliberations, Cecil Collier, another of the Jamaica High Commission's Welfare Counsellors with whom I had worked during the 1960s in the days of St John's Interracial Club, rose to speak. He looked in the direction where I was seated and immediately a chill went straight through me. He then said: "*Will Gloria Cameron, please join us here on the platform?*"

Although I had experienced my fair share of surprises, I had to will my feet to take me to the platform. It was as though the muscles had contracted causing me to move gingerly. Mr Collier introduced me as one who had served the Lambeth Community in the true tradition of the early public-spirited African Jamaican women. In his conclusion, he said: "*She has led the way in establishing a measure of social concerns, cultural development and care for young children by reaching out beyond the dividing line of race and class*".

I was then invited to be the recipient of the Prime Minister's Medal of Appreciation for outstanding services in the field of Community Development. The appreciation that was shown and expressed about my work in the community made me inexpressively happy and thankful.

I still recall how proud I felt on that day, barely six weeks after the false allegations were directed against me. I left that gathering with restored dignity and a renewed feeling of worth; in fact, I was walking taller than ever! It may have been my imagination, but it seemed to me that every Jamaican in that hall was walking taller too!

The Labour Party annual autumn conference had just ended. I watched the closing deliberations on television, catching a glimpse of some of the familiar faces of people I knew. Simultaneously my thoughts shifted to the ex-parent of the nursery who had been recently elected as a Member of Parliament, whose image I could not see among the joyous throng of dignitaries and party adherents.

Becoming locked in deep thoughts, I reflected on what our serving Member of Parliament told me only a few weeks earlier, when I discussed my plight with him. Those words have since rang in my ears, even to this day. "*Why did you offer nursery places to that family? You have upset an awful lot of people...*".

Throughout the months of my ordeal, I had heard nothing from this family. I wondered how aware they were that by my reaching out to help in their childcare needs – for which they paid, contrary to the rumours that they did not – had provided their opponents with a whip to beat my bare back? I could feel my disappointment and sense of rejection jostling within me for prominence. However, I soon revised my thinking about people who were willing to pass by on the other side. I always believed that there were still good Samaritans around.

A few days later, I received a telephone call. Surprise, surprise, it was my erstwhile parent! He informed me that a number of people at the conference had asked him to contact me with a view to offering his support to my plight. He wanted me to provide him with detailed information as to what I thought could have precipitated the allegations that were being made against me. I told him that I was not all together clear about any legitimate reason for the sudden allegations of mismanagement and dishonesty which lead the parents and staff to record a vote of 'no confidence' in me.

These were the same staff, who until recently were committed to their work and showed interest and care in what they did. Now their discontentment seemed to have had no bounds. In a tone of voice that appeared to be coming from someone in a desperate haste, he said, *"I will not be able to represent you, as you know, I am no longer in legal practice, I am now a politician."*

He continued, *"Do inform me of any developments. You can reach me at the office".*

He then gave me the telephone number, which straight away I recognised as that for the House of Commons. I replaced the receiver on its cradle and took a long deep breath. That in effect was a cross between a deep breath and a sigh.

Sitting on the step, I allowed my imagination to roam. Of course, I felt quite perplexed. However, I learnt two things from that conversation. Firstly, that he knew far more about what had happened and secondly, I had not been arrested for any indictable offence, so why did he think I needed the services of a solicitor? His approach to my plight left me feeling ill and absolutely rejected. I came to the conclusion that the three people with whom I had spoken were closer to the pulse of what was happening within the Social Services Directorate but they, however, felt the need to remain tight lipped and leave me to stew in the sauce that their colleagues had brewed.

Little did I know that this was a revelation to prepare me for what was to come! Somehow or other, a lightening flash statement revealed a man who I was convinced knew more about the Social Services 'witch hunt strategy', but did not care to soil his hands with what might set him apart from his colleagues.

The Management Committee, in its desire to retain the premises, sought advice as to the organisation's legal position in the matter. The advice was that action could be taken by issuing an injunction against Linda Bellos, the Leader of the Council, for illegally entering and handing over the premises to a preferred group. I was vociferously encouraged to lead the action but the financial commitment needed to take such an action was not readily available. In the meantime, the sustained attack on my character and the false allegations made against me personally, rather than at the organisation, changed the direction of my focus.

I soon lost interest to lead a cause for the same people who, if our action were to succeed, would become the beneficiaries. I therefore took seriously the advice of my family and legal advisor that I leave the struggle for the organisation's retention of the premises to the other officers and pay due attention to the innuendos which were directed at me. At this stage, the Management Committee, through the Chairman, wrote to the Chair of the Social Services Committee asking the Council to justify its action for ignoring the usual covenants and conditions contained in the user clause binding the organisation to use the premises for the objects stated in the constitution. The Committee drew attention to the fact that no breach of the covenant had occurred and that no steps had been taken to activate the procedure prescribed in the relevant statute. The Committee in its conclusion stated that: *"unless we receive some justification by return of post, it is our intention, in accordance with the advice received, to apply to the High Court for relief by way of an injunction".*

Swiftly on the Council's receipt of the above correspondence, the Assistant Director of Children and Young Persons, whose responsibility it was to periodically inspect the day-to-day aspect of the children's care, wrote to the Council's Chief Solicitor: *"You may by now have had some discussion with the CCCVS... concerning a reply to WIPAG's letter of 22nd September. It would be helpful to us, and members of the Directorate's Committee if the following points could be clarified concerning WIPAG's 30 years lease".*

Given the somewhat unusual circumstances surrounding the Council's decision to enter the building, is an application to the High Court for relief by way of an injunction likely to succeed?

Is there any legal way under the current terms of the lease that this could be speedily revoked without a lengthy court battle, should the organisation decide to act against the Council? *"We are due to hold a briefing soon and as a number of issues raised are likely to have legal implications or require legal advice, we would very much like you to attend. I hope you will be able to join us".*

Three days later, the CCCVS sent this reply to the Assistant Director, Children and Young Persons Officer. It read:

I am surprised that you should unilaterally write to the Council's Chief Solicitor on this matter without first consulting me. I can understand your anxiety but as I understand it, I am still the lead officer on issues pertaining to voluntary organisations. I will have to enquire from the Director whether there has been an un-negotiated change. Meanwhile, I will be grateful for an explanation and an assurance from you as to the basis of your conduct.

The following day, the Assistant Director responded with a letter to the Director. It read:

In recent weeks the Finance and Race Relations Officers have expressed concern at the lack of briefing and consultation over the above organisation. I have attempted to respond to this and felt some responsibility to do so, as the senior officer involved with the organisation. As a consequence, I have borne the brunt of the written criticism arising from communication difficulties. To my knowledge no direct correspondence has gone from either the Race Relation Officer or CCCVS's line manager, the Senior Assistant Director, identifying him as lead officer, with responsibility for briefing on the WIPAG matter. He does not now feel that it is appropriate for me to make managerial decisions on this matter without first consulting him. He has now instructed my Secretary to suspend all briefing meetings that I had asked her to arrange.

I do not therefore have any desire for line of responsibility and accountability to be blurred – so I await your instructions.

Replying direct to the CCCVS, the Assistant Director wrote: *"Clearly we have different perceptions of our respective roles and responsibilities. I therefore feel that the proposed action I have identified in my memo to the Director of Social Service will ensure that there is no further clouding of managerial accountability"*.

The Assistant Director's role eventually became restricted to WIPAG's operational practice issues and her involvement together with that of the Finance and Race Relation Officers in relation to WIPAG ceased.

It therefore followed that the CCCVS was, with all intents and purposes, the 'single hatchet man' within the Directorate destined to meet out the Council's punishment to the black community by manipulating the demise of WIPAG. It was not, however, difficult to recognise that he was not the sole protagonist involved in the fast developing fiasco. Throughout all this, the Director of Social Services' response remained muted. In the meantime, I sweated it out waiting anxiously on edge to be given an opportunity to meet with the Director or any other senior person within the Council.

CHAPTER 14

THE PORTENTS

The Police Visit

Day by day, I could sense that some troubles were awaiting me. I could feel the effects of loneliness, tiredness and periodical lapses of confused mind overtaking me. I knew that my world would never be the same again – what I did not know was the nature and the magnitude of that change. I woke up and peered through the window on to the road, the area around was deserted and silent, so why am I feeling so uneasy? I had learnt to trust my intuition but became overwhelmed with the feeling that that day was likely to be filled with surprises.

I got dressed with a precision, as though I was keeping an appointment, made myself a cup of tea and returned to my room. Hearing the patter of raindrops on the window, I walked over and low and behold, to my utter amazement, I was startled by the crunchy sounds of footsteps on the gravelled path. Leading towards the entrance door were two pairs of feet. From the vantage point of the upstairs bedroom window I could get a below the knee glimpse of the trousers cuffs and regulation type style of the shoes. The gait of the wearers suggested that they were Police Officers.

I went downstairs and said to the girls, *"The plot thickens, they have called in the Police"*, then I moved towards the door – the bell by then had been activated.

Two Police Officers, one in full uniform, identified themselves as 'City of London Police Fraud Squad'. As soon as they entered the house, the Detective Constable (DC), whom I later learnt would be conducting the investigation, informed me that they had come to conduct a search of the premises to remove items of equipment, documents, files and financial statements that, according to complaints they had received, had been removed by me from the WIPAG Day Nursery premises.

I assured them that I had not removed anything at all which did not belong to me, except for the financial records that were taken to the Organisation's firm of auditors for safekeeping. I showed them a large box with old documents relating to the history of the organisation that we were in the process of compiling and a camcorder that I had always kept at home for safekeeping. The organisation's mini-bus was parked in the drive. I offered them the key and showed them my books, all with my name and date of purchases inscribed within.

During this time both officers listened carefully, they looked as uneasy as I was. I then beckoned to them, with a wave of my arm – I said *"Be my guest, go wherever you please"*, although I was aware that if the officers had a sworn warrant they were obliged to conduct the search unhindered. I called one of the organisation's trustees to inform him of what was happening. I was desperate to talk with someone. One of the officers decided to take away the box with the documents and the camcorder, showing no interest in the mini-bus.

As I closed the door behind them, the fear of the unknown ripped through me with intensity. Those moments are etched on my memory even today. Except for the thundering of my heart, not a word had passed between the family members in the presence of the Police, not a word was spoken long after they had gone, our eyes expressed the general feeling of fear.

I leaned over the table in the kitchen and noticed that my hands were trembling, my head shook in disbelief, I cried out, *"This could not be happening to me, how could they?*

Mother gazed at me. She showed signs of immense distress and the girls were clearly in a state of shock. I went upstairs to my room, followed by the girls. Mother joined us later; she sat herself down on the bed and beckoned us to kneel. There she led prayers in a powerful strong and vibrant voice. She asked God for his protection from the enemies who had encamped against us. She was explicit in her prayer and she asked the God of love for things.

That night I could not sleep, I did everything to distract myself from the helplessness that engulfed me. Haunted by the possibility that they may return I could not relax. I walked towards the girls' rooms. I tried to read but could not concentrate and I made cups of tea. Swallowed by a feeling of utter defeat, I gave way to an emotional outburst. As the warm tears trickled down my cheeks, I asked myself how I could counter such malicious allegations especially when they emanated from a source that should be regarded as efficient and official. I so wanted to make my contribution to the society in the field of providing Day Care by being accessible to the children during their formative years. I wanted those under-fives with whom I came in contact to become well-balanced individuals going off to their schools full of confidence, ready to take on their primary education with enthusiasm and purpose. But now, all these expectations that I had harboured over the eleven years of working towards the establishment of the nursery had been absolutely derailed.

Two weeks later, just past lunchtime, the doorbell rang. A feeling of unease swept over me. It was the Detectives from the

Fraud Squad returning to seize whatever they could find. On this occasion, they decided to take the computer and all the discs. I told them that the machine was the personal property of my young son whose course assignments were recorded there on, but they took it away.

The Descending Cloud

The destructive intention of my pursuers had now become clear, as were the implications. The awful news had been circulated in a dramatic form by the Ethnic Press – *"Fraud Squad Swoop on Nursery Papers"*. *"Police had removed documents missing from the Brixton Nursery"*.

With this developing situation, I sought the help of a fellow Justice of the Peace who was also a Solicitor. His advice to me was that because of the nature of the allegations I should inform the Lord Chancellor's Office because it might be appropriate at some early stage for me to tender my resignation from the position as Justice of the Peace for the Inner London Commission.

I followed the procedure and arranged to meet with the Chief Clerk. At that meeting, I assured him that the allegations were false. I asked to be relieved from all the immediate sittings that were scheduled. He asked me to inform the Commission the instant I realise that charges would be made against me. He expressed his sympathy to me for being caught in such an unpleasant situation and gave me his best wishes. About three weeks later, much before I had any more contact with the Detectives, I received a letter from the Chief Clerk of Inner London Commission stating that they had been informed by the Police that it is their intention to prosecute me for fraudulent offences.

Needless to say, I was crippled with fear, anxiety and shame. Reluctantly, I tendered my resignation as a Justice of the Peace. Realising how tainted my reputation had become, together with the onset of depression, I set about to resign from the other bodies on which I served in a voluntary capacity.

These were:

The West Lambeth Area Health Authority
The Society of West End Theatres
Lawrence Oliver Awards Panel
HM Rochester Youth Borstal
African Peoples Historical Monument Foundation (Black Cultural Archives)

From day-to-day feelings of indignation, sadness and loss enveloped me. I could not bring myself to read in details the misinformation and lies that were being circulated to the Charity Commission, officers of the Borough Council's Social Services Directorates, other Directorates, Members of Parliament, Councillors and NALGO alleging the nursery was being mismanaged.

The complaint in the form of a document, which I shall call the 53 points allegation, signed by a community activist and composed by some of the parents and staff from misinformation given to them by my part-time Secretary was damming and humiliating. It is a personal denouncement of me, set out in the most vitriolic terms.

I suffered great difficulty to confront the negative things that had been said about me with acute pains compounded by the fact that this was made public. I was in no position to get the community to recognise that the information was untrue. The Black Press, The Voice, which purports to be the voice of the ethnic community did not publish the organisation's side of the story but maintained a biased reporting stance in favour of the Council and the community activists.

Preparing for Battle

Recognising the reality of my situation, I set out with the help of my 'three angels of mercy' to find a firm of Solicitors to represent me in the forthcoming legal battle. Two firms of Solicitors disclosed that taking my case would pose, in their estimation, a 'conflict of interest'. Whilst in the throes of finding a reputable firm that was willing to represent me, I was contacted by Anthony Rampton, one of the few philanthropists around at the time, who had devoted his help both in human and financial terms to the black community efforts. He also was one of WIPAG's Day Nursery formidable patrons. He settled the legal costs incurred by the organisation's officers for the earlier legal advice they received and introduced me to a firm of high repute in the legal field. In addition, he settled the costs of all the work executed prior to the granting of my legal aid application. The Solicitor having been briefed, we awaited a call from the Police to inform us of their next move.

The information came to my Solicitor two weeks prior to Christmas 1987 that I was required to attend Holborn Police Station on the morning of 7th January for questioning. On that morning, the Reverend Hewie Andrew, a Methodist Minister who is well known for his community involvement, particularly in state education and supplementary education schemes for young people, arranged to hold a service aimed at strengthening my faith at the Lambeth Mission Methodist Church.

It was gratifying to see the number of people who joined my family in prayer. My pleasant surprise, however, was to see one community project leader among the congregation, Rene Webb of the Melting Pot Foundation. Surprised because I was well aware of the sanction that might be imposed on anyone that is seen to offer support to my plight. More so, a project leader who receives grant-aid from the Council. That would be treading on very dangerous grounds. My concern was not at all unfounded. Months later, his long standing project folded, his grant-aid was discontinued in much the same way as many others.

On my way to meet the Solicitor soon after the service, a quiet anger rose in my stomach. I was not angry about being interviewed; I was more pained and bewildered about something else. I was not quite sure of what! Perhaps it was about the general unfairness of the false allegations against me and the unwillingness of the Social Services Directorate to carry out its own assessment.

CHAPTER 15

INTERROGATION

I met with my Solicitor at the appointed time and we walked to Holborn Police Station, a stone's throw away. I was invited to take the stairs to the upper floor. I asked to use the ladies room when we got to the top of the stairs, and as soon as I was shown to the room, and before entering, there was a sudden movement which could not have escaped my notice. The officer from the rear moved over to my left. I glanced back to see them standing like sentinels on guard on either side of the door. My fear was complete but the presence of my Solicitor kept me calm. I was then ushered into a small room; I felt the outside world vanish with an immediate hush. A deafening silence persisted while one of the officers played boyishly with the tape recording system and the other flicked nervously with the papers on the table. He then sat motionless, my solicitor sat next to me. My heart pounded wildly.

After recording my name and address, the main Investigating Detective asked, *"So you are a Justice of the Peace, aren't you?".*

"That was in the past" I replied.

"and OBE?"

"No, MBE", I replied.

"I will have to see about that", he stated firmly.

I stared him straight in the eyes and looked at him with surprise. He continued, *"As a diabetic you are prone to forgetfulness. I understand that you do not manage your condition very well so I hope you will be able to deal with the line of questioning we are about to follow. If you are not sure of the answers, we will give you time to think".*

I immediately informed him that I was diagnosed with a mild form of diabetes that required dietary adjustment; I was not insulin dependent and did not suffer from marked memory lapses. He then tried to assure me that he was only trying to help me. I thanked him graciously.

His line of questioning regarding the £10,000 that the CCCVS reported missing from the nursery funds was approached by using an intimidatory strategy. While he posed the questions, his colleague kept tapping the table to the rhythm of his voice. This clearly indicated to me that his intention was to disrupt my thoughts.

The main officer questioned, *"On ..., you visited the bank. Agreed?"*

"Yes" I replied.

"You signed a form to remove £10,000 from the deposit account. Agreed?".

I hesitated. He then showed me a form. I noticed my signature but at the time, I did not notice that it was not a withdrawal form but was, in fact, a transfer from the deposit account to the current account.

He continued, *"You then withdrew £10,000 cash and left the bank".*

"I did not", I replied firmly.

The other Detective hurriedly pushed his chair further away from the table, raised both his fisted hands and banged the table with all his might, jolting me into continuing what I had to say in a flash.

I asked, *"Am I such an irresponsible person to withdraw £10,000 cash from the bank, put it in my flimsy handbag and walk down Brixton Road? Why would I want to take such a risk? Why would I want to carry out such an idiotic act?"*

They looked at each other, his red rimmed eyes peered at me with disgust. I was then questioned about various amounts of money spent over a two year period and was expected to recall what those payments were for.

When it came to my salary, which was the same figure every month because we no longer received the statutory annual pay awards, the Detective would not accept that I was able to identify my salary over an eighteen-month period.

The main Investigating Detective seemed to have prided himself in speaking with a patronising haughtiness. The monthly contribution that I received from my grown up children who were part of the household was questioned. He would frown and asked. *"Why were they paying cash? Why not pay you by cheque?"*

He accused me of practising nepotism, because my daughter, a qualified nursery officer, worked for WIPAG. His scornful sneers were so hurtful, his naivety of the Brixton scene at the time was so obvious, it made me cringe.

Towards the end of that day's interrogation, I felt a knot of anger gathering in my heart but knew very well that his insensitive approach to this use of remarks and innuendo were probably aimed at provoking an unpleasant atmosphere. His many attempt to humiliate and scare me into thinking that they had an abundance of evidence to prove that I had been fraudulent during the course of my work, washed over me like water over a duck's back. My strategy was to act with a good deal of civility towards them. I have been around long enough to know the realities of big versus small, so although my heart was filled with fear and utter resentment I kept in mind the great biblical drama of David and Goliath: Will history repeat itself? I wonder!

The day's interrogation came to an end and I was remanded on bail in my own recognisance to return two weeks later. During this waiting time, my Solicitor called to say that the Fraud Squad wanted to launch an investigation into my daughter's fraudulent involvement in WIPAG's affairs. The following day, one of my daughters received a letter from Lambeth Council Social Services Area 5 Office, where she worked as a Senior Clerical Officer in the Adaptation and Aids team for over nine years. This letter informed her that a decision had been made to suspend her from duties until an allegation of fraud against her has been investigated. At this point in time, my daughter was nearing completion of maternity leave. She was further warned that she should not at any time enter the premises unless with the permission of someone in authority.

This unexpected development sent shock waves within the family - my daughter had never worked for WIPAG and had no involvement whatsoever in the administration of the nursery. As a fully paid up member of the NALGO, she sought help from the Union Branch Secretary but he was eternally indisposed and over the ensuing 18 months he was unable to offer any form of support. For the first time since my ordeal had started, I saw my daughter totally demoralised.

Following sharply was the indication that my youngest daughter who was a Senior Nursery Officer at the nursery was also wanted for questioning.

The second date for attending the Bow Street Police Station for further questioning dawned and I met with my solicitor and we made our way to the Police Station. The Police had on display before my eyes a number of cheques and transfer requests dating from the previous 3 years that they had retrieved from the bank. They asked me to identify each, giving an explanation of how the amounts were spent. This proved difficult for me, except for the recurring figures that represented wages – salaries and utility bills. This exercise took up most of the morning and early afternoon. No mention of the missing £10,000 was made, so my Solicitor enquired. The DC leading the investigation quickly said, *"This line of questioning will not be pursued".*

He yawned, stretched his arms upward then mentioned that they would be seeking guidance from an accountant as to how much money is missing from the organisation's funds. At one point during this tense day, it was said they needed to have a second opinion as to whether there is a prima-face case. The lunch break was imminent so my Solicitor and I were told to return in an hour's time for the completion of the interview.

That one-hour break seemed like an eternity. Needless to say, I could hardly swallow the smallest parcel of food. I felt sick to the core of my being. On our return, while activating the revolving entrance door of the station, the DC was positioned just inside, had I made a couple more steps I would have been standing on his toes. He faced us and commenced to caution me, *"Gloria Cameron, I am arresting you ... Anything you say will be used as evidence against you".*

My jaw dropped involuntarily, everywhere went dark and everything around me was spinning. I held on to a nearby desk tightly for support. My solicitor moved towards me, held my hand and helped me to a chair. We were told that it would be sometime before they could decide what the charges would be because they had to confer with someone else.

Both detectives returned about two hours later with the charge sheet. Three charges of theft were registered against me in relation to 18 months' salary (£18,000), a grant of £25,500 for equipment and Petty Cash of £8,000.

I was then fingerprinted by a burly heavy-handed female Police Officer who held and squeezed my thumb so hard, leaving it hanging limp as though it was no longer a part of my body. I saw red, something snapped inside me. At that juncture I lost control of my composure, I was angry and annoyed at being subjected to such humiliation. The process left me feeling foul, dirty and near suicidal. The same Police Officer then reached for a camera, my grief and anxiety grew to an enormous level. My Solicitor intervened and objected to any photograph being taken. There was a short conversation and he was presented with a form that he duly signed.

I was ever so frightened. I felt that my whole world had collapsed. With all the necessary documents signed, we walked through the rotating door. I was completely exhausted.

The long interrogation and preferment of criminal charges had taken its toll. Emotionally and mentally wounded, I knelt on the pavement and cried out to the Lord for help. I so wanted to be in touch with mother earth. I called on my ancestors, I prayed to the superior being and because I am only human, I was explicit in that prayer. I asked the God of Love for things. My children and constant supporter, Sister Amelda, who had come to collect me, gaped in wonderment on witnessing my emotional state. She hugged me and covered my mouth with the palm of her hand to silence the hysterical sound that was bouncing through the chill air of the very quiet area.

I was helped on my feet and literally carried to my son's waiting car. On that day, I strongly suspected that the Police had not submitted the evidence and or complaint they had received to the Crown Prosecution Services. Their role in the Criminal Justice System was to scrutinise the papers before any charges were preferred. That day in particular left me feeling the full injustice of how the law was being misrepresented by these egotistic detectives.

The crisp April air whipped through the open window of the car as we drove along the Strand towards Trafalgar Square.

I could not clear my thoughts of the gruelling I had experienced during the day. The music, 'Greatest Love of All', emanating from the car radio, caused my skin to tingle. The words, 'Let the Children's laughter remind us what it used to be', directed my mind to the children at the nursery, the sounds which I so enjoyed, that then seemed forever lost to my ear. A deep sense of loss overwhelmed me! I wanted to get home as quickly as possible to see my mother, the rest of the family and the few supporters who, I understand, were waiting to see me.

The news that I had been charged was circulated at a meeting held at the Town Hall on that same night. A group of people attended to seek information about the Council's involvement and handling of the WIPAG crisis. The close liaison between the Detectives and the Council's CCCVS facilitated swift communication of the news that I was charged. He in turn made an announcement that I was charged on three counts of dishonesty, which prohibited him from answering questions on the matter that was deemed sub-judice.

I felt that there was something unexpected and strange about the Police decision to charge me, something wrong about it. The decision left me chilled and afraid. Some people who heard the announcement were at my home to commiserate with me and to express their dismay and disappointment. I sat, motionless, for a while trying to collect myself and to get in tune with the reality of it all. Half paralysed with fear and humiliation, I could not muster the strength to communicate with the visitors. My children embraced me trying very hard to hide their tear stained faces. My mother massaged my shoulders and arms as she had normally done; her touch was like balm to my tired limbs and a comfort to my troubled mind. She produced a Bible and asked one of the visitors to read from the Psalm of David No.18, followed by a strong prayer which marked the beginning of a 'Prayer Circle' that grew within various groups, spreading further afield and continuing throughout the eighteen months of the Police investigation.

That night I closed my eyes and said a silent sobbing prayer, my prayer was not to God but to my dear Papa. It seemed the more urgent thing for me to do at the time. I could sense his presence around me quite strongly. He loomed high in my consciousness. A strange phenomena.

My Daughters' Interrogation and Charges

Now an even worst nightmare was beginning. The Police indicated a date on which they wanted to interrogate my daughters. The night before that date was a terrible one for me. I woke up that morning of the appointment feeling totally wretched and besieged. Together with the Solicitor, I accompanied the girls to Holborn Police Station. A colleague met me there and we waited in a restaurant nearby positioning ourselves where we could see anyone entering or leaving the main entrance to the Station. We waited for a considerable time, perhaps for about three hours, during this time drinking cups of tea and trying to subdue the fear and agony that overtook my body. My anxiety was reaching a high pitch, when I saw them together with the Solicitor emerging from the rotating door. Their grim faces conveyed the results of what must have been a harrowing experience.

The Solicitor explained to me what had taken place. Neither of the girls was able to verify anything that was put to them by the Detectives because they, in fact, had no dealings with the financial administration of the nursery funds. The Detective showed my older daughter a WIPAG cheque that he retrieved from her bank. She could not at the time of the interview remember why or when she was given the cheque. At that time, the Detectives had in their possession all the numbered receipts which they collected from the Firm of Auditors, together with the financial records, including Petty Cash Book. They could have identified all the items of purchases against the numbered receipts but they chose to ignore the facts. Notwithstanding the transparency of the transactions, she was arrested and charged with theft.

My younger daughter who was an employee of WIPAG was charged with colluding with me to steal the £25,500 grant given for the purchase of equipment. It was later communicated to the detectives that the cheque given to my daughter was a reimbursement for a purchase she made for the nursery. The receipt was clearly marked but he shrugged his shoulder with the phrase, *"Purchase aye"*.

A feeling of terror literally overtook me. I clutched the arm of the chair so tightly that I could see my knuckles changed in colour. Fear and misery reduced me to helpless tears. One of the girls in a quivering tone said, *"You have got to be brave Mom, that's how we will get through this"*.

You never want to look helpless in front of your children and you never think you are going to show them such weakness but I did and it was terribly difficult.

It was inevitable that a complicated court case was looming. However, the Support Group set up by a very loyal colleague and a few parents and staff became overrun with many who could not respect the confidentiality that my situation demanded. On the other hand, there were those who were terrified in case they were asked to take responsibility for repaying the tens of thousands of pounds which the CCCVS claimed had gone missing from WIPAG's funds.

Because I no longer had the energy to defend myself against the gossip, lies and slander, I asked for the disbandment of the Support Group and sought solace in the confines of my home. I communicated only with a few people who had earned my trust. I literally shut down and entered a strange world of detachment. The lessons I had taught my children about trust, love, care, community life and respect for people had now become empty rhetoric. I had no comfort to give them. There was nothing I could do.

News that the organisation's Treasurer was arrested and charged for dishonest handling of funds sent me realing in pain and dismay. It was indeed the last straw in the entire saga.

Desperation Whilst Awaiting Trial

The burden of the imminent court appearances for the trumped up charges had taken its toll and left me with a feeling of total disillusionment. Only the organisation's documents could verify what I had to say as the truth but these were maliciously removed from the filing cabinet in my office. This possibly took place in my absence on the first day of the temporary closure of the nursery when the Leader of the Council, ordered council workers to deactivate the alarm system to the premises. This thoughtless action allowed the disgruntled parents and staff to take over the premises and contents for their own use. The Social Services Department provided supervision in the person of a day care officer from his department.

Eighteen months of Police investigation and community bad mouthing left me feeling mentally and physically paralysed. A dreamlike state would overtake me at nights and during the morning, my emotions often spiralled to unbearable levels. I searched for answers to the many questions that plagued my mind: why were my daughters implicated? They had no financial responsibility for the organisation's funds. One of them did not even work for the organisation.

On a particular grey December morning, a week before I was due to appear at Bow Street Magistrates Court, I found myself on the platform of the East Brixton Railway Station. I stood there looking down at the rail line, oblivious of the throng of people milling around in the rush hour melee. Now I felt that I was within weeks of possible incarceration, because of the conspiracy of others to cover up their own foul deeds, I had no employment prospect and no financial support. Caught in the clutches of despair, I reasoned that it would be ultimately better for me to end my life in Brixton, to make it possible for that uncaring community to behold my broken form.

I cannot recall how long I stood there contemplating to jump at the sight of an oncoming train, I really don't know. However, I remember having a desperate need - a need to talk with someone, not anyone, someone whom I could communicate with, someone of substance. My shattered trust at that time generalised itself to exclude most people. I turned out of the station and willed my feet to take me somewhere. Before long, I was at the front door of a lady to whom I was introduced a few months earlier. She was the leader of a prayer group and I felt that entering her abode could help me to dispel the hopeless, shaky faith that I had developed in God's promised power. Her greeting was warm and spontaneous, gradually calming my fears and immersing me in a tranquil, spiritual, serene mood. Her leading message to me was conveyed through these never forgotten lines:-

"Come before God with a clean heart and conscience
Ask for his help in prayer and trust him absolutely
He will make your innocence shine like the dawn
The justice of your cause: like the noonday sun"

Even at that time of my collapsed faith, I sent my urgent heartfelt prayer to God, the ruler of the universe. Full of the assurance that no one person in this world had been designated heirs to false accusations, I shook myself out of the self-pity mode – directing my thoughts to the Lord.

By the early afternoon, I returned home feeling less burdened and able to converse with the rest of the family who now were unemployed. It seemed that the conspiracy was contrived to isolate us from the community - socially, financially and materially.

However, there were some days when my spirit soared high above the distraction of the negative interlude. At such times, I could acknowledge the glorious sunny days, stroll in the garden, notice the gorgeous colours of the flowers and a chance to sniff their wonderful fragrances. On days when the allure of the clear blue sky above stood out like an endless canopy, I would muse at the colourful birds flittering around and emitting their familiar sounds as they enjoyed the expanse of space and freedom. Trips to Brighton – about 40 miles away from home - were frequent. Mother, the girls and myself would get out of the house to bask in the sunshine, breathe in the fresh sea air and savour the sight and sound of the foaming waves lapping on to the seashore. All those daily experiences served to excite the dormant artistic flair in me. There is something quite lovely about a clear beach. No wonder some people chose to acquire their homes in close proximity, just to enjoy the piece of the private shoreline that comes with them.

CHAPTER 16

THE LEGAL SAGA BEGINS

The First Court Hearing

On the morning of the first court hearing, I woke up much earlier than I needed. Gazing out of my bedroom window, I thought of the frightening day ahead of us. A fine mist floated like pale water over the garden below, blurring my eyes, as I tried to focus on the trees just as I had done many mornings before. Today, they seem to have turned into illusory shapes that stood against the sombre sky farther afield in the neighbourhood gardens. The early morning light had a purplish colour obscuring the basis of the trees so that only their peaks were visible. All around this wintry landscape lay silent, as though the world had stopped. Nothing seemed to be moving on that cold Tuesday morning in January 1989. Everything was washed in a vast sea of bewilderment. I have experienced numerous ups and downs in my life, but this ordeal I was due to face in hours chilled me through and through.

We waited on the pavement a little way from the entrance to the Bow Street Magistrate Court that serves, although not exclusively, the business area of London. The charges laid against us were of the type usually heard by this court. Unlike our local South Western Magistrates Court that was considered inappropriate for such a high profile drama to be staged, Bow Street has dealt with most of the much publicised, high-ranking criminal cases in the country.

We stood there as the mild showers sprinkled over us waiting for the main door of the court to swing open. Precisely as the doorman released the latch, a van drove up and out came DC Taber, the main Investigating Police Detective. He unloaded a push trolley piled high with enormous ringed binders and stacks of rolled papers neatly tied with coloured ribbons.

My stomach moved involuntarily when I saw his hefty cargo. I thought, *"O Lord I must have done something of which I am oblivious"*. I asked myself, *"Am I insane?"*

The sheer volume of the documents frightened me. I reasoned that, perhaps, he was delivering all the court's documents for that day's court hearing. I, however, realised much later that the documents were extensively duplicated and the figures inflated, to give an appearance of abundance of documentary proof.

Having registered our arrival to the appropriate person, we were seated at the end of the corridor from where we were later ushered to sit in the dock. I leaned forward as I sat uncomfortably in the dock. My two daughters sitting either side of me with a custody officer seated at the end. It felt unreal, an experience I had never had before. I am supposed to be in my right senses, yet everything around me seemed so unreal. I could not get a grip on it. I prayed that God would hold my shattered nerves together and help me to maintain the dignified composure that characterised my whole person. Earlier I had swallowed the prescribed dose of Natracalm to provide me with an air of natural calm.

I felt the presence of Papa strongly. His voice resonated in my sub-conscious state; his message was clear and precise. *"This has nothing to do with you 'Glo'"*. He always called me 'Glo' when he wanted to reassure me. *"It is only a bad dream, a dream that is experienced by some people, some of the time"*.

I snapped out of Papa's reassuring words to hear my name as if it was coming out of space, followed by the thudding dull words of the young, eager but polite representative of the Crown Prosecution Service. Addressing the Magistrate, she emphasised the serious and grave nature of the offences that the defendants had committed. She stated that in view of the exhaustive investigation that had been launched, it would be necessary for the prosecution to ask the court for an adjournment as there was a possibility that further charges may be made and whether a fourth person should also be charged. That fourth person turned out to be the organisation's Treasurer who was arrested and charged with theft. This sent me reeling with agony. I could not understand how such a baseless allegation could succeed.

In response to my Solicitor who asked for a time scale for the case to be properly heard, the Magistrate assured him that the case had been given due priority owning to the fact that the investigating Detectives from the Fraud Squad Division had preferred charges without prior submission of the papers to the Crown Prosecution Service. In continuation, she informed the Court that, at a recent meeting with the Detectives, they were advised as to the nature of the further evidence they were required to obtain.

As the announcement of the adjournment was pronounced, everyone was on their feet. Frozen and glued to my seat, I remained seated. I felt so confused and alone my Solicitor came over to us, whispered a few encouraging words and with a few supporters, we walked towards the front door of the building. Not feeling physically able, I asked them to wait, while I sat in the foyer to compose myself. I must not become openly emotional. I must try and keep the girls strong.

We had planned to walk to Covent Garden underground station but soon had to change our minds. As I walked out of the door, cameras were clicking from across the road and along the right side of the building. I moved back quickly in shock to the court's main door. By then, like a reflex action, one of my colleagues, John Franklin, former Community Relations Officer for Southwark, who was a little over six feet tall, moved over to shade me from view while two others, simultaneously tackled the camera men who were determined to get the picture at all cost. No one uttered a single word during this brief encounter with the photographers. We hailed a taxi to take us to the station. Humiliated, shaken and in despair, we arrived home safely.

I recounted the day's event to mother who was facing the most uncertain time of her eighty-two years of life. I had to transmit positive vibes to her at all times.

During the period between the adjournment and our second appearance at the court, Detective Taber, in his quest to accumulate more evidence to prove his hypothesis, visited a number of WIPAG former staff, among them the former administration officer who was in our employ for over five years. She had moved on three years earlier to a larger organisation that offered her career advancement. However, we had maintained a good working relationship so periodically she had returned to offer In-service Training to my Secretary in maintaining the highly developed system that was entrusted to her.

On the second day of the Bow Street Magistrate Court hearing, we were informed by the representative of the Crown that it was evident from the volume of the papers that this was not a minor case which could be put together overnight, particularly since the documents kept by the organisation were sadly deficient. She continued to emphasise to the court that efforts were being made to have the Crown Prosecution Service's opinion as to whether there was a 'prima facie' case to answer. At this point in the proceedings, eighteen months had elapsed, charges had been preferred, yet the Crown Prosecution Service had not been presented with the documents relating to the case.

Legal arguments on both sides were presented to the Magistrate and a decision made to remand the case to the Crown Court for hearing. Amidst the departure of the Magistrate from the courtroom, my hazy and blurred vision recognised the identity of the learned clerk. She had on a number of occasions served the Juvenile Court sitting on which I had adjudicated during my twelve years of service. I dropped my gaze, ashamed and frightened, though at the same time I instinctively knew that I had done nothing to deserve this exposure.

My role had had a dramatic change; I was in the dock with my daughters on criminal charges. *"This time I know what to expect"*, I murmured and gritting my teeth, I closed my eyes tightly and managed to hold back some of the pain.

The Remand to Southwark Crown Court
The case was set to be heard at the Southwark Crown Court, estimated to last for five weeks. The CCCVS must have been bathing in reflective glory, he would have thought that all his Christmases had come at once.

My daytime hours drifted away during the long wait. I had no employment, few friends and nothing else to do but to stay at home, brood over my fate and look forward to the next appointment with my Solicitor. At the end of each day, a dreamlike quality of the evenings became evident, ushering me to a less than restful sleep.

The nights were especially hard to bear. Sorrow, despair and uncertainty merged like a dark cloud over me preventing me from indulging into any discussions. The silence in our home had a death like aura, our expressive pleas to the Lord giving us a source of strength.

As the date for the hearing approached, the meetings with my Solicitor became more frequent and on my introduction to Mr Thomas, my Counsel (now Lord Thomas), I found him thorough and particularly challenging. He cautioned, *"There are three people whom you should not lie to - your priest, your doctor and your legal advisor. The results could be quite devastating. I want you to think carefully about all those allegations and charges and tell me if you have done any of these things that have been alleged. I will leave you to think about it".*

There I was, left sitting comfortably in a room, deep in my thoughts, examining every aspect of what had been said about me over an eighteen-month period. I could not regard any aspect of the allegations as a true reflection of any action that I had undertaken during my years of working in the community. I duly conveyed this to the QC, honestly and resolutely. I suppose he felt the need to prepare me for the likely consequences of the detractors' allegations. He warned, *"It is possible that although you have had no previous criminal conviction you could be sentenced to prison for at least eighteen months. So be sure of what you are telling me, I really do not want any surprises when I go to court".*

My heart by then was racing at an unimaginable pace. I was quite terrified. All of a sudden I was convinced that something terrible was about to happen and that the entire fabric of my life was about to be completely torn apart. I had never experienced such desolation and abandonment of this magnitude. My girls and I were sailing towards a terrifying unknown territory.

CHAPTER 17

CROWN COURT HEARING

On the morning of the Southwark Crown Court hearing, I woke up in deep thoughts about the possibility that I might be required to give evidence in the case for my defence. I really had not been able to focus on this aspect of the process, as any attempt at facing up to the many falsehoods inherent in the charges against me would leave me consumed with pain and confusion. In fact, to most things, my answer would have been, *"I don't know" or "that is not true".*

I could not stand the 'what ifs' any longer so I quickly got out of bed, dressed in my track suit and walked briskly around the garden. Then I found myself strolling along Peaks Hill. It was early spring of February 1989 and the dawn wind blew cold. I shivered a little as I watched the daylight peeping through the branches of the tall leafless trees. I tried to think of how Papa would have looked at my situation. I believe that he would have taken things in his stride, treating the day just like any other day. While Papa had become a less important mentor, he remained a sort of checkpoint in my life as to how to behave when caught in a tight spot. I could almost hear his reassuring voice. On my way back to the house the sun was rising. I found myself repeating Marcus Mosiah Garvey's chant – One God, One Aim, One Destiny.

The house was alive with music. Family members were getting ready for the big frightening day, most of them had never seen inside of a court of law before and viewed the coming experience with trepidation. Mother kept her eyes on me throughout. She knew that part of my calm composure was an attempt to help the girls stay strong. My groans and sighs gave my true feelings away. That morning my mother wept, the tears trickled down her cheeks and splashed onto her huge bosom. She rubbed her large dark hands along the length of my arms, moaning and groaning as she held all three of us closely.

The mood in her room was electrifying and sad, exposing the helplessness that had overtaken our household. A large tear rolled down my cheek as we bade goodbye to Momie.

We arrived at the court in good time, early enough to witness the arrival of many others. We reported our presence to the appropriate court officer and on our way to the designated area where we were instructed to wait, we came upon the CCCVS. He stared at me with an evil grin. I felt really small and a little bewildered.

I expected that he would have been flanked by his officers from the Social Services Directorate and his community supporters but 'no', he was in the company of a junior clerk from the Directorate. I soon gathered that he was appearing as the main Crown Prosecution Witness together with three members of my former staff. These four names that appeared on the list seemed so unreal. I thought, *"What on earth can these people prosecute me about. What do they know about the administration of the nursery?"*

With a sickening realisation, I saw that my suspicion of a conspiracy was well founded. Now I knew that without a doubt.

Gradually a number of people began to gather along the corridor to the courtroom. The two investigating detectives busily got their avalanche of prosecution documents in place.

The smaller in stature seemed quite pleased with himself. The legal team arrived. The area around the courtroom buzzed with the movements of the solicitors, Barristers and QC, all attired in their traditional Crown Court outfits that gleamed in the morning light.

When WIPAG's Treasurer entered the courtroom, a lonely smile played on her sad and questioning face as she walked in accompanied by her father and Barrister. One cannot imagine the agony I felt at that moment.

We were then ushered in and seated in the custody seats with an officer sitting at the end of the row.

All four of us, the accused, were now sitting in the Dock. The twelve members of the jury, all but one were white, were being seated. I looked around and recognised a few members of WIPAG's Management Committee and, of course, my two 'Sisters of Mercy', Amelda Inyang and Mavis Clarke-Best. My heart thumped vigorously. With blurred vision, I sat in the dock nervously like a little child who has been placed on a chamber pot. My husband did not attend any of the Court hearings. The tears had now welled up in my eyes and soon cascading down my cheeks involuntarily - there was this sensation of wanting to fall asleep.

"Court stand", was the command from the court usher. The female judge, Her Honour Valerie Pearlman, entered and took up her position in the large ornate chair on the raised platform – the learned clerk came into my focus, seated strategically with a mound of documents and ribbon-tied rolled papers laid out before him. I soon recognised the Crown Prosecutor bedecked with his wig and displaying a haughty, aloof air.

The proceedings had truly began.

Throughout the preliminary hearings, we had entered pleas of "Not Guilty" despite the Detectives' offer that if I pleaded "Guilty" they would dismiss the case against the girls. They knew that I love my girls dearly but no plea bargaining tactics that they chose to engineer had any place whatsoever in my determination to assert our innocence. The Crown Prosecutor rose on his feet to open the case for the Prosecution.

I closed my eyes and counted to ten, took a deep breath and tried my utmost to compose myself.

He described me to the court as an overbearing woman who intimidated her staff by shouting at them and reducing them to tears. This I believe was a way of creating a stereotype of the frightening type of black woman that is often portrayed. He presented the case exactly as he was coached by the Detectives – tens of thousands of pounds had been systematically milked from the charitable organisation's fund. This had played no small part in Mrs Cameron's procuring and maintaining a large house in upmarket Purley in Surrey. His presentation was eloquent and forceful and one could sense that he believed every word he uttered.

The CCCVS was the first Crown Prosecution witness.

The Council's CCCVS – Crown Prosecution Witness

He stated in a loud precise tone his name and professional position in the Social Services Directorate. His testimony was centred around his strong belief that grant aid given for the organisation's purchase of equipment was not spent for the purpose intended. He further intimated that he strongly suspected that other finance had been similarly milked from the organisation's funds. Shown the inventory of the equipment which was compiled by a Local Authority Officer and the Police soon after the closure of the nursery, he sought to justify his claim that I did not purchase the exact number of the items as per the pro-forma invoice.

The organisation's accounts, prepared by the Treasurer and checked and certified by an eminent firm of auditors, were submitted to him six months earlier. The accounts were presented to the Court. It displayed an itemised account of all the equipment that was purchased. It also showed that purchases during the period under review had far exceeded the amount of grant-aid given to the organisation.

The CCCVS paid scant regard to the information the document imparted, instead he maintained that by my substituting certain items for others, without his prior consent, I had committed an offence. I listened to his irate exchanges with the defence Barrister. The contrast between his explosive demeanour and the sombre still courtroom could not have been more dramatic. My daughter's grip tightened around my index finger momentarily and then released again. *"Oh Mom"*, she said out of the corner of her lips, eyes steadfastly gazing at the CCCVS in the witness box.

I followed her gaze and observed that he had a permanent angry look. Under cross-examination, he was encouraged to respond to questions put to him by the defence counsel. Not wanting to co-operate, he turned to the Judge and wailed, *"I need legal representation"*.

The Judge gave him the assurance that as a Crown Prosecution Witness he would be legally guided when it became necessary.

The next question to him from the defence met with his reluctance to reply, perhaps a fear of perjuring himself. He turned to the Judge and asked, *"Must I answer that question?"* The Judge nodded in the affirmative.

When his confrontation with the defence revealed his utter ignorance of what is factual compared with what is hearsay, he became even more irate. This brusque behaviour led the Judge to dismiss him from the courtroom in order to address the jury and at the same time give him the opportunity to cool off.

In order to establish the validity of the CCCVS's claim that the organisation was in debt, testimonies were sought from our suppliers of goods. Representatives from two companies presented accounts of our financial dealings with them. Their records showed that they had received payments by cheque soon after the delivery of the equipment. British Telecommunication and the utility companies all showed records that bills were settled prior to the closure of the nursery.

An officer from the Greater London Fire Service was asked to give the court the benefit of his experience in the handling of pro-forma invoices. He explained that a pro-forma invoice is made up of items of equipment for which current prices are sought from companies and submitted to would-be funding bodies as an indication of approximate costs. These could not be perceived as a final itemised document as the items could be subjected to changes as a result of price increases and changes in circumstances. In our case, the grant was received five months after the pro-forma invoices were submitted. The conclusion of his testimony coincided with the lunch period.

I listened helplessly and in despair when the Judge announced that for us the lunch adjournment should be spent in the cell. My Solicitor's shoulders jerked, it seems involuntarily and gradually settled in its former position. He informed the Judge that there was no need to confine us over the lunch period but she decided on a remand in custody because, as she explained, she wanted to avoid us making any trouble. Within minutes of the lunch adjournment, we were ushered to a cell. The click, click sound from the warden's heavy bunch of keys reinforced our most unwelcome arrival, as if to say, '*You have no choice Gloria and company, you had better adjust to the inevitable*'.

We sank back on the wooden bench in the dark filthy cell that was littered with dirty plates and left over food on the floor – lying there it seemed, for a long time. The lock in the door clicked again and a rather large woman, rather dismissively, placed a tray with four plates containing mashed potatoes and sausages on the bench next to us. No words were spoken and this helped to increase our contempt and justified us ignoring the most unattractive mound of what looked like food unfit for human consumption.

This was a very low point for me.

I pondered over the Crown Prosecutor's description of me – I am not an overbearing woman. I flinched when I heard him describing me as such. The girls talked, laughed and teased me about my new personality with which I had been endowed, the hideous black woman fraudster and tormentor of vulnerable people – we laughed at ourselves, we laughed at our own misfortune to be where we were.

They then started to give vent to their pent up frustration by exercising on the concrete floor, heaving and slapping the walls with the palms of their hands and the sole of their feet; a way, I suppose, to expel their pent up emotions. I studied their distraught mood as I sat there faced with the reality of our situation. The constant banging soon brought the click clanging sound of the keys in the lock, *"Are you ok?"* the warden asked.

"Oh we need to go to the toilet please", we all chanted in unison.

She pointed to the door across the corridor. I went first and it was sickening to behold the state of the much vital amenity. I held my breath and quickly relieved myself. The girls also had the same experience.

On the second day of the case, three former members of my staff were called to the witness box. They were all speculative about what they were alleging, each on a different plain. My part-time Secretary, being the person who furnished the CCCVS with false documentary proof of my milking the organisation's funds, was seen by the Police as a natural witness to call. However, when she stepped in the witness box on that day of my trial, her face was shielded by her bowed head, barely revealing her small sunken eyes. Her voice had vanished. It had quite simply vanished.

Confronted by the array of legal representatives and the Judge, she retreated into silence. She croaked and muttered inaudibly. On more than two occasions the Judge asked her to demonstrate how she would act if one of her children was running towards danger.

"Would you call out to the child?", the Judge asked.

"Yes", she replied.

"Demonstrate how you would do that", said the Judge.

The loss of voice persisted. The Judge was evidently concerned about this main prosecution witness.

On the following day, she was again in the witness box. She admitted to defacing the Petty Cash Book by changing figures and scribbling on a number of pages and photocopying documents from the files that she handed to the CCCVS, other staff and a few parents. Asked by the Defence Counsel why this was necessary, she replied, *"The parents wanted to know how the grant was being spent".*

He continued, *"So, why did you not inform Mrs Cameron about the parents concern?"*

In a barely audible tone she replied, *"Oh, she would have sacked me".*

This response induced a wry smile and raised eyebrows from persons in the courtroom. She told the court that I did not at any time make entries in the Petty Cash Book. This was solely her responsibility.

The receptionist's testimony was short. She seemed quite traumatised. When asked if she had ever been reduced to tears as a result of my hostility towards her she said, *"Never".*

She was further asked, *"Have you ever witnessed Mrs Cameron behaving in a manner to cause distress to staff and parents?"*

She replied, *"Never"*.

She testified that she knew nothing about the financial administration of the nursery. Asked if she had anything more to add, she said, *"Mrs Cameron has been a kind lady to me – always ready to help when one is in difficulties"*. She was dismissed from the witness box.

The third witness made clear her resentment of me. In a bold forthright voice, she told the court that I was diabetic, had special food at lunchtime and named the vegetables I ate but said she did not think that I was being consistent with my diet. She expressed her dislike of me because I behaved as though the nursery belonged to me. She could not produce any evidence to substantiate the allegations of fraud brought against us.

I listened attentively to these women who were brought to the court as prosecution witnesses. Noticeably absent was the one complainant who was so convinced that I acted fraudulently that she wrote to the CCCVS stating that if he did not act against me in accordance with their complaint she would report the matter to the Ombudsman or ask for a Judicial Review. Also absent was the parent who was responsible for the assembling and distribution of memos, notices, letters and the fifty-three point allegation of dishonesty that she sent to the Directorates within the Council, Members of Parliament, Councillors and individuals.

Why were these two women not part of the Crown Prosecution witness team?

The Detectives, in their desperation to assemble a team of witnesses for the prosecution, lost sight of the precarious route in which they trod. Their attempt was to throw vulnerable people together, then coerce and give them someone else's baggage with the hope that they could deceive the court of law.

On the third day of the hearing, the CCCVS returned to the witness box. As he took the witness stand, I silently repeated an exhortation of my Yoruba ancestors:

"Leave the battle to God and rest your head upon your hand
The prayer need not be long, if your faith is strong"

From the outset of his cross-examination, he looked quite nervous. His refusal to co-operate in furnishing the defence team with relevant responses to their questions bore heavily against the court's inclination to accept him as a reliable prosecution witness. The untruth of his allegations had begun to bear down on him with excruciating effect. His face rippled with creases and it was amusing to watch the mean expression of irritation on his face. His behaviour continued to deteriorate under cross-examination and being warned by the Judge for a second time, he was asked to leave the courtroom.

His ignorance and bombastic approach to what was a serious matter had completely overshadowed his professional judgement. He left the witness box in a surly indignant mood. The DC was ashen faced as he followed his main witness out, in a brave attempt to pacify him and appeal for calm. Looking in my direction, he tried very hard to muster a smirk.

The Jury was asked to retire. A legal argument began between the learned gentlemen. I soon discovered that listening is an important art. You learn not simply to listen to what people say, it's what people do not say that is important. If you listen hard enough, you can hear the most amazing things going on behind the speaker's voice; it is like a secondary sound track. I saw that there was an ocean of darkness but an infinite ocean of light and love had begun to flow over the darkness.

It was gratifying for me to remember that there were the prayer circles of light in homes and places of worship in the

UK and abroad true to the tradition of my African ancestry. Those lights had spread their beams.

After a short adjournment, the court was reconvened and the CCCVS was summoned to retake his position in the witness box. This time he seemed a lot calmer, like a kettle that was boiling at the highest temperature and after the current is switched off, gradually, the hissing subsides. He stood in the box, brought his hand up to his face and sniffed. Thoroughly humbled, he faced the Judge.

At that moment I saw a ray of sunshine breaking through. Here was a chance to compose myself. I noticed the look of bewilderment registering on the faces of the Investigating Detectives – small worry lines had appeared over the forehead of the stern, steely eyed, no nonsense Judge. The CCCVS's pursuance of a relentless campaign against me was near subsiding. On this occasion he seemed to have come to terms with the reality of the situation that he had contrived, as society's mirror confronted him with unsparing severity.

In the hushed atmosphere of the courtroom, amidst the sober stares of the Judge, Jurors, Prosecution and Defence Teams, his hopes and dreams of deceiving the court receded. He exchanged embarrassed glances with the Investigating Detectives, then in a thoroughly deflated tone he said, *"Mrs Cameron is a highly respected member of the community whose integrity was never doubted by the Council. It was the parents and staff who insisted on an investigation. As a Senior Officer I had a duty to deal with..."*

The Clerk's eye shot up in surprise. The QC for the defence rose to his feet, *"Thank you..., that will be all your Honour"*, he said.

The Chief Prosecution Witness, the Council's CCCVS, stood in the dock, under oath and shifted the blame on to the people who were the victims of his plot. The gasps in the court were audible. The CCCVS was dismissed immediately from the witness box and he crept away to the exit of the courtroom in a docile manner.

My gran-gran would have said, had she been around, *"Because it rained on the day the egg was hatched, the foolish chicken swore he was a fish"*.

The Adjournment

Astonishingly, the Crown Prosecutor closed the case for the prosecution by inviting the Judge to agree an adjournment for two days. In his address, he told the court *"I am no accountant but it is clear that the sum does not add up. I would like to give an accountant the opportunity to check the figures presented to the court"*.

The Judge took a deep breath and acceded to his request.

On hearing this, I was absolutely amazed and then delighted. With the adjournment agreed, we left the courtroom at lunchtime and walked on to the court precinct. As we did so, we were confronted by a group of my former staff who began to jeer and shouted, *"Prison for you, prison for you, thief, thief"*.

Theirs were the faces of the younger staff whom I had employed as assistants in order to prepare them for a career in childcare. They giggled and behaved as though it was carnival time. They made me an object of ridicule and disrespect. My acute anger and shame rose like a bile in my mouth. I was tempted to lash out at the ringleader but I shrugged my shoulder and hurried away purposefully from the scene with sweat streaming down my face.

As the embarrassment consumed me on that cold February afternoon, we continued on our way to London Bridge railway station. On reaching there, we stopped for a drink. I must have drunk about two litres of water to quench the anger I felt bubbling inside me.

The evening before the final day of the hearing found us feeling a little relieved but still nervous. The telephone rang incessantly but this call was one that had an absolute calming effect on all of us. My defence lawyer's voice conveyed some upbeat information which brought on a flood of joy. I passed the receiver to the girls to give them the opportunity to hear for themselves. He informed us that the report from the accountant who checked the figures for the Crown Prosecutor has found that within a few pounds it was possible to account for the organisation's funds. He told us that the legal team would be meeting with the Judge in chambers before the court resumed so we should have a restful night and report to the court an hour later than usual.

I was so happy to know that the court was nearer to the truth that no money was stolen from the organisation's funds. This was the reason I was glowing with confidence that the court would not rubber stamp the CCCVS's lies and intrigues as the investigating Detectives did.

CHAPTER 18

I HAVE SURVIVED

I arrived at the Southwark Crown Court as scheduled feeling as though I was riding on a slowly gathering crest of the ocean's waves. I felt that at the end of the ride, the mystery of the CCVSO's allegations would be solved and my freedom assured.

The strands of hair on my head stood on end as I took an almost leisurely walk down the aisle of the courtroom. An air of expectancy buzzed. The main DC, a small man in structure, tip toed humbly around the courtroom with shoulders hunched as he seemed to have acquired a stoop. The legal practitioners, having concluded their meeting with the Judge in chambers, were in the process of taking their seats.

I sat with my daughters and the Treasurer of the organisation with the Defence Barrister in the custody seats. The Usher signalled the commencement of the court's proceedings by her usual command, "Stand please". The Judge entered, took her seat and we all sat simultaneously.

The Crown Prosecutor, Bruce Houlder, rose to address the court. He said that as a result of investigation carried out during the adjournment, he did not propose to offer any further formal evidence in the case. Mr Houlder continued, "*A fairly extraordinary turn of events had taken place*". This phrase immediately brought many people to the edge of their seats.

At first sight", he continued, "there appeared to be very considerable cash withdrawals from the account of the organisation which seemed to correspond with deposits being made into Mrs Cameron's personal bank account. I have become quite concerned about some of the figures in the Prosecution's report and it was difficult to understand how that conclusion was reached. In addition, the Prosecution only took account of eight salary payments over two years to come to his conclusion that money was missing. A computer had also made a number of errors that we do not understand. The Prosecution had also utterly failed to add up correctly the Petty Cash book; how they could conceivably arrive at the figures they have put in the charges has not yet been explained. The result is that we have formed a view that within a few pounds it was possible to account for all the organisation's funds.

At this stage the Judge announced in a kindly apologetic human voice, *"Will all four of you please move out of those custody seats and sit over there"*, pointing to the seats across the aisle near where the Press representatives were seated.

Her Honour then remarked that the case had caused her, the most enormous concern. It was a quite appalling injustice that any defendant should have to face worrying allegations and eighteen months of anxiety over what appears to be a prosecution witness statement that did not, on inquiry, support the allegations. I hope there will be an investigation as to how this has happened.

My stomach was now in knots. I averted my eyes from the Judge to focus my attention on the Jury comprising the one black male who was grim faced, nervously flicking his papers.

Then came Judge Valarie Pearlman's chilling pronouncement. Her piercing words rang out amidst the pristine silence of the courtroom – loud, clear and sustained.

"You all have been found 'not guilty' and there is not a stain on the character of each of you. Defence cost for each of the defendant to be paid out of central funds"

A rush of relief flooded over me. I was sitting almost next to my rock and agile supporters Amelda and Mavis. Three members of the Management Committee waited outside the courtroom. In a dreamlike trance, I noticed that Amelda was sitting upright, absolutely still. Listening and watching with silent intensity, her right palm placed against her lips, the portrait of a true African-Caribbean sister, she understood her people so well! The tears trickled down her cheeks rapidly. Mavis released her emotions with distressing sobs that one usually expected from a frightened child who had lost her mother and suddenly found her. That emotional outpouring was certainly a sign of joy and relief.

The Defence Council, Mr Martin Thomas QC (now Lord Thomas), in his comments concluded that the family had been through a nightmare.

"What has emerged is that a small and tightly organised group of people were desperate to destroy Mrs Cameron and her family and the work they had built up but they have not heard the last of it yet".

Although the judicial process had been completed, the DC rose to his feet and asked the Judge to consider another charge relating to one of my daughters. He claimed that she used a cheque card belonging to Lloyd's Bank knowing that she would have incurred an unauthorised overdraft. Like Shylock in Shakespeare's Merchant of Venice, he was determined to secure his pound of flesh even if it was to be taken nearest to the heart.

My subdued relief was immediately thrown into turmoil. The Judge looked shocked; there were gasps in the courtroom. I was shaking terribly. I felt like an iceberg tingling from a sudden increase in temperature. The learned clerk was now rummaging through the papers before him, then asked the DC to identify the relevant papers as, *"I have not received any documents relating to the matter you have just mentioned. Where are they".*

He looked directly at the DC.

The Crown Prosecutor looked directly at the DC.

The DC just heaved both shoulders in response.

The Judge then said, *"This, together with all matters, are now dismissed".*

As the usher commanded, *"Court rise",* the Judge left the courtroom followed by the learned clerk. The sobs soon died away and were replaced by the sound of movements and excited conversation.

Whilst conversing with our legal practitioners, the two DCs walked towards me, the former now seems more diminutive. He stopped and bowed his head to me revealing a sullen facial expression. I simply ignored his attention.

A number of reporters were there from the National Press so they expressed the wish to interview me. I made one comment to the effect that I was relieved but not surprised by the verdict and hoped that someone would reinstate the day care provision for the benefit of the children in Brixton.

I began my career with a passion for service to the community. This passion was severely tested with these false allegations but was revived with the utterances of the presiding judge - *"You all leave this courtroom with not a stain on each of your characters".*

Those words of assurance have continued to ring in my ears and give me a comfort that no financial compensation could ever replace. I therefore walked out of that courtroom with a range of emotions. Firstly, as a towering tree – erect, strong and rooted. It was a sensation of looking back with a sense of pride, holding my head up high while some people around me had theirs bowed.

Outside, in the courtyard, everyone was giving their commiseration and best wishes for our gradual return to normality. At that time I also felt as light as a feather. It seems I was floating on air. But, whether as a tree or a feather, I was conscious that there were pieces for me to pick up from this awful experience.

Throughout my ordeal, there was this constant belief that the truth would not be killed off, neither would it be trampled on. My fervent prayer was that the truth would pass from one mind to the other and manifest itself. "That day had dawned".

I held the girls close to me, it was ever so difficult to express my feelings in words, I just held them close and maintained eye contact; our eyes were watery. But as we faced each other, a slow weary smile appeared and glowed across the face of the organisation's Treasurer – a young woman of such immense moral stature. That smile graciously acknowledged the importance and the meaning of 'truth'.

For me, morning had broken, like the first morning, heralding for us, the accused, the beginning of our escape from living in the deepest valley where the mountain stood high above us like an endless towering barrier. Mountain-top-time, in the life of the 'Cameron family' had re-appeared. As a family, we are now able to attest to the fact that over time 'truth' can prevail, certain struggles can go forward and certain faiths can be kept.

Fortunately, there are fair and all pervasive laws that aim to give protection to those who are abused unjustly. In our case the openness and fair-mindedness of the Presiding Judge, the wisdom and integrity of the Crown Prosecutor, our Queen's

Counsel and legal team all successfully averted what could have been a catastrophic ending to the dreams, ideals and uprightness of the Cameron family.

In the days following conclusion of the case, the family met to look through a number of letters and cards sent by well-wishers, to cheer us up and to remind us that we were not alone. The sentiments expressed were greatly appreciated and served to uplift our spirits and gave us cause to smile again. We were, however, overtaken with uncontrollable laughter when a member of the family brought out some of the press reports that were circulated during this ghastly period. Those reports, we remembered, were scanned with nervous tensions and shame. Now we were gleefully displaying our copies, but, at the time, each of us kept our findings and thoughts secret – trying our utmost, then, to avoid causing each other any pain.

After the Case was Resolved

Shocked by the onslaught on my character and dignity, the mental wounding of my daughters and the Treasurer of the organisation, I needed to return to Jamaica to mend my broken spirit. I would often sit at home staring into space, too stunned to even think of anything in particular. My family so wanted me to be strong again. They would often say, *"Pull yourself together mom, it is not the end of the world"*. I would sometimes use this throwaway line, *"Well, it looks and feels like that to me"*.

Then amidst my confusion to find a way forward, out of the blue, my children presented me with an airline ticket for a six months stay in Jamaica, giving me the opportunity to start dismissing the negative inheritance bestowed on me by the CCCVS and those vindictive and uncaring parents and their supporters.

It was a truly happy homecoming, returning to many people with whom, as youngsters, so much was shared – ideology, expectations, lifestyles, etc.

The peculiar gold Jamaica sunset threw its twilight shadows across the window, etching the outlines of the bougainvillea edging which grew up and over the perimeter of the garden's wrought iron fencing. I looked out at the tranquil sky, the heat and then the humming of the air conditioning system reminded me that I was away from London. But this reminder only brought back sad memories of my family who had endured so much anguish through no fault of their own. I thought deeply about the organisation's young Treasurer who had just completed her training and imagined the anxiety, uncertainty and threat that the whole episode must have posed to her professional pursuits.

The idyllic ambience of the green luscious surroundings, not forgetting the blue sparkling Caribbean Sea, reignited a form of attachment so acute that part of me wanted to remain in the land of my birth. But alas, my children were missing me. Concerned for my well-being, Jenny, my youngest daughter, arrived in Jamaica four months into my six months stay, to persuade me to return to London.

I did not realise how enormous my fear of living in London had become; that ever present feeling of being hounded. My reluctance to meet anyone outside of the immediate circle became stronger as time went by.

I had a duty to return, particularly to see my mother, who was close to her 85th birthday. So I whispered a fond farewell to the place and people whose love and understanding helped to lift my spirits out of the doldrums of despair. I returned to London, reliving the wonderful time spent in Jamaica, a time that I will always remember as long as life lasts.

I returned home feeling rested but somewhat in trepidation. Being out of work for such a long period my financial position was acutely grave making our everyday life quite difficult. All three of us were still out of employment. My pension had not yet started, I could not cope with the deflated feelings that the benefit system imposed on me, and there was absolutely no help nor support from my husband.

Fortunately, my son Chris was able to take on my living expenses over an eighteen months period. During this time of re-adjustment to normal life, mother became more and more unsettled desperately wanting to return to Jamaica. She had often pleaded, *"Please don't let me die in this cold country – you go out at night and return at night".*

Much thoughts were given to mother's desperation to return home, so plans were put in motion to find a suitable environment to place her. Fortunately, the Kingston Moravian Church was in the process of establishing a Golden Age Home. Their agreement to accommodate mother warmed my heart because she would be among church members whom she knew and we felt that her physical and spiritual needs would be abundantly met.

Frank and I escorted mother on the journey to Jamaica. Her nine and a half years with her family in London drew to an end. Mother spent a happy, enriched, idyllic life for three years among the church community – friends and family members visited her regularly. We were delighted to learn that the results of her health checks were good. Our telephone conversations were remarkable in that alertness, humour and happiness shone through, leaving me feeling comfortable.

However, in a matter of a few weeks, after one of the medical reports, we received a frantic telephone call from the Matron; mother had had an accident by slipping as she walked across the floor in her room resulting in a severe fracture of the femur.

Jenny and I, together with her six month old baby Ayanna, travelled to Jamaica to see Mother. The medical team had cancelled the surgery on two occasions – they were now saying it is because of her advanced age. On our arrival on the Island, we hurried to the hospital, with the help and assistance of a very dependable longstanding friend, Steve Higgins, who had prepared us to witness the deterioration in her health. We were given permission to play a tape-recorded re-arrangement of "The Lord's my Shepherd" by my son, Chris, at her bedside. She kept repeating my name. Oh, it was so moving!

She passed on the following morning at the age of 94 years. This ended the honeymoon period of mommy's exceptional health. That is why the finality of her passing was such a hard blow.

The day of the funeral coincided with the Nation of Islam's much celebrated Day of Atonement. One of my granddaughters who had converted to this faith sent a tribute to be read at the funeral service. This was ably presented by my friend, Gerlin Bean.

I stood there at the lectern and delivered my prepared eulogy. I had cause for mourning, not only because she was my mother and was no longer with us, not because she was there cradled in a casket rather than in my arms, but because I was forced to deprive her of the pleasure of dying in a hospital closer to her grand-children whom she loved so much. This has left me with an inexpressible sadness.

Immediately after my return from Jamaica, I became pre-occupied in finding some sort of employment. I was now facing a time of life when the struggles of youth are distant, when security becomes the main priority, but I had no job and no one on which to depend. I became obsessively concerned about how I would be able to manage financially. Having attended a number of interviews which fell short of a job offer, I learnt that an organisation was looking for someone to undertake some research in the needs of the black elderly for the '1990

Trust'. I applied for the position, attended an interview, and was verbally offered the post.

A few days later, I was invited for a second interview with the Chairperson of the Trust. On that occasion, I was met with probing questions about my work within the black community. His wide-eyed scrutiny and a kind of negative signal did much to warn me that my tarnished reputation had played a major role in the behaviour of the interviewer rather than my ability to demonstrate my understanding of the requirement for doing the job. I was therefore not surprised to learn later that the Chairperson had vetoed the decision to offer me the position.

This experience of rejection was short lived. Fortunately, I was appointed, some months later, to serve as a lay member of the Department for Education, Special Education Needs Tribunal. This was established as a result of Part 3 of the 1993 Education Act. This placed duties and responsibilities on Education Authorities and Schools to make provisions for pupils with special educational needs. Serving as a Lay Member was not only satisfying but very enjoyable in that I regarded its administration as a fair, just and accessible system for dealing with disputes between parents and Local Authorities.

My three years term had come to an end. Not wishing to continue commuting to the City, I opted to remain at home. With the arrival of three grandchildren in close succession I took on their daily care – well, this gave me a new lease of life. I enjoyed every minute of the day with those beautiful beings. Soon it was time to visit the playgroup with them, then Kindergarten, school run, school concert, sport days – the busy glamorous grandmother as some teachers remarked. I thoroughly enjoyed looking after, nurturing and loving them all. This autumn all three will enter University. I am proud, very proud of their achievements.

The greatest sadness I have had to endure was not the loss of a career, the premature loss of a salary cheque, the unfinished journey, which stopped short of me realising my dreams to establish a landmark for children in care in the borough, but it is suffering the trauma of being falsely accused and degraded. On reflection, I have come to realise that very little has changed in some of my peoples' underdeveloped minds and perceptions; despite the Pan-Africanism and Cultural Awareness Programmes. One can only pray that as a people we begin to refrain from harbouring grudges and jealousies that lead to painful irreparable damages to those around us.

The trauma I experienced in 1987-89 had far-reaching effects on my physical and psychological being. My people relationship zeal had waned. Unlike others who had experienced similar trials, I had reached aged sixty and I began to question the efforts I had made in attempting to reach out to my community. I had developed the disease of old age – 'resignation'. My life with Herb had highs and lows. His struggle to deal with a diagnosis of hypertension by way of prescribed medication resulted in a stroke that caused immobility to the left side of his body. Following a long hospitalisation and nursing care, he sadly succumbed to his illness three years later.

Now after so many eventful years of successes and failures, the focus of my attention is firmly set on my seven children, eleven grandchildren and two great grandchildren. I am comforted that my tribulations and fight for survival have made it possible for their own futures to be more assured than when I first came to the UK. I count my blessing every day and give thanks, looking forward to the joys of retirement.

I had survived.